FAITH AND WEALTH

BY THE AUTHOR

The Story of Christianity, Volume I
The Early Church to the Dawn of the Reformation

The Story of Christianity, Volume II
The Reformation to the Present Day

A History of Christian Thought, Volume I
From the Beginnings to the Council of Chalcedon in A.D. 451

A History of Christian Thought, Volume II
From Augustine to the Eve of the Reformation

A History of Christian Thought, Volume III
From the Protestant Reformation to the Twentieth Century

FAITH
AND WEALTH

A History of Early Christian Ideas on the
Origin, Significance, and Use of Money

JUSTO L. GONZÁLEZ

1817

Harper & Row, Publishers, San Francisco

New York, Grand Rapids, Philadelphia, St. Louis
London, Singapore, Sydney, Tokyo, Toronto

FAITH AND WEALTH. *A History of Early Christian Ideas on the Origin, Significance, and Use of Money.* Copyright © 1990 by Justo L. González. All rights reserved. Printed in the United States of America. No part of this book may be used or reproduced in any manner whatsoever without written permission except in the case of brief quotations embodied in critical articles and reviews. For information address Harper & Row, Publishers, Inc., 10 East 53rd Street, New York, NY 10022.

FIRST EDITION

Library of Congress Cataloging-in-Publication Data

González, Justo L.
 Faith and wealth : a history of early Christian ideas on the origin, significance, and use of money / Justo L. González.—1st ed.
   p. cm.
 Includes bibliographical references.
 ISBN 0-06-063317-4
 1. Wealth—Religious aspects—Christianity—History of doctrines—Early church, ca. 30-600. I. Title
BR195.W4G65 1990
261.8'5'09015—dc20   89-45742
                        CIP

90 91 92 93 94 BANTA 10 9 8 7 6 5 4 3 2 1

Contents

PART III: CONSTANTINE AND BEYOND

RETROSPECT

Acknowledgments

In some ways, this book is a surprise to me. As I have stated in the Introduction, a few years ago I would not even have thought of writing a book such as this. Yet now I am convinced that the issues with which it deals are not only fundamental to an understanding of early Christian theology but are also among the most urgent theological issues of our day. My first word of gratitude must go to those who have led me to this conviction. Unfortunately, in most cases I do not know their names, for they are legion: a Mexican woman sharing her pain and her hope with other Christians in a dilapidated building; a Colombian young man risking his life daily by speaking the truth over the radio; an Afro-American student challenging me on the relevance of my field of studies; and many, many more. To them goes my first word of gratitude and my sincere plea for help as we all seek to be faithful.

On the more academic side, I take this opportunity to thank the library staff at Columbia Theological Seminary, and in particular its Associate Librarian, Dr. Christine Wenderoth, for their joyful and patient assistance in many difficult bibliographical searches.

Finally, it is customary to thank one's spouse for inspiration, support, and patience. In my case, however, I must thank Catherine for that and much more. The history of doctrines is also her field of expertise, and therefore her careful reading of my manuscript in its various stages of development has saved me from many errors and significant omissions.

JUSTO L. GONZÁLEZ

Abbreviations

AmJPhil	American Journal of Philosophy
AngTheolRev	Anglican Theological Review
ANF	The Ante-Nicene Fathers American Edition, 10 vols. (New York: Scribner's, 1908–11)
Ant	Antonianum
Aug	Augustiniana
BAC	Biblioteca de Autores Cristianos (Madrid: La Editorial Católica, 1944–)
CH	Church History
CInscLat	Corpus Inscriptionum Latinarum (Berlin: Akademie der Wissenschaften, 1862–)
CQR	Church Quarterly Review
CSEL	Corpus Scriptorum Ecclesiasticorum Latinorum (Vienna: Academia Litterarum Caesarae Vindobonensis, 1866–)
EuA	Erbe und Auftrag
FOTC	The Fathers of the Church (Washington: Catholic University of America, 1947–)
JQR	Jewish Quarterly Review
JRH	Journal of Religious History
JRomSt	Journal of Roman Studies
JStNT	Journal for the Study of the New Testament
JST	Journal of Theological Studies
LCL	The Loeb Classical Library: Greek and Latin Authors (Cambridge, MS : Harvard University Press, 1912–)

NPNF	The Nicene and Post-Nicene Fathers, American Edition, 2 series, 14 vols. each (New York: Christian Literature Co., 1886-1901)
PG	Patrologiae cursus completus . . . series Graeca, ed. J.-P. Migne, (Paris: Garnier, 1857–91)
PL	Patrologiae cursus completus . . . series Latina, ed. J.P. Migne, (Paris: Garnier, 1844–)
RevBened	Revue Bénédictine
RIntDrAnt	Revue internationale des droits de l'antiquité
RScRel	Recherches de Science Religieuse
TheolQuar	Theologische Quartalschrift
ZntW	Zeitschrift für die neutestamentliche Wissenshaft
ZKgesch	Zeitschrift für Kirchengeschichte

Whenever possible I have quoted translations that are readily available, such as those in *ANF, NPNF,* and *FOTC.* Since parentheses and brackets appear often in such translations, I have marked my own additions and comments with braces—{ }—not with square brackets as is customary.

It is regrettable that most of the translations of ancient Christian writers are riddled with sexist language. I have used those translations in order to facilitate the work of readers who wish to read the quotes given in their larger context. The reader should note, however, that most often such sexist language results from the translators' use of English and does not appear in the original Greek or Latin.

¹/Introduction

The study of history has always involved a bipolar relationship between the past and the historian's own perspectives and interests. The same is true for the history of Christian thought. During the debates following the Reformation, several Protestant theologians at Magdeburg began publishing a history of the church (commonly known as the *Centuries* of Magdeburg) in which they tried to show that Lutheranism was most faithful both to the original Christian proclamation and to the best of Christian tradition. This work drew a number of refutations, of which the most significant was the work of Cardinal Cesar Baronius, *Ecclesiastical Annals*. Both in the *Centuries* of Magdeburg and in the *Annals* of Baronius, the issues raised and the questions asked of ancient texts were determined by the polemics surrounding the Protestant Reformation. Yet both works opened up previously unexplored fields and thus gave birth to the modern discipline of church history. The polarity between the sixteenth-century concerns of polemicists—both Protestant and Catholic—on the one hand, and the ancient texts of earlier times, on the other, led to a new reading of those ancient texts and through it to a better understanding of them.

Twentieth-century historians are not exempt from that polarity. Our vantage point may limit our understanding of ancient texts, and in that case part of our task is to make certain that we do not lose the insights of earlier generations of historians. On the other hand, that vantage point may also enrich our understanding of those texts by prompting us to pose new questions to them.

Nowhere is this as clear as in matters having to do with the economic views of early Christians. Until relatively recent times, scholars have paid scant attention to the economic teachings of the early church or, indeed, to the economic teachings of any Christians but the most recent. When I first read the letters of Ignatius of Antioch, some thirty-five years ago, I was fascinated by what Ignatius had to say about the meaning of communion and about the unity of the church; I was so fascinated that ever since that time I have spent most of my professional career studying the history of Christian thought.[1] During the first twenty years of that study, I paid much attention to the development of the doctrine of the Trinity, to Christology, and to eschatology, but I gave little or no attention to issues of wealth and its use.

Only in the last ten to fifteen years, prompted by new developments in theology and in the life of the church, have I begun asking different questions of the same texts and paying more attention to texts dealing specifically with the economic and social order. I have become increasingly convinced that such matters, far from being tangential to the life of the early church, were central to it, and that without a proper understanding of them we have a truncated view of that life.

The most important factor leading to this awareness—at least in my case—has been the development of liberation theology. In Latin America and other parts of what is commonly known as the Third World, Christians involved in the struggle for social justice are claiming that the issues in which they are involved are theological issues, deeply rooted in Christian doctrine and Christian tradition. With sound scholarship and cogent arguments, they claim that the best way to understand the God of Scripture is not through philosophical discourse but by doing justice, and that this justice includes matters such as land tenure, the distribution and management of wealth, and food for the hungry. They are not simply affirming the commonplace, that Christians ought to be concerned about these matters. They are saying also that the Christian faith and the Christian God are radically misunderstood when theology does not place these concerns at its very heart. And they are also saying that economic realities and agendas both influence and are influenced by seemingly abstract theological discourse.

At this point, liberation theologies draw on another development that has led them along with the entire theological enterprise to ask new questions and develop new methodologies. This is the growth of the social disciplines, particularly sociology and economics. These relatively new disciplines have affected the way we read all of history. Thus, for instance, a history of the Roman Empire written today can no longer deal with cultural and military matters without paying significant attention to trade, the ownership of land, and the systems of production and finance. The same is true with the history of Christianity, which is increasingly researching and debating the social composition of the church at various stages in its history.[2]

For many reasons such attempts at sociohistorical research are problematic. Foremost among them is the nature of the evidence. Written materials by their very nature reflect certain social and cultural strata, and those whose names, occupations, and economic conditions are mentioned are not usually representative of the entire community. Archeological material is fragmentary, scarce, and hardly representative of the empirewide community that was the church. Sweeping descriptions of the social reality of the church at any point during its early centuries are apt to be misleading oversimplifications. There is still much research to be done in that field before it is possible to paint the larger picture. On the other hand, this type of research has yielded valuable, though fragmentary, conclusions, and I have sought to take them into account in the present work.

This book does not add to the rapidly growing body of literature on the sociological and economic profile of the early church. It is not a social history or an economic history of Christianity during the first four centuries of its existence. It is rather a history of the views that Christians held on economic matters, particularly on the origin, significance, and use of wealth. The central question in the pages that follow is not how rich or how poor Christians were at a given time and place, but rather what Christians thought and taught regarding the rights and responsibilities of both rich and poor. Clearly, the two questions are entwined and cannot be entirely separated, for whatever Christians taught on these matters presumably had something to do with the economic and social conditions of their communities. Yet the focus here is on the history of Christian ideas on social and economic relations and not on the history of such relations themselves. One could say that this book falls within the field of the history of doctrines, which has long been my field of interest, with the difference that now, instead of studying what Christians said about the Trinity or the eucharist, I am investigating what they said on the origin and use of wealth.

Unfortunately, this aspect of Christian doctrine has usually been ignored by historians of theology, and it is even less known by the church at large. This may be one of the reasons why, when the Catholic bishops in the United States issued their pastoral letter on the U.S. economy, or when John Paul II issued the encyclical *Solicitudo rei socialis*, so many Christians, Catholics as well as Protestants, questioned the wisdom of church leaders straying from the field of theology in order to make statements on economics. The truth is, as the pages that follow amply show, that from the earliest time economics was a theological issue, and it still is. Thus part of my purpose in the present study is to make known some of the patristic material on issues such as the proper distribution and use of wealth, land tenure, and the rights of the poor.[3]

After some deliberation, I have decided not to deal directly with the issue of Christian attitudes toward slavery. There is no doubt that slavery is also an economic issue and that it is impossible to understand the Roman system of production, at least in some sections of the empire, without taking slavery into account. On the other hand, in the period that most interests us here, the importance of slavery as a means of production was declining, and workers who were technically free but whose freedom was increasingly limited came to occupy the place of slaves. That is the context behind my discussion of slavery. I have tried to clarify the nature of ancient slavery and its place in the economy of the Roman Empire. What I have not tried to do is review the legislation, both civil and ecclesiastical, regarding slavery, nor to survey ancient Christian attitudes toward slavery.[4] Given the declining role of slavery as a means of production during the early centuries of the Christian era, such a discussion would have tended to drift away from economic matters. Contrary to our common assumption, slaves in the Roman Empire were not always poor nor always powerless. As economic historian M. I. Finley has stated, slaves "did the same kind of civilian work as their free counterparts, in the same ways and under the same conditions, despite the formal difference in legal status."[5]

Finally, a word about the subtitle of the present work. I had originally considered *Christianity and Economics in the First Four Centuries of the Christian era* and eventually decided against it because that use of the word *economics* would have been anachronistic and therefore confusing. When the ancients spoke of *oikonomía*, they understood something very different from what we understand today by its derivative *economics*. Xenophon's *Oikonomikos* was a treatise of practical and ethical advice on managing a rural household, including lands and slaves. Eventually the word *oikonomía* came to mean simply "organization" or "management." In that sense Demosthenes applied the term to the management of a city, Quintillian to the organization of a poem, and Tertullian to God's trinitarian "self-management."

If the ancients had no word for our modern concept of economics, it was because they also lacked the concept. As we shall see, they did have definite ideas about how society should be ordered—for instance, whether there should be private property or not. They also understood the connections between the availability of commodities and price fluctuations. They speculated on why money is valuable and the connections between monetary value and societal conventions. What they did not do was link all this together into a coherent view of economic phenomena and their behavior. Much less did they see any connections but the most obvious between government policy and economic order. Not until the time of Diocletian did the Roman Empire have anything that even remotely resembled a budget. Even then, they apparently had little understanding of the connection between inflation and money supply. Thus while rulers were often concerned about the plight of the poor—for the threat they posed, if for no other reason—their only remedies were stopgap measures such as doles.

The early Christians possessed no better understanding of the workings of the economy than did the rest of their contemporaries. They knew—and often experienced—the gap separating the rich from the poor, and they saw that gap deepening as time progressed. But they lacked the instruments of social and economic analysis that we usually associate with the term *economics*.

For this reason I have preferred to speak of views on "faith and wealth" rather than of "economics." Strictly speaking, the ancient Christians, like all ancient Romans, had no economics. They did, however, have a strong sense of wealth and of the degree to which its distribution—or lack of it—affected people. They also had a strong sense of faith and an equally strong conviction that somehow these two crucial issues, faith and wealth, must be related.

As we read what the ancients said about faith and wealth, we may disagree with their understanding of the mechanics of economics. We may be able—we should be able—to improve on their understanding of the forces and counterforces at work in economic systems. Yet we must now allow that to obscure the main thrust of their message: that issues of faith and wealth cannot be separated; that we cannot hide behind our technical knowledge of the workings of the economy in order to avoid asking the crucial questions; that ultimately the crucial questions on the economy are questions of ethics and of faith.

While this study focuses on the major theologians of the church during the first four centuries of its existence, in order to understand their views we must first look at the background in which they worked. This is the purpose of the two chapters of Part One. To understand that background we shall look first, in Chapter 2, at the three main intellectual currents that influenced the nascent church: Greek, Roman, and Jewish. Chapter 3 outlines the manner in which the economic life of the Roman Empire was organized and how it evolved from the early days to the fourth century. The order of Chapters 2 and 3, however, is dictated by chronological rather than methodological reasons; it would be awkward to return to the ancient Greeks and to Jewish law after following the economic development of the Roman Empire throughout the fourth century. Thus the order should not be understood to imply that theological reflection is based first on ideas and only secondarily on the concrete realities of economic life.

In Parts 2 and 3 I have followed the chronological development of Christian views on faith and wealth. The obvious and necessary point of division between those two parts is the radical change of religious policy that took place under Constantine. Finally, in a brief conclusion, I summarize the major findings of the entire essay and suggest some themes for further inquiry and reflection.

NOTES

1. I have summarized the results of those studies in a textbook, *A History of Christian Thought*, 3 vols. (Nashville: Abingdon, 1970–1975; revised edition, 1987).
2. The bibliography on this subject is extensive. See U. Benigni, *Storia sociale della Chiesa* (Milano: Francesco Vallardi, 1906); E. A. Judge, *The Social Patterns of Christian Groups in the First Century* (London: Tyndale, 1960); P. Hinchcliff, "Church and Society before Nicea," *CQR* 165 (1964):39–50; P. Kowalanski, "The Genesis of Christianity in the Views of Contemporary Marxist Specialists of Religion," *Ant* 47 (1972): 541–75; A. J. Malherbe, *Social Aspects of Early Christianity* (Baton Rouge: Louisiana State University Press, 1977); R. M. Grant, *Early Christianity and Society: Seven Studies* (New York: Harper & Row, 1977); G. Barraclough, ed., *The Christian World: A Social and Cultural History* (New York: Harry N. Abrams, 1980); E. A. Judge, "The Social Identity of the First Christians: A Question of Method in Religious History," *JRH* 11 (1980):201–17;

W. A. Meeks, *The First Urban Christians: The Social World of the Apostle Paul* (New Haven: Yale University Press, 1983).

3. Three anthologies of patristic texts on these subjects are W. Shewring, *Rich and Poor in Christian Tradition* (London: Burns Oates & Washbourne, 1948), which includes only six selections from the period we are studying; A. Hamman, *Riches et pauvres dans l'église ancienne* (Paris: Grasset, 1962); and R. Sierra Bravo, *Doctrina social y económica de los padres de la Iglesia* (Madrid: COMPI, 1976). The latter has more abundant selections, although sometimes without sufficient context.

4. That task has been well done by H. Gülzow, *Christentum und Sklaverei in den ersten drei Jahrhunderten* (Bonn: R. Habelt, 1969).

5. M. I. Finley, *The Ancient Economy*, 2d ed. (Berkeley, and Los Angeles: University of California Press, 1985), p. 65.

PART I

BACKGROUND

2/The Wisdom of the Ancients

Long before the advent of Christianity, people in the Mediterranean basin had reflected on the meaning of wealth and the manner in which it should be acquired, employed, and distributed. Greeks, Romans, and Jews had all considered and debated these matters, and on such sources the ancient Christian writers drew for their own reflections.

The Greeks

From ancient times, one stream of Greek thought favored common property. The Pythagoreans—at least the most advanced in that religious-philosophical sect—held their goods in common. According to Aristotle, Phaleas of Chalcedon was the first to propose a redistribution of land in order to achieve equality, and a number of ancient constitutions—most notably those of Sparta and Crete—contained similar provisions.[1]

In 392 B.C., Aristophanes wrote the comedy *Ecclesiazusae* or *The Assembly of Women,* in which he made fun of such proposals. In the comedy, a group of women, made up as men, appears at the Assembly and manages to gain power on its promise to save Athens. Its proposal, which Aristophanes considers ridiculous, is explained by the group's leader, Proxagora:

I want all to have a share in everything and all property to be in common; there will no longer be either rich or poor; no longer shall we see one man harvesting vast tracts of land, while another has not ground enough to be buried in, nor one man surround himself with a whole army of slaves, while another has not a single attendant; I intend that there shall only be one and the same condition of life for all. . . .

I shall begin by making land, money, everything that is private property, common to all. Then we shall live on this common wealth, which we shall take care to administer with wise thrift. . . . [2]

The senselessness of the proposal in Aristophanes' view is made manifest when Proxagora spells out its supposed benefits: "The poor will no longer be obliged to work; each will have all that he needs, bread, salt fish, cakes, tunics, wine, chaplets and chick-pease."[3] And then this senselessness work itself out in the rest of the comedy, which draws out some of the bawdy consequences of the commonality of men and women included in the proposal.

The first great social utopia in the Greco-Roman world is the *Republic* of Plato. It is significant that, although written some twenty years after Aristophanes' comedy, Plato proposes essentially what Aristophanes ridiculed. Could it be that the comedian knew of the philosopher's views that long before their publication? Or is it rather that such ideas were fairly common in ancient Greece? It is impossible to tell.

In any case, Plato's dialogue begins with a discussion between Socrates and two young men on whether happiness is really the lot of the just. The two challenge Socrates in this regard, arguing that the just are misunderstood and mistreated by those who do not understand or envy virtue. In contrast, the cunning unjust—those who are not found out—enjoy all the benefits denied the just. What then is the reward of the just? demand the two youths. They know that Socrates believes in life after death, but that is not an answer they find acceptable. What about happiness here, in this life?

Socrates never answers their question. Instead, he enlarges it by asking the question of a just state. Such a state is happier than an unjust one. The implication is that the just individual, like the just state, derives happiness from inner harmony. Yet the point that Socrates explicitly makes is that even though such a state is nowhere to be found, except perhaps in the realm of pure ideas, one can live according to its principles. Thus the subject of Plato's dialogue is the just state.

Plato asserts that not all people are equally suited for various positions and functions in the state. He recognizes three orders of people: the rulers, the defenders (called "helpers" in the quote that follows) and those who perform manual labor—farmers and artisans.[4] These differences are congenital and cannot be changed. "While all of you in the city are brothers, we will say in our tale, yet God in fashioning those of you who are fitted to hold rule mingled gold in their generation, for which reason they are the most precious—but in the helpers silver, and iron and brass in the farmers and other craftsmen."[5]

That these differences are congenital does not mean that they are necessarily hereditary, and therefore rulers must not allow themselves to be swayed by family considerations when assigning various places to the next generation.

And as you are all akin, though for the most part you will breed after your kinds, it may sometimes happen that a golden father would beget a silver son and that a golden offspring would come from a silver sire and that the rest would in like manner be born of one another. So that the first and chief injunction that the god lays upon the rulers is that of nothing else are they to be such careful guardians and so intently observant as of the intermixture of these metals in the souls of their offspring, and if sons are born to them with an infusion of brass or iron they shall by no means give way to pity in their treatment of them, but shall assign to each the status due to his nature and thrust them out among the artisans or the farmers. And again, if from these are born sons with unexpected gold or silver in their composition they shall honor such and bid them go up higher . . . [6]

This distinction is crucial for understanding the commonality of goods that Plato describes in the *Republic*. It does not include all citizens but only those of the two higher classes, the rulers and the soldiers or "guardians." In other passages, Plato implies that the distinction between guardians and rulers is not immediately apparent, and that it is only as they mature that some of the guardians will give proof that they are truly fit to rule.[7]

Declaring some fit to be guardians or even rulers is not intended to provide them with comforts or rewards. Members of the two higher orders will be fed by the state,[8] but their reward will consist in neither money nor praise. On the contrary, they rule because by so doing they avoid the pain of being ruled by those who are of lesser quality.[9] In consequence, those who simply wish to rule are the least qualified to do so.

The state originates from the necessity of joining with others in order to have various needs met.[10] This, however, does not mean that those who meet material needs ought to be valued more highly than others. On the contrary, of the three rewards that can be sought—profit, victory, and wisdom—profit is the least worthy.[11] While in a number of passages Plato acknowledges that material needs are important, and even that those destined to be philosophers need to taste the rewards of profit and victory, in many other places he attacks the quest for gain as corrupting both the individual and the society:

For there are some, it appears, who will not be contented with this sort of fare or with this way of life, but couches will have to be added thereto and tables and other furniture, yes, and relishes and myrrh and incense and girls and cakes—all sorts of all of them. And the requirements we first mentioned, houses and garments and shoes, will no longer be confined to necessities, but we must set painting to work and embroidery, and procure gold and ivory and similar adornments, must we not? . . .

Then shall we not have to enlarge the city again? For that healthy state is no longer sufficient, but we must proceed to swell out its bulk and fill it up with a multitude of things that exceed the requirements of necessity in states . . . [12]

And so, as time goes on, and they advance in the pursuit of wealth, the more they hold that in honor the less they honor virtue. May not the opposition of wealth and virtue be conceived as if each lay in the scale of a balance inclining opposite ways?[13]

The corrupting power of the quest for material goods is the reason behind Plato's insistence on community of goods among the ruling classes.[14] By having all goods in common and all their basic needs met they will be free from that corrupting power.

Plato's fear of political corruption is also the reason for what has often been singled out as the most extreme instance of his communism: that all women are to be common to all men, and vice versa. Plato's goal was not promiscuity nor was his underlying reason what we now call "free love." His goal was the good of the state. By precluding monogamous unions, he sought to prevent fathers from treating their own children with special consideration and from trying to pass on to them their wealth or authority. Unions for procreation were to be strictly regulated, and only the offspring of the "better" should be allowed to live. Here Plato used the example of the breeding of hunting dogs and fighting cocks. How this is done—or even that it is being done—should be a secret known only by the rulers. One way would be to determine unions by lot and to make certain that the lots turn out as the rulers have devised—in other words, by cheating.[15] Later, in the *Laws*, written some forty years after the *Republic*, Plato moderates these extreme views, allowing for marriages in the more traditional sense.[16] Still, both in the *Republic* and in the *Laws*, the goal is the good of the state.

For the same reason, Plato has no patience with the chronically ill. The resources of medicine should be employed only for those who can become productive again. Those who cannot be cured should not be treated lest they prolong a wretched existence and beget equally wretched children. "Such a fellow is of no use either to himself or the state."[17]

In the *Laws*, Plato gives further details on the economic order of his ideal state. There he takes for granted that this state will hold, besides the various classes of citizens already mentioned, slaves and foreign merchants. As in the *Republic*, the commonality of goods is limited to the ruling classes. Those who work the land will not do so in common, for that would be "beyond their birth, breeding, and education."[18] The land as a whole is indeed the "common property of the whole society,"[19] and "he who shall vend house or land assigned him, or purchase the same, shall suffer the fitting penalties for his act."[20]

In order to manage this state, there shall be a prescribed number of hearths. Every man will have only one male heir. In order to keep this number fixed, extra sons are to be distributed among those who have none. If too many male offspring are born, the extras will be sent off to establish a new colony. Among the owners of these hearths there will not be strict equality, but the state will determine the minimum lot

of each, and some will have up to four times that much. Citizens will be
allowed to rise or descend along this scale of wealth, but none will be
allowed to fall below the level of poverty; if any manage to surpass the
upper limit, the excess will be the property of the state.[21] The reason
here is that both penury and excessive wealth corrupt the state, the one
inciting to crime and the other to sloth and luxury.[22]

There will be division of labor, always regulated by the state, but
citizens will not be permitted to engage in trade or crafts, either directly
or through their slaves.[23] In order to perform these tasks, foreigners will
be encouraged to come to the city, with the proviso that, except under
extraordinary circumstances, they will not be allowed to remain for
more than twenty years. Plato shared the negative view of trade and
crafts common in antiquity. He saw them as necessary but also as corrupting those who practice them:

Internal retail trade, when one considers its essential function, is not a mischie-
vous thing, but much the reverse. Can a man be other than a benefactor if he
effects the even and proportionate diffusion of anything in its own nature so
disproportionately and unevenly diffused as commodities of all sorts? This, we
should remind ourselves, is the very result achieved by a currency, and this, as
we should recognize, the function asigned to the trader. Similarly, the wage
earner, the tavernkeeper, and other callings, some more and some less reputa-
ble, all have the common function of meeting various demands with supply and
distributing commodities more evenly. What, then, can be the reason why the
calling is of no good credit or repute? . . .

There are not many of us who remain sober when we have the opportunity
to grow wealthy, or prefer measure to abundance. The great multitude of men
are of a completely contrary temper—what they desire they desire out of all
measure—when they have the option of making a reasonable profit, they prefer
to make an exorbitant one. This is why all classes of retailers, businessmen,
tavernkeepers, are so unpopular and under so severe a social stigma. . . . For
purposes of commerce a man sets up his quarters in some solitary spot remote
from everywhere; there he entertains the famished traveler and the refugee
from tempests with welcome lodging, and provides them with calm in storm and
cool shelter in heat. But what comes next? Where he might treat his customers
as so many friends, and add a hospitable banquet to the entertainment, he
behaves as though he were dealing with captive enemies fallen in his hands, and
holds them to the hardest, most iniquitous, most abominable terms of ransom.[24]

Buying and selling on credit are to be strictly forbidden.[25] The one
exception is that of an artisan who works on the basis of being paid
when the work is completed, This in itself may be considered a form of
credit. But if the person ordering the work does not pay immediately,
there will be a surcharge of 100 percent; after a year this will be raised
to a penalty of 16.66 percent per month! Quite clearly, this exorbitant
rate is understood as a penalty rather than as interest on a loan.[26] Other
loans, from friends and at no interest, are allowed; they do not have the
authority of a contract, and their repayment will not be enforced by
law.[27]

Finally, in Plato's ideal state only the government will possess precious metals or currency that could circulate beyond its borders. Those residing in the state will use a local currency for their normal transactions. If any need to travel abroad or to import something necessary for the state, the government will issue them a sufficient amount of common Greek currency, with the proviso that travelers returning to the state must exchange any such currency they have not spent in return for the local coin.[28]

Quite clearly, what all this means is that Plato's ideal state is a regimented one in which the common good, as determined by an intellectual elite, takes precedence over individual desires or inclinations. The purpose of Plato's insistence on the commonality of goods—limited as it is to the ruling classes—is not distributive justice but the proper ordering of the state. Extreme poverty is to be banned from this ideal society, not so much because it in itself is evil as because it threatens the stability of the state. The ruling classes are to have things in common for two reasons: first, because by so doing they will avoid the envy and strife that would also threaten stability and preclude good government; second, because the rulers are to be philosophers, and true philosophy can be done only when one is unconcerned about the material necessities of life.

On a number of matters concerning the ordering of society, Aristotle disagrees with Plato. He agrees on an elitist view of the state and its government and would readily exclude from citizenship, not only slaves and aliens, but also artisans, whom he compares to children in their ability to undertake the duties of citizenship.[29] But he strongly rejects the notion of common property.[30]

He offers a number of reasons why property should not be held in common. The first is the typical conservative argument that the present system, tried by experience, should not be abandoned lightly. "Let us remember that we should not disregard the experience of ages; in the multitude of years these things, if they were good, would certainly not have been unknown."[31] This does not mean that one should not seek to improve the order of society but simply that this should be done within the framework of the existing order. "The present arrangement, if improved as it might be by good customs and laws, would be far better, and would have the advantage of both systems."[32] Also, this does not preclude one from putting one's goods at the disposal of one's friends, just as the Spartans, while each having their own, use of each other's slaves, horses, and dogs as if they were their own.[33]

Furthermore, common property would destroy the possibility of liberality, which requires that those who share with friends or guests share of what is really theirs.[34] The pleasure of owning something would be gone, people would spend their time complaining about those who apparently work less and receive more rewards, and this wasted time and effort would hinder progress.[35]

The lack of private property would also lead to the mismanagement of the whole,

For that which is common to the greatest number has the least care bestowed upon it. Every one thinks chiefly of his own, hardly at all of the common interest; and only when he is himself concerned as an individual. For besides other considerations, everybody is more inclined to neglect the duty which he expects another to fulfil.[36]

However, Aristotle's main objection to Plato's proposal is its conception of the state and its function, in which the state, by overregulation, exceeds its bounds:

The error of Socrates must be attributed to the false notion of unity from which he starts. Unity there should be, both of the family and of the state, but in some respects only. For there is a point at which a state may attain such a degree of unity as to be no longer a state, or at which, without actually ceasing to exist, it will become an inferior state, like harmony passing into unison, or rhythm which has been reduced to a single foot. The state, as I was saying, is a plurality.[37]

Thus, as in so many debates on similar subjects since that time, the issue dividing Plato and Aristotle is the question of the proper function of the state. Plato supports the ideal of common property because he believes that this will produce a better state. Aristotle rejects it because he believes that a state, by its very nature, must have a variety that Plato's plan tends to destroy.

Aristotle does not, therefore, favor the unlimited accumulation of wealth. He expects that every state will include "three elements: one class is very rich, another very poor, and a third in a mean."[38] Of these three, the two extremes produce negative effects both on individuals and on the state. Therefore, excessive wealth is to be avoided just as much as excessive poverty, and the middle class is the real strength of a city.

Those who have too much of the goods of fortune, strength, wealth, friends, and the like, are neither willing nor able to submit to authority. The evil begins at home; for when they are boys, for reason of the luxury in which they are brought up, they never learn, even at school, the habit of obedience. On the other hand, the poor, who are in the opposite extreme, are too degraded. So that the one class cannot obey, and can only rule despotically; the other knows not how to command and must be ruled like slaves. Thus arises a city, not of freemen, but of masters and slaves, the one despising, the other envying . . . But a city ought to be composed, as far as possible, of equals and similars; and these are generally the middle classes. Wherefore the city which is composed of middle-class citizens is necessarily best constituted.[39]

Thus although Aristotle rejects Plato's outline of a communistic state, he also rejects the notion that the acquisition of unlimited wealth is good. On the contrary, he distinguishes between proper management of the gifts of nature (economics) and the art of getting rich (chrematistics). Although he uses the latter term in more than one sense, he usually condemns those who practice it. It is one thing to manage one's patrimony so it will yield at its highest; it is another to be engaged in trade and money lending in order to accumulate wealth.

There are two sorts of wealth-getting . . . ; one is a part of household management, the other is retail trade; the former is necessary and honourable, while that which consists in exchange is justly censured; for it is unnatural, and a mode by which men gain from one another. The most hated sort, and with the greatest reason, is usury, which makes a gain out of money itself, and not from the natural object of it. For money was intended to be used in exchange, but not to increase at interest. And this term interest, which means the birth of money from money, is applied to the breeding of money because the offspring resembles the parent. Wherefore of all modes of getting wealth this is the most unnatural.[40]

Distributive justice, argues Aristotle, does not consist in flat equality, but in proportional distribution according to merit. To give people with unequal merit an equal share of goods or honor would be unjust, just as it would be unjust to give unequal shares with no basis on merit. "This, then, is what the just is—the proportional; the unjust is what violates the proportion." When there is injustice, "the man who acts unjustly has too much, and the man who is unjustly treated too little, of what is good."[41]

Much more could be said about Aristotle's views on the problems that have become the subject of economic theory and discussion at a later time, such as monopolistic practices, the fluctuation of prices and how they can be controlled and manipulated, and various theories regarding the value of money. On these issues, however, Aristotle offers little more than anecdotes or passing references whose interpretation varies greatly. A number of these references appear in the *Economics,* a pseudo-Aristotelian work that may or may not report faithfully what the master did in fact teach.

On the basic issue of the proper ordering of the state, the cynics appeared to agree with Plato—at least the later cynics, for the doctrines of the founders of the school are difficult to ascertain—but in fact were quite distant from him. They did believe that the notion of private property should be abolished, as did Plato. They also declared that family and marriage had no place in the ideal society, as Plato had declared in the *Republic* but not in the *Laws.* But they carried their iconoclasm much further than did Plato, advocating the abolition of the state itself. In contrast to Plato, whose goal was the creation of an orderly state, their vision was that of a primitive, "natural," simplicity, returning to the primal stage, which had no state and no law.

On the issues that concern us here, the doctrine of Epicurus—like that of the cynics, much maligned by the later development of its name—adds little to the traditional words of wisdom. He rejects the endless strife after ever-greater wealth, as well as the extremes of poverty, for "poverty, when measured by the natural purpose of life, is great wealth, but unlimited wealth is great poverty."[42] Desire after what one lacks destroys the joy of what one does have.[43] Desires fall into three categories: the natural and necessary, the natural and unnecessary, and the unnatural and unnecessary.[44] Presumably, one should seek to satisfy only the first category, and the second in certain circumstances; but great wealth belongs to the third and therefore must be avoided. Finally, Epicurus rejects the notion that things ought to be the common property of all. However, his reason for rejecting it is not—as in the case of Aristotle or Aristophanes—that common property is not good for the state or for the economy in general. He thinks rather that placing things under common ownership is a sign of mistrust. Friendship and trust, he argues, should be such that the commonality of goods is not necessary.[45]

The doctrines of particular Stoic teachers in the first generations are difficult to ascertain, since all that remains are fragments and several of these are attributed to more than one philosopher. Apparently Zeno of Citium envisioned a state similar to that of Plato's Republic. Significantly he no longer spoke of a Greek city but of a universal state, "all peoples being a single flock on a single pasture."[46] In this universal Republic—the title also of his written work, now lost—people would share common clothes, a common table, and a common marriage.[47] In that state, no coin will have to be issued, presumably because, all things being the common property of all, there will be no place for trade in the traditional sense.[48] Other fragments, however, take for granted that the philosopher will own certain things and will be a citizen of a particular polis. Some have interpreted this apparent discrepancy as an indication that Zeno changed his views on the matter.[49] It appears more likely that Zeno is speaking on one instance of the ideal state and on the other of the philopher's life while in the present society.[50]

Zeno also insists on the common idea in Greek philosophy that wealth can be a hindrance rather than an aid to wisdom. He quotes with approval the episode of Crates and the shoemaker. According to the story, Crates was reading aloud Aristotle's dedication of a book to the king of Cyprus, where the philosopher told the king that, due to his great wealth, he should be able to devote himself to philosophy. Noting that the shoemaker was listening attentively, Crates said that he was better suited for philosophy than the king of Cyprus.[51] Zeno also agrees with Crates' commentary at the market, to the effect that buyers and sellers all envied each other, for each wanted what the other had. In contrast he, Crates, neither sold nor bought and was therefore free.[52]

In the present order, where there is no such community of property, the wise have to find principles whereby to order their lives. Some of the Stoics—Ariston of Chios among them—apparently held that virtue is the only good and that everything else is either bad or indifferent.[53] Naturally, such a view would make it difficult to arrange one's daily life, where choices must constantly be made among things that in this case would be indifferent. Others Stoics—probably Zeno among them, and certainly the later Stoics—introduced a distinction between things that are to be preferred and those that are to be rejected.[54] Thus, while declaring health and material goods to be ultimately indifferent, the Stoics were able to establish a scale of values among such goods. In this scale, wealth is among the goods that are to be sought, although they are not necessarily connected with virtue. Such wealth, however, must be limited, for excessive wealth—and in particular the quest for it—goes against nature. Also, the wise must abstain from all means of attaining such wealth, save the three means appropriate to the philosopher: governing, teaching, and writing good books.[55] In any case, in the quest for material goods, as in all of life, one must be careful not to take away what belongs to others, just as a runner in the stadium must make every effort to win but not by tripping or shoving others.[56]

The later Platonists had little to add. Generally, they paid less attention to Plato's vision of an ideal state and more to personal economic morality within the established order. Also, as Middle and Neoplatonism grew more inclined to mysticism, it showed an increasing disdain for those who paid too much attention to the world of material reality.

Plutarch repeated common statements about the vanity and the corrupting power of wealth, although with more eloquence than others. The constant and unending quest for wealth is a disease that stems, not from a real need for money, but from an inner disorder.

Certainly in the case of sufferers from thirst you would expect the one who had nothing to drink to find his thirst relieved after drinking, while we assume that the one who drinks on and on without stopping needs to relieve, not stuff, himself, and we tell him to vomit, taking his trouble to be caused not by any shortage in anything but by the presence in him of some unnatural pungency or heat. So too with money-getters.[57]

Insofar as the happy life is concerned, the rich are no better off than those of more modest means, for even the richest can buy no more of the real necessities.[58] Indeed, they are worse off, for there is a corrupting power in excessive wealth. This, says Plutarch, is why Lycurgus ordered that no tools other than saw and ax be used on the doors and roofs of houses. Lycurgus was not legislating against other tools; he ordered this "because he knew that through such rough-hewn work you will not be introducing a gilded couch." In such a house, the simple furniture and dinnerware will force the owner to serve unpretentious meals, and this in turn is important because "all manner of luxury and extravagance follow the lead of an evil way of life."[59] The avaricious are morally disgusting, for as "vipers, blister-beetles, and venomous spiders offend and disgust us more than bears and lions, because they kill and destroy men without using what they destroy, so too should men whose rapacity springs from meanness and illiberality disgust us more than those in whom it springs from prodigality, since the miserly take from

others what they have no power or capacity to use themselves."[60] Like
so many others before him, Plutarch condemns the lending of money
on interest. Money lending goes against the fundamental principles of
nature, "that nothing arises out of nothing; for with these men interest
arises out of that which has as yet no being or existence."[61] But most of
all, those who are tempted to borrow should see the senselessness of it:

Borrowing is an act of extreme folly and weakness. Have you money? Do not
borrow, for you are not in need. Have you no money? Do not borrow, for you
will not be able to pay . . . Being unable to carry the burden of poverty you put
the money-lender upon your back, a burden difficult for even the rich to bear
. . . Live by teaching letters, by leading children to school, by being a door-
keeper, by working as a sailor or a boatman; none of these is so disgraceful or
disagreeable as hearing the order "Pay up."[62]

Plutarch does not support Plato's grand project for a state that
would regulate the economic life of its people. On the contrary, he generally speaks in individualistic terms and has little or nothing to say on
the role of government in the economy. He comes closest to this in his
treatise on *Precepts of Statecraft,* where he declares that "there are also in
public life ways which are not dishonourable of helping friends who
need money to acquire it."[63]

Philo of Alexandria was a Jewish contemporary of Jesus who eagerly
sought to reconcile the best of Jewish and Platonic traditions. He represents a further stage in the development of Platonism with regard to
the issues that interest us here. In him we find, to a degree perhaps
paralleled only by Seneca—to whom we shall turn shortly—an astounding combination of great personal wealth with eloquent passages disparaging riches.[64] Philo was a rich member of a distinguished family in the
Jewish community of Alexandria. His brother was a tax collector or
publican so wealthy that he was able to cover nine gates in the Temple
in Jerusalem with precious metals and to loan enormous sums to Herod
Agrippa. Philo himself was sufficiently concerned about the wealth of
his coreligionists that when they were despoiled he went on an embassy
to Rome to seek redress.

And yet we find passages by Philo that advocate the renunciation
of wealth, as when he praises the Essenes because "they have become
moneyless and landless by deliberate action rather than by lack of good
fortune."[65] Elsewhere he calls for "the mind . . . of those who provide
themselves with no property that has its place among things created,
but renounce all these on the ground of ultimate association with the
Uncreated, to possess Whom, they are convinced, is the only wealth."[66]

The reasons for this discrepancy may be debated. It is true that in
a long tradition of eastern Mediterranean texts aristocrats spoke of the
evils of wealth, and Philo is certainly an heir to that tradition. However,
a further reason made it easier for Philo to combine his personal wealth
with his stated contempt for riches. Platonism was taking this direction

in his time. Plato had contrasted the mortal body with the immortal soul. Now that contrast became starker. Platonists considered the soul the seat of happiness and virtue. The body and its well-being could contribute to those goals, but ultimately it was the soul and its life that counted. Within this context, the important issue regarding wealth was not whether one has it or not but the role of the will. Inner attitude mattered more than outer wealth. The Essenes were to be applauded, not because they were poor, but because they accepted poverty voluntarily. Those who renounced all property were to be lauded, not so much for their renunciation, as for the mind that led to such an action. True wisdom and virtue became inner matters. The problem with wealth was not wealth itself but its tendency to draw one away from wisdom and to ephemeral things.

Thus we see in Philo a development in which, while the traditional harsh words about wealth and avarice are repeated, they no longer have the same significance, for what is now important is the inner life of the soul. It is possible to be virtuous and wealthy and at the same time to speak wisely of the evils of wealth, because the life of wisdom and virtue has been interiorized and individualized.

By the time of Plotinus, this development in the direction of individualism and interiorization has reached such a point that Plotinus hardly deals with economic matters, not even in Philo's ambivalent manner.

In short, as we conclude this brief overview of Greek ideas on wealth and its distribution, it should be apparent that much of the debate had to do with how the ideal state ought to be ordered. Many agreed with Plato that common property should be the rule in such a state. Aristotle, on the other hand, argued for private property. All agreed, however, that there should be a limit to the wealth held by any individual. Not to set such limits would corrupt both the state and the individual. On this basis, calls for moderation in the accumulation of riches, and pejorative comments about the rich, are fairly common in Greek literature. As time goes by, however, this tends to become a literary cliche, so that some who write the most disparaging lines about wealth are also among those who hold much of it.

The Romans

We find in Latin writers also the notion of an ideal order in which all things are held in common. For them, however, this order existed only in a bygone and irretrievable golden age of simplicity, and the very authors who bemoan its demise[67] have little to say about restoring it.[68]

The most influential Roman writers do look to the past for guidance. The past they refer to, however, is not the remote golden age of

simplicity and common property. It is rather the times of the early republic, which had been built, as they thought, by honesty and hard
work. In this sense, all the great writers of Roman antiquity are conservative. They look back to a time when agriculture was the main source
of wealth and when the land was cultivated by citizens who were also
landowners. Many of their writings adopt a moralizing tone, bemoaning
the erosion of traditional values.

The opening of Cato's treatise on agriculture is typical:

It is true that to obtain money by trade is sometimes more profitable, were it
not so hazardous; and likewise money-lending, if it were as honourable. Our
ancestors held this view and embodied it in their laws, which required that the
thief be mulcted double and the usurer fourfold; how much less desirable a
citizen they considered the usurer than the thief, one may judge from this . . .
The trader I consider to be an energetic man, and one bent on making money;
but, as I have said above, it is a dangerous career and one subject to disaster.
On the other hand, it is from the farming class that the bravest men and the
sturdiest soldiers come, their calling is most highly respected.[69]

Yet, although agriculture is the morally preferred source of wealth
and the most noble activity, and although they claim that abandonment
of the land is one of the root causes of Rome's malaise, Cato and many
who held similar theoretical views in practice preferred to live in the
city. Of the great authors who devoted works to the praise and practice
of agriculture—the *scriptores de re rustica*—only Columella actually lived
in the countryside. And not even he worked the land with his own
hands.

While a moralizing tone enters their works, such morality is understood in the sense of the traditional Roman virtues. Moral scruples do
not preclude Cato, for instance, from recommending that old slaves, like
old oxen, be sold when they are no longer useful.[70]

In general, little in Latin writings favors common property. On the
contrary, it can be argued that one of Rome's most characteristic contributions to the Western world was its understanding of private property.
In the ancient Greek constitutions attributed to Solon and Lycurgus, for
instance, ownership of land was not absolute. In ancient Rome, where
each small farmhouse was surrounded by its farmland, and each dwelling included the altars to one's ancestors, the notion of property developed a sacred quality that it had lacked in ancient Greece. For Romans,
ownership in the full sense included the right to use, to enjoy, and even
to abuse one's property. This was the main reason Romans felt that any
tax on their lands was inappropriate, and also why all such taxes were
considered signs of conquest. For similar reasons, the right to leave one's
property to one's heirs was also fundamental in the Roman legal and
economic system.

In many ways the most Roman of Romans, and certainly the most
articulate and typical exponent of these ideas, was Cicero. The issue of
the inviolability of land ownership over against the need for agrarian

reform and the redistribution of land among the citizenry of Italy was one of the main bones of contention in Cicero's confrontation with Catilina. Cicero considered Catilina's proposal of agrarian reform a menace to the state. Against Catilina's proposal, he firmly held that the main function of the state was precisely the preservation of private property. The importance of private property is such that the sum total of all private wealth is the wealth of the state.[71] The very notion of an "equality of goods" (*aequitatio bonorum*) denotes the ruin of the nation, argues Cicero, and the primary responsibility of those in government is to protect the rights of private property.

The man in an administrative office, however, must make it his first care that every one shall have what belongs to him and that private citizens suffer no invasion of their property rights by the state . . . For the chief purpose in the establishment of constitutional state and municipal governments was that individual property rights might be secured . . .

The administration should also put forth every effort to prevent the levying of a property tax, and to this end precautions should be taken long in advance . . .

But they who pose as friends of the people, and who for that reason either attempt to have agrarian laws passed, in order that the occupants may be driven out of their homes, or propose that money loaned should be remitted to the borrowers, are undermining the foundations of the commonwealth: first of all, they are destroying harmony, which cannot exist when money is taken away from one party and bestowed upon another; and second, they do away with equity, which is utterly subverted, if property rights are not respected. For, as I said above, it is the peculiar function of the state and the city to guarantee to every man the free and undisturbed control of his own particular property.[72]

Although Cicero repeats the commonplace that happiness is based on virtue and not on riches, he also says that those who decide to seek great wealth should have the right to do so, as long as they hurt no one in the process.[73] And even this last injunction is not final, for the wise and virtuous can dispossess the useless or unproductive on the grounds that this is best for the common good.[74] Thus it is clear that Cicero's defense of property is more a defense of the propertied classes—he himself owned at least fourteen large farms—than a defense of a legal or moral principle.

Finally, it may be illuminating to quote the manner in which Cicero classifies and evaluates the various occupations:

Now in regard to trades and other means of livelihood, which ones are to be considered becoming to a gentleman and which ones are vulgar, we have been taught, in general, as follows. First, those means of livelihood are rejected as undesirable which incur people's ill-will, as those of tax-gatherers and usurers. Unbecoming to a gentleman, too, and vulgar are the means of livelihood of all hired workmen whom we pay for mere manual labour, not for artistic skill; for in their case the very wage they receive is a pledge of their slavery. Vulgar we must consider those who buy from wholesale merchants to retail immediately;

for they would get no profits without a great deal of downright lying; and verily, there is no action that is meaner than misrepresentation. And all mechanics {artisans} are engaged in vulgar trades; for no workshop can have anything liberal about it. Least respectable of all are those whose trades cater for sensual pleasures: "fishmongers, butchers, cooks, and poulterers, and fishermen," as Terence says.[75]

This passage and those that follow it are significant, for they epit-omize the aristocratic Roman view of the social order. Menial work—indeed, the very need to work for a living—was considered degrading. Significantly, agriculture is not mentioned by Cicero among the "vulgar" or "sordid" occupations, for there was still an echo of the ancient tradi-tion of Roman citizens as free farmers.[76] Cicero himself was a farmer only in the sense that he owned vast estates and that he apparently invested most of his wealth in agriculture. Still, he could not bring him-self to declare the actual work of agriculture to be demeaning, unless it was work for hire, which in his mind approached slavery. Wholesale trade was respectable, but retail was not.[77] The occupation of those who provide for the physical needs of society—fishmongers, butchers, and so forth—are sordid. The text continues on to tell us that the occupations requiring the use of the mind—artists, architects, lawyers, and so forth—are more respectable than mere work for hire. At this point, it is significant to remember that, although most of Cicero's income came from his investments, he was also a lawyer.

Cicero is the conservative *par excellence*. His manner is proper and his speech polished. He defends the order of the state, particularly since he believes that the main function of the state is to protect private prop-erty, and he owns much of it.

Seneca is part of the same tradition. He too is wealthy, and yet he speaks eloquently of the sorrows of wealth and of the folly of seeking it. For two reasons the wise should eschew the quest after wealth: it pro-duces anxiety, and it brings about a sort of slavery. He quotes Epicurus approvingly, "He who needs riches least, enjoys riches most," and then he comments:

He who craves riches feels fear on their account. No man, however, enjoys a blessing that brings anxiety; he is always trying to add a little more. While he puzzles over increasing his wealth, he forgets how to use it. He collects his accounts, he wears out the pavement in the forum, he turns over his ledger—in short, he ceases to be a master and becomes a steward.[78]

These are the words of a fabulously rich man who has no financial cares and who therefore can speak of the folly of those who worry over money. Fortunes, he declares elsewhere, "are the greatest source of hu-man sorrow," and this to such a point that "we must reflect how much lighter is the sorrow of not having money than of losing it." Poverty, he contends, should be welcome, for "the less poverty has to lose, the less chance it has to torment us." It is not more painful for a bald-headed man than for one with a head full of hair to have a hair plucked. Likewise, both the poor and the rich suffer a loss equally, and, since the rich is more likely to lose money than the poor, the poor is more fortunate![79]

This may sound like good moral advice for those whose financial resources are quite adequate and who run the danger of being enslaved by their quest after greater wealth. Yet, as a general view of the comparative lots of the rich and the poor, or as a moral guideline for the way a society should be organized, it leaves much to be desired. It is literature written by the wealthy to be read by the wealthy. Therefore, while the author speaks eloquently of the evils of wealth, these are mostly the evils it brings upon its possessors and not upon those who are dispossessed. As a result, on occasion poverty is extolled as a blessing—although not one to be actively sought!

Pliny the Elder deplores the growth of latifundia, large landed estates, as causing great harm to the state,[80] and he speaks of the folly of wealth gathered only to be displayed. According to him, the first crime was committed by the person who wore the first ring,[81] and it made no sense that so many hands must be worn out scratching the earth so that a single finger be adorned.[82] Yet the elder Pliny himself had great wealth and land holdings, and by his time efforts to limit the growth of latifundia or the wealth of the rich were a thing of the past.

Such efforts, and attempts at agrarian reform, had been a subject of discussion and even the cause of civil war in earlier times. According to tradition, Romulus had allotted two *jugera* to each citizen—that is, the amount of land that could be plowed in two days with a single team of oxen. At the beginning of the republic, the allotment for plebeian citizens had been established at seven *jugera*. Later, it was decreed that five hundred *jugera* was the limit of land that a senator could possess. All these laws, however, soon were forgotten, much to the chagrin of authors such as Pliny and Columella,[83] who saw in the growth of latifundia the main reason for the decline in agricultural production.

In these matters, as in all others, the evolution of Roman law and practice was toward protecting property rights. Significantly, even attempts at strict economic regulation under Diocletian and Constantine in the third and fourth centuries A.D. dealt mostly with the marketplace and did not seek to limit the growth of latifundia. In the second century, jurist Marcianus had affirmed that certain things are by nature the common property of all and are not therefore susceptible of private ownership. Yet these common things are only the air, running waters, the sea, and the seashore.[84] Nor could one put up a building that would cut off the wind and prevent a neighbor from winnowing grain[85] or use fishing lights that could confuse sailors at night[86] or withhold food from sale in time of famine.[87] It was also commonly held that no one should harm another in order to gain greater wealth.[88]

Apart from such limitations, however, the rights of property owners were the backbone of Roman law. There were practically no limits on private contracts.[89] The right to dispose of one's property by will had few limits, and even a moderate tax of 5 percent met stiff resistance[90] until it was finally abolished by Justinian in A.D. 531.[91] In sale transactions, it was legal for both seller and buyer to deceive each other.[92] The right of an owner, not only to use, but also to abuse or destroy property—with some limitations in the case of slaves—was guaranteed by law and tradition. Indeed, ownership was traditionally defined as the right to use, to enjoy, and to abuse—*jus utendi, jus fruendi, jus abutendi.*

The one point at which the law did consistently limit property rights was interest on loans. Although Roman moralists repeatedly condemned the practice of lending money on interest, the practice itself was established and regulated by law. Since the earliest times, the maximum rate had been fixed at 1 percent simple interest per month, and this was generally the legal limit throughout the history of Roman legislation. Compound interest was forbidden, although ways were often found to circumvent this regulation as well as those limiting the rate of interest.[93] Especially when the lender could claim that significant risk was involved, such as in shipping enterprises or in agriculture, interest rates could exceed the established limit, sometimes rising as high as 50 percent.[94]

In short, the rights of private property, and the owners' right to use it as they saw fit, was the backbone of the Roman legal system. Neither Roman law nor Roman philosophy explored communal property as had some ancient Greek constitutions as well as Plato and other Greek philosophers. Roman writers did continue the tradition of declaring that riches were a source of anxiety and that therefore one should not seek them. Yet the very writers who penned such lines accumulated wealth in quantities that the earlier Greeks could never have dreamed, and some like Cicero were convinced that the protection of private property was both the principal function and the highest interest of the state. The taxation of free citizens was traditionally considered tyranny and eventually came to be accepted only as an evil necessity. It would never have occured to a Roman that taxation could or should be used as a means to redistribute wealth or to promote social policy, although it is clear to us now that the Roman system of taxation did promote the concentration of wealth in ever fewer hands. As to the poor, it was not the business of the state to be overly concerned for their needs, except in cities such as Rome and Constantinople or in times of famine, when their numbers and desperation could produce civil unrest.

The Jews

The third tradition, besides the Greek and the Roman, from which early Christianity drew its views on the economic order of society was Judaism. Like the ancient Romans and most peoples of antiquity, the

Israelites attached great significance to the land in which their ancestors were buried. This is why in Genesis 23 it is so important for Abraham to own the land in which Sarah is to be buried. For the same reason, when Joseph sees death approaching, he asks that his body be interred with his ancestors.[95] Likewise, his father Jacob charges his sons:

I am to be gathered to my people; bury me with my fathers in the cave that is in the field of Ephron the Hittite, in the cave that is in the field of Mach-pelah, to the east of Mamre, in the land of Canaan, which Abraham bought with the field from Ephron the Hittite to possess as a burying place. There they buried Abraham and Sarah his wife; there they buried Isaac and Rebekah his wife; and there I buried Leah.[96]

On this basis, the land and its possession held a significance that went beyond the merely economic. This, however, did not lead to the doctrine of absolute property rights that ruled in Roman tradition and jurisprudence. The land was sacred, not only because it held the sepulchers of the patriarchs of Israel, but also because it was God's land. It had been God's land to give at the time of the conquest, when God said to Joshua, "Now therefore arise, go over this Jordan, you and all this people, into the land which I am giving them."[97] And it remained God's land even while Israel had possession of it: "The land shall not be sold in perpetuity, for the land is mine; for you are strangers and sojourners with me."[98]

Thus, in contrast with Roman law, Hebrew law set definite limits on what one could do with one's property. One clear difference was that Jewish law did not permit the abuse of property, be it land, animals, or slaves. Just as rest was ordered for humans and beasts alike every seventh day, so was the land to be left fallow every seventh year.[99] This included not only annual crops such as wheat but also vineyards and olive trees. According to rabbinical interpretation this precept, like the year of jubilee, was a reminder to Israel that the land ultimately belongs to God.[100] Whatever the untended land would produce on its own the poor could gather as food, and whatever the poor did not take was to be left for the wild animals. It is not clear how regularly this was practiced, yet it appears again in the covenant of Nehemiah.[101] It clearly was practiced during the period of the Maccabees,[102] and there are indications that it was practiced, if not generally, at least occasionally, until the second century A.D.[103]

God's ultimate ownership of the land also meant that part of its produce had to be reserved for God, both directly through tithes and other similar duties, and indirectly by making it available to the needy. A hungry or thirsty traveler could go into any field and eat grain and grapes, as long as nothing was taken beyond what was needed.[104] Likewise, the poor, the orphan, the widow, and the sojourner had a right to a portion of every crop. This included the edges of a field of grain, any fruit that had dropped to the ground, and all that the harvesters left behind after passing through the field once.[105] This commandment was so important, and raised so many questions, that an entire tract in the Talmud, *Pe'ah*—literally, "corner"—was devoted to elucidating its scope and application.[106] According to the Talmud, although the amount of *Pe'ah* left for the poor would depend on the size of the field, the number of the poor in the community, and the size of the crop, it should never be less than one-sixtieth of the entire crop.[107] It was also made clear that not only the crops specifically mentioned in Scripture but all produce of the land was subject to *Pe'ah*.[108] In the case of crops that require special expertise or equipment to harvest, such as date palms, the owner was responsible for harvesting the *Pe'ah* and then distributing it to the poor.[109]

Although all these laws were based on God's ownership of the land, the rabbis constantly kept in mind God's special concern for the poor. For instance, it was true that any traveler, no matter how poor or how rich, could take produce from a field or orchard and eat it; the rabbis debated whether, if the traveler in question had property and found it necessary to take from that portion of the produce reserved for the poor (for instance, if the field had already been harvested and all that remained was the gleanings), restitution must be made to the poor. Some argued that the traveler was poor at the time, in the sense of having need of the gleanings. Others insisted that restitution must be made, for otherwise the truly poor would be cheated out of their just portion.[110]

Eventually, such issues led to debates over every conceivable detail: If a harvester's hand is pricked by a thorn, and a handful of grain falls to the ground, can it be picked up, or does it belong to the poor? If grain falls into an ant hole, does it belong to the owner of the land or to the poor?[111] It would be easy to ridicule such discussions as unwarranted legalism; but the main point should not be obscured, that all these debates and regulations were an attempt to safeguard the rights of the poor, and that their fundamental premise was that the poor do have rights—rights that limit the power and authority of those who own the land.

A further source of support for the poor was a special tithe collected on the third and sixth years of each seven-year cycle.[112] This was a religious duty, again illustrating God's particular concern for the poor. Indeed, in later Judaism, when the Temple was no longer standing, the term *hekdesh*, which had originally referred to property consecrated to God or dedicated to the needs of the Temple, came to mean property consecrated for synagogues or for the poor. And *zedakah,* whose original meaning was "righteousness," came to mean charity.

Hebrew legislation dealt with the inevitable loss by some of their ancestral lands and sought ways to remedy that situation. This was the reason behind the prohibition to sell land in perpetuity, to which reference has already been made. Significantly, the prohibition did not apply to houses in cities, which could indeed be sold in perpetuity.[113] But for fields and houses in villages, a number of procedures were offered so that title could revert, if not to the original owner, to the next of kin.

If all this failed, there was the law regarding the year of jubilee. The jubilee, intended to take place once every fifty years (or after seven periods of seven years each), was a time when all land reverted to its original owners, debts were canceled, and Israelite slaves were to be set free. Naturally, this meant that the value of a piece of property had to be reckoned according to how much time was left before the next jubilee.[114] Whether or not this was ever practiced is not clear.[115] It did, however, remain at least as an ideal to which prophets could point and which Jesus would apparently apply to his mission.[116]

In short, the Jewish understanding of property differed radically from that of Roman law. While the former tended to be absolute, with few limitations set on it, Jewish property rights were limited by the rights of God, by the rights of the property itself, which must not be abused, and by the rights of the needy—the poor, the sojourner, the orphan, and the widow. Along these lines the commandment against stealing is to be understood, not as a safeguard for the rights of private property, but rather as a safeguard against abuse that would destroy life.[117]

At the same time, however, since these views were based on God's direct ownership of the Holy Land, some rabbis came to the conclusion that most of the laws regarding agriculture and the limits on land ownership and use were applicable only within the Holy Land. Jews outside its borders were not bound by them. [118] This may be one reason Philo—whom we have discussed among the Greeks, for he belongs to both traditions—could show great respect for the Law and yet order his own economic life according to very different principles.

Toward usury, on the other hand, the law of Israel evinced the same condemnation found in the Greco-Roman tradition, plus a call for compassion for the poor who have to borrow: "If you lend money to any of my people with you who is poor, you shall not be to him as a creditor, and you shall not exact interest from him. If ever you take your neighbor's garment in pledge, you shall restore it to him before the sun goes down; for that is his only covering, it is the mantle for his body; in what else shall he sleep?"[119]

As time went by, means were found to circumvent this prohibition, and therefore later Jewish jurists took pains to clarify its meaning and scope. The Mishnah, for instance, declares that it is permitted for someone who rents a courtyard to another to offer the renter a lower rate if the rent is paid in advance, but that it is not legal to do the same in case of a sale.[120] Likewise, the rabbis said, it is forbidden to buy produce to be delivered at a certain date and on a fixed price before the market price is known. Such a purchase of what today we would call "futures" would risk becoming usury if the market price of the commodity increases, since in that case the net result would be that the purchaser advanced money to the seller and then made a profit by virtue of having made that advance.[121]

Finally, a word must be said about two Jewish sects whose use of wealth differed from that of their coreligionists: the Essenes and the Therapeutae. The Essenes, who are much better known since the discovery of the Dead Sea Scrolls, practiced commonality of property. Philo speaks of a spirit of sharing (*koinonía*) that is beyond description and then depicts their life as follows:

First of all then no one's house is his own in the sense that it is not shared by all, for besides the fact that they dwell together in communities, the door is open to visitors from elsewhere who share their convictions. Again they all have a single treasury and common disbursements; their clothes are held in common and also their food through their institution of public meals. In no other community can we find the institution of sharing roof, life and board more firmly established in actual practice. And that is no more than one would expect. For all the wages which they earn in the day's work they do not keep as their private property, but throw them into the common stock and allow the benefit thus accruing to be shared by those who wish to use it.[122]

Apparently those who joined the sect surrendered increasing portions of their wealth to the community, until they had surrendered all.[123] In contrast to other Jews, who insisted on charity, not only towards Jews, but also towards Gentiles, the Essenes had strict rules forbidding their association even with other Jews and excluding from their community any who suffered from a number of physical or mental disabilities, for instance, the blind, the lame, and the retarded.

The Therapeutae also surrendered their possessions, although in their case the main purpose was not shared communal life, but rather ascetic contemplation.[124] In spite of the presence of such groups, however, the mainstream of Jewish tradition insisted that, while charity should be significant, one should not dispossess oneself for its sake.[125]

Quite naturally, as the Christian movement emerged, it was influenced first of all by its immediate Jewish environment. Thus much of what we shall see in the early stages of the movement will be clearly derived from Jewish tradition. As time went on, however, and the church expanded among the Gentile community, the influence of Greek and Roman authors became more marked. Of this too we shall see indications in the chapters that follow.

NOTES

1. Aristotle, *Politics* 1264–72, from The Basic Works of Aristotle, ed. R. McKeon (New York: Random House, 1941). All quotes from Aristotle are taken from this edition.
2. Aristophanes, *Ecclesiazusae* 589–99, from *The Complete Greek Drama*, ed. W. J. Oates and E. O'Neill, Jr. (New York: Random House, 1938).
3. Ibid. 604-9.

4. In the *Republic* (455–57), both men and women are included in each of these categories, although we are told that males are superior in every human activity. Later, in the *Laws* (759a and 828b), Plato would declare that women are not fit for the manly functions in society, except for the priesthood. Plato, *Republic*, trans. Paul Shorey, in *The Collected Dialogues of Plato*, ed. E. Hamilton and H. Cairns. (Princeton: Princeton University Press, 1961). All quotes from Plato are taken from this edition.

5. *Rep.* 415a.

6. *Rep.* 415b.

7. *Rep.* 540a–b: "At the age of fifty those {guardians} who have survived the tests and approved themselves altogether the best in every task and form of knowledge must be brought at last to the goal. We shall require them to turn upward the vision of their soul . . . devoting the greater part of their time to the study of philosophy . . . but when the turn comes to each, toiling in the service of the state and holding office for the city's sake."

8. *Rep.* 420a.

9. *Rep.* 347c.

10. *Rep.* 396c.

11. *Rep.* 582b–c.

12. *Rep.* 372e–373b.

13. *Rep.* 550e.

14. *Rep.* 417b: "But whenever they {the guardians} shall acquire for themselves land of their own and houses and coin, they will be householders and farmers instead of guardians, and will be transformed from the helpers of their fellow citizens to their enemies and masters, and in so hating and being hated, plotting and being plotted against, they will pass their days fearing far more and rather the townsmen within than the foemen without—and then laying the course of near shipwreck for themselves and the state."

15. *Rep.* 459–61.

16. *Laws* 773.

17. *Rep.* 407e.

18. *Rep.* 740a.

19. Ibid.

20. *Rep.* 741c.

21. *Laws* 744–45.

22. *Laws* 919b–c.

23. *Laws* 846–47, 919–20.

24. *Laws* 918.

25. The prohibition on interest: *Rep.* 556b; *Laws* 742c–743d. The prohibition on any kind of sale on credit: *Laws* 849e, 915e.

26. *Laws* 921b–c. Cf. Glauco Tozzi, *Economistas griegos y latinos* (Mexico City, México: Fondo de Cultura Económica, 1968), pp. 91–92.

27. *Laws* 915e.

28. *Laws* 742a–b.

29. *Pol.* 1277b–1278a.

30. At the same time, he agreed that for a state to exist its members must have something in common, at least a common place. But his point is that "our present condition" is better than "the proposed new order of society." *Pol.* 1261a.

31. *Pol.* 1264a.

32. *Pol.* 1263a.

33. Ibid.

34. *Pol.* 163b.

35. *Pol.* 1263a.

36. *Pol.* 1261b.

37. *Pol.* 1263b.

38. *Pol.* 1295b.

39. *Pol.* 1295b.

40. *Pol.* 1258a–b. In order to understand Aristotle's comments on the term *interest,* one must remember that in Greek this is *tókos,* which means "offspring." In the *Nicomachean Ethics,* 1121b (from McKeon), Aristotle condemned those who take "anything and from any source, e.g. those who ply sordid trades, pimps and all such people, and those who lend small sums at high rates." Here, in contrast to the *Politics,* it is not interest as we know it but only usury that is rejected. Also on the matter of trade, the *Nicomachean Ethics* nuances what Aristotle has said in the *Politics.* For instance, in *Nic. Eth.* 5.5 there is a discussion of the positive results of trade. Here the example is that of a shoemaker who needs a have a house built. He must find a way, through trade, to pay for the builder's work with the results of his own work as shoemaker. What Aristotle appears to reject is trade as an occupation.

41. *Nic. Eth.* 1131b.

42. *Vat. fragm.* 25, in *The Stoic and Epicurean Philosophers,* ed. W. J. Oates (New York: Random House, 1940). Other texts from Epicurus are quoted from this source.

43. *Ibid.,* 35.

44. *Frag.* 29.

45. Diog. Laert., *Lives* 10.11 (*LCL*).

46. Plutarch, *De Alex. virt.* 329 (*LCL*).

47. However, in another reference, we are told that he held that "women should be the common property of the wise" (Diog. Laert., *Lives* 7.131). Cf. 7. 121.

48. Diog. Laert., *Lives* 7.33.

49. So Tozzi *Economistas* (n. 26 above), p. 182.

50. On this ideal city according to Zeno, see Diog. Laert., *Lives* 6.85.

51. Quoted by the fifth-century anthologist Joannes Stobaeus, *Flor.* 95.21, in *Stoicorum veterum fragmenta,* ed. J. von Arnim (Lipsia: B. G. Teubner, 1905). All references to Stobaeus are from this edition.

52. *Flor.* Ibid., 5.52.

53. Sextus Empiricus, *Adv. math.* 11.64–67, *LCL.*

54. Stobaeus, *Ecl.* 2.84.18. Cicero, *De fin.* 3.50–54, *LCL.*

55. N. Festa, *I frammenti degli Stoici Antichi* (Bari: Laterza, 1932–1935), 1:23–24. These are opposed to demagoguery, teaching for a charge, as the sophists do—in contrast to accepting whatever the students pay our of gratitude—and the writing of pernicious books.

56. A theme later taken up by Cicero in *De off.* 3.10. 42, *LCL.*

57. *De cupid. divit.* 3, *LCL.*

58. *De cupid. divit.* 8, *LCL.*

59. *De esu car.* 2.2, *LCL.*

60. *De cupid. divit.* 6, *LCL.*

61. *De vitando aere alien.* 4, *LCL.*

62. *De vit. alien.* 4, *LCL.*

63. *Praec. ger. reip.* 13, *LCL.* This, after he has declared that rulers ought not to favor their friends. The context shows that, while Plutarch objects to rulers applying the law in ways that benefit their friends, he does not have the same qualms in economic matters.

64. A subject that has been discussed by D. L. Mealand, "Philo of Alexandria's Attitude to Riches," *ZntW* 68 (1978): 258–64. This article has produced a lively discussion: T. E. Schmidt, "Hostility to Wealth in Philo of Alexandria," *JStNT* 19 (1983):85–97; Mealand, "The Paradox of Philo's Views on Wealth," *JStNT,* 24 (1985):111–15; F. G. Downing, "Philo on Wealth and the Rights of the Poor," *JStNT* 24 (1985):116–18.

65. Philo, *Quod omnis probus* 77, *LCL.*

66. *De plant.* 66, *LCL.*

67. A theme that appears already in Pindar, *Ol.* 2.70, but which the Latin poets developed. Vergil, *Georg.* 1.126, *LCL; Aen.* 9.569, *LCL;* Ovid, *Met.* 1.132, *LCL;* Horace, *Epod.* 16.49, *LCL.* Cf. Seneca, *Ep.* 90.41, *LCL.*

68. There is on occassion the hope that the golden age, usually associated with Saturn and with agriculture, will return. So Ovid, *Ep.* 4, *LCL.* The Epicureans, in contrast

with the theory of a primal golden age, held to a theory of progressive ascent, so that the golden age lies in the future. On this entire issue, see K. F. Smith, "Ages of the World (Greek and Roman)," in *Encyclopaedia of Religion and Ethics,* ed. J. Hastings (New York: Charles Scribner's Sons, 1931), 1:192–200.

69. Cato, *De agri cult.* 1, *LCL.*

70. *De agri cult.* 2, *LCL:* "Sell worn-out oxen, blemished cattle, blemished sheep, wool, hides, an old wagon, old tools, an old slave, a sickly slave, and whatever else is superfluous. The master should have the selling habit, not the buying."

71. Cicero, *De off.* 3.15, *LCL.*

72. *De off.* 2.21–22, *LCL.*

73. *De off.* 1.20–21, *LCL.*

74. *De off.* 3.6, *LCL.*

75. *De off.* 1.42, *LCL.*

76. *De off.* 1.42, *LCL:* "But of all the occupations by which gain is secured, none is better than agriculture, none more profitable, none more delightful, none more becoming to a freeman."

77. *De off.* 1.42, *LCL.* "Trade, if it is on a small scale, is to be considered vulgar; but if wholesale and on a large scale, importing large quantities from all parts of the world and distributing to many without misrepresentation, is not to be greatly disparaged. Nay, it even seems to deserve the highest respect."

78. Seneca, *Ep.* 14, *LCL.*

79. *De trang. anim.* 8, *LCL.*

80. Pliny the Elder, *HN,* 1.18.

81. *HN* 1.33.8.

82. *HN* 1.2.158.

83. *De re rust.* 1.3, *LCL.*

84. *Dig.* 1.8.2, in *Corpus Juris Civilis,* ed. C. M. Galisset (Paris: Cotelle, 1867). All references to Roman jurisprudence, except the *Codex Theodosianus,* follow this edition.

85. *Cod. Theod.* 3.14, in *Theodosiani Libri xvi,* ed. Th. Mommsen (Berlin: Weidmann, 1962). All references to the *Codex Theodosianus* are from this edition.

86. *Cod. Theod.* 47.9.

87. *Cod. Theod.* 10.27.

88. *Dig.* 2.15.8; 12.6.14.

89. Paulus, *Sent.* 1.1.1–4.

90. Pliny the Younger, *Pan.* 37, *LCL.*

91. *Cod. Theod.* 2.33.

92. *Dig.* 4.4.16.4.

93. *Dig.* 3.5.37; 12.6.26.1; 26.7.7.8.

94. *Cod. Theod.* 2.33.

95. Gen. 27:30.

96. Gen. 47:29–31.

97. Josh. 1:2.

98. Lev. 25:23.

99. Exod. 23:10–11; Lev. 25:2–4. Also on every seventh year, Israelites who had been enslaved by other Israelites because of debts were to be see free.

100. *Sanh.* 250, affirms that God said, "Sow for six years, and let the land lie fallow for the seventh year, so that the earth may know that the land is mine."

101. Neh. 10:31.

102. Mac. 6:49, 53.

103. R. deVaux, *Ancient Israel* (New York: McGraw-Hill, 1965), 1:174–75. Whether this law should be applied in modern Israel, and how, has been a subject of discussion among rabbis from the outset of the Zionist movement. See M. Simon's introduction to the *Berakoth* in *The Babylonian Talmud,* ed. I. Epstein (London: Soncino Press, 1948), *Seder Zera'im,* p. xxi. All references to the Talmud are from this edition.

104. Deut. 23:24–25: "When you go into your neighbor's vineyard, you may eat your fill of grapes, as many as you wish, but you shall not put any in your vessel. When you go into your neighbor's standing grain, you may pluck the ears with your hand, but you shall not put a sickle to your neighbor's standing grain."
105. Lev. 19:9–10; 23:22; Deut. 24:19–21.
106. Although most of the rabbinical legislation on the portion of the harvest that belongs to the poor is under the heading of *Pe'ah,* the rabbis listed several categories of produce that must be left for the poor. Besides the "corner" (*pe'ah*), there were gleanings (*leget*), whatever was missed or forgotten by the harvesters (*shikhhah*), grapes that fell to the ground (*peret*), and small clusters of grapes that were not harvested (*'olelot*).
107. *Pe'ah* 5–6. In this case, as in most other references to rabbinical tradition, it is difficult or impossible to determine the exact date of these dispositions and interpretations of the law. Many of them are post-Christian and should be read as illustrating the views of Jews during the first centuries of the Christian era, and as perhaps reflecting views that already existed at an earlier time.
108 *Pe'ah* 6–7.
109 *Pe'ah* 18.
110 *Pe'ah* 25–26.
111 *Pe'ah* 22–23.
112 Scholars disagree as to whether this was an actual practice or merely a principle that was never followed. See R. Gnuse, *You Shall Not Steal: Community and Property in the Biblical Tradition* (Maryknoll, N.Y.: Orbis, 1985), p. 129 n. 51.
113 Although even in that case a seller had the opportunity to buy the house back during the first year after the sale. Lev. 25:29–30.
114 Lev. 25:8–55 (vv. 19–22, however, refer to the sabbatical year on which the land will lie fallow); 27:16–25; Num. 36:4.
115 See Ezek. 46:17, which seems to take for granted that there will be a year of jubilee.
116 Isa.61:2–3; Luke 4:18–19.
117 Such is the thesis of Gnuse, *You Shall Not Steal* (n. 112 above), as he concludes, "The ethos of Israel called for a sharing of property according to human need. Theft was the deprival of the things necessary for a meaningful life—it was the Canaanite way of doing business" (p. 85).
118 *Talm. Kidd.* 180.
119 Exod. 22:25–27. Cf. Lev. 25:37; Deut. 23:19–20. In this latter text, the distinction is made between lending to another Israelite (which should be done without interest) and lending to a foreigner (in which case interest is lawful).
120 *Mishnah. Baba Mezja* 5.2., trans. H. E. Goldin (New York: Hebrew Publishing Co., 1933).
121 *Mish. B. Mez.*
122 Philo, *Quod omnis probus* 85–87, *LCL.* Cf. Josephus, *De bel. Iud.* 2.7, *LCL.*
123 R. Mullin, *The Wealth of Christians* (Maryknoll, NY: Orbis, 1983), pp. 37–38.
124 Philo, *De vit. cont.* 1.1; 2.13, 18.
125 One proposed measure was to give a fifth of one's possessions to the poor, and there was a tendency to frown upon larger gifts. Cf. H. Polano, *The Talmud* (London: Frederick Warne, 1978), p. 298.

3/The Roman Economy

The first centuries after the advent of Christianity coincided with the high point of the Roman Empire. Augustus, the first emperor, died in A.D. 14. By then, every shore of the Mediterranean was under Roman rule or control, as was all of Europe west of the Rhine and south of the Danube. Eastward, the empire extended along the southern coast of the Black Sea and inland from Syria and Palestine to the northern reaches of the Euphrates and the edge of the Arabian desert. During the next century and a half, Roman power also reached into Britain in the north, into Armenia, inner Syria and Mesopotamia in the east, and at some points also across the Rhine and the Danube. Thus by the middle of the second century the Roman Empire had achieved its greatest extension. Although after that time decline would set in, the prestige of the empire would last for centuries.

This empire took from its Hellenistic predecessors the notion that human existence at its best is "civilized" existence—that is, quite literally, "citified" existence. The greatest invention of antiquity, from the point of view of both Greeks and Romans, was the city. When Aristotle described humans as "political animals," he did not mean merely, as we would interpret his words today, that humans are by nature involved in politics; he also meant that the essence of the human is best seen in that highest of human creations, the polis.

Agriculture

In spite of such views, the fact remains that the backbone of economic life for the Roman Empire was agriculture. Few technical advances were made; the crops, tools, and techniques remained practically the same. What did change was the ownership of land, the distribution of crops, and the nature of the labor force.[1]

Long before the time of Augustus, as early as the third century B.C., some of these changes had begun to take place, largely as a result of the military and political conquests of the Roman Republic. At the time of those conquests, the Roman legions were composed exclusively of Roman citizens, most of whom were also farmers. The officers, members of the higher orders of senators and equestrians, generally were able to leave their lands in charge of others who managed them during their absence. The rank and file of the army, however, owned small farms of five to eight acres, which they were obliged to leave unattended when they went to battle. Upon returning, many found their lands in such a state that they simply sold or abandoned them and settled in the cities. Since Roman conquests were also flooding the markets with slaves, richer landowners were easily able to buy up these abandoned lands, join them to others, and create larger holdings, which they exploited with slave labor.

We know of the management of these properties through the works of two first-century authors, Columella and Pliny the Elder. Both decry the growth of latifundia and the use of slave labor.[2] Their reasons, however, have to do less with the injustice done to slaves than with the moral and economic decay that this produces in agriculture. Pliny looks back to former times when the land was cultivated by free citizens, and when agricultural labor was a sign of honor.[3] Columella exhorts his readers to be kind to their slaves, so that they in turn will be more productive.[4] Still, by Columella's time it is clear that he is not speaking of the owner of the land doing the physical labor. Land that is not cultivated by slaves will normally be leased out to those who till it. During periods of intensive labor such as the grape harvest, free laborers will be hired. Furthermore, in spite of all the romantic allure that these authors find in the land, Columella takes for granted that a well-managed property will be under the supervision of a manager, probably a trusted slave. This means that the owner will either reside away from the property or will be absent for prolonged periods. Pliny deplores the change in values that this represents, with people preferring the easy life of the city over the hard work of the countryside.

Slave holding in the Roman Empire was concentrated in Italy, where slaves may have made up as much as a quarter of the entire population. This was mostly because the majority of the slaves captured during the early wars of conquest had been brought to Italy. In the provinces, slaves may have comprised a tenth of the total population. After military expansion ceased or slowed down, the main sources for slaves were foreign markets, infants abandoned—"exposed"—by parents who either did not want them or could not afford to raise them, and the poor who had to sell themselves or their children into slavery. Also, as punishment for massive revolts such as those of the Jews in A.D. 66–70 and A.D. 132, thousands of the rebels and their families were deported and sold into slavery.

The lot of slaves varied greatly. Members of the upper classes often employed trusted slaves as managers of their estates. Following the same pattern, some imperial slaves were employed as high-ranking managers and bureaucrats. Many were artisans working in shops side by side with free laborers and under similar conditions. A master could give a slave a *peculium*—an amount of property which the slave could employ and invest freely, but which remained the ultimate property of the *paterfamilias*.[5] In some cases, this was a fairly small amount, allowing the slave to set up a trade. In other cases, the *peculium* was much larger, and under its provisions some slaves in turn owned other slaves. Some slaves were assigned functions requiring special trust, such as the care and education of children or various forms of domestic work.

The institution of the *peculium,* however, should not obscure the harsh realities of slavery. Under old Roman law—the practice began to change around the year 200—slaves were not allowed to marry or have a family, for their procreation was a matter for the master to regulate. On some latifundia a significant part of the labor was performed by chained gangs of slaves. The work in mines and quarries, notoriously harsh and unhealthy, was performed mostly by slaves. If a slave killed a master, all the slaves of the deceased were executed, no matter whether or not they had been present at the time.

On the other hand, except in some areas of North Africa, where there were substantial numbers of black slaves, slavery was not normally connected with race or national origin. The main exception was immediately after a conquest or a bloody revolt, when the market was flooded with slaves from a particular region. Slaves who bought or received their freedom had the status of a freedman or woman, in which they still owed a measure of allegiance to their former masters. This, however, was true for one generation only, for the son of a freedman was a full citizen. (The status of daughters, as was the case of all females, depended on whom they married.)

Some former slaves amassed vast fortunes. A typical, though fictitious, example is Trimalchio, the rich freedman so masterfully described in the *Satyricon*. He is the quintessential parvenu who makes crass ostentation of his wealth and achievements, perhaps in rebellion against and hatred for the unbreachable wall that separates him from his social superiors. If the author of the *Satyricon* is Petronius, as many believe, the contrast is even more striking between Trimalchio and his creator, dubbed "the arbiter of elegance." As described in this satire, Trimalchio may be as rich as Petronius, but the two will never be at the same level.

The reason is evident. The institution of slavery normally tries to justify itself on the basis of the supposed inferiority of the slave. If such

P lautus
× Davby

justification is not based on race, it must be based on a personal defect. In ancient times, it was possible for anyone to become a slave through a bad turn of fortune, such as being defeated and captured in battle. But it was considered indecent to speak of such possibilities in polite company, just as it would have been indecent for Petronius to have described Trimalchio as wise, polished, and temperate, for this would have brought into question the very presuppositions on which slavery stood.[6] The reservations of Columella and Pliny regarding slavery had nothing to do with moral considerations. They were simply asserting that other and better ways might be found to secure agricultural labor. One of the reasons this was true was that by their time, the first century A.D., the empire was changing once more, for it had almost reached its maximum extension. The rapid territorial conquests of earlier times, which had provided large numbers of slaves, many of them skilled agricultural laborers, had almost ceased. The price of slaves thus began to rise. Free citizens were not willing to work the lands of the rich. At the same time, lands were readily available in the provinces. The result was that large-scale agriculture became less profitable in Italy. While medium and small farms subsisted, much land held by the rich was left fallow. Others turned their latifundia into pastures. Land cartage was so expensive that it was cheaper to bring wheat to Rome from Egypt or Sicily than to cart it any great distance within Italy itself. Animals raised on inland pastures, on the other hand, required no cartage, for they could be walked close to market before being slaughtered.

Italy, a land that had originally become rich through its agriculture, now found itself unable to support its own population. Columella complained: "In this Latium, land of Saturn, where the gods taught their own descendants the art of agriculture, we now must hold auctions for the carting of wheat from provinces beyond the sea."[7]

It was not only wheat that the provinces grew. Since wine and oil produced greater revenues than grain—about five times as much for wine as compared to wheat—large vineyards and olive groves supplanted grain fields throughout the newly acquired provinces.[8] Although olive trees took much longer to produce and therefore required a long-term investment, once they were in production they were quite valuable. At one point, at least in Syria, olive groves in production were taxed at a rate almost five times that of vineyards.[9] In some areas, wheat became simply an extra crop that was planted among olive trees. While the trees were small the land could be kept almost in full production. Eventually, wine and oil from the provinces offered stiff competition to similar products from Italy, where labor was more expensive.

An even more serious threat was the shortage of wheat for the army and the cities, both of which, if not properly fed, could be sources of unrest. Several measures were taken in order to promote the production of wheat. In Sicily and Egypt, the main suppliers of wheat for Rome, agricultural production came under increasing government supervision.

In A.D. 92, Domitian issued an edict ordering that half the vineyards in the provinces be destroyed and that no new ones be planted in Italy.[10] Apparently the purpose was to promote grain production. The landed aristocracy raised such an outcry that the emperor rescinded his decree. These events may lie behind the outraged words of Revelation 6:6: "A quart of wheat for a denarius, and three quarts of barley for a denarius; but do not harm oil or wine." From that point on, several emperors tried to promote the production of grain, generally to no avail. Soon a large amount of wheat for the armies in the east was regularly imported from what is now southern Russia. Still, since the needs of the empire took precedence over local requirements, outlying provinces often suffered famine, especially those in Greece, Asia Minor, Syria, and Palestine, where agricultural surplus was either small or nonexistent.

The greatest landowner in the empire was without any doubt the emperor. At first a distinction had been made between what belonged to the emperor as a citizen—his patrimony—and what belonged to the state—the *aerarium* and the *fiscus*. That distinction, however, was progressively blurred and eventually disappeared in all but in theory.[11] The imperial lands included those formerly belonging to conquered kings or to cities whose resistance to Roman advance was punished by confiscation of property.[12] In Egypt the emperor, as the successor of the pharaohs, became the owner of most productive land. Imperial lands also included property confiscated from wealthy foes of the emperor. Although some of this land was sold to other wealthy landowners, and some (usually not the best) was granted to veterans upon retirement, no single landowner's holdings even approached those of the emperor.

Imperial lands were usually managed by *procuratores*, who normally did not supervise agricultural work but rather leased the land, or large portions of it, to *conductores*.[13] These in turn entered into contracts with the actual workers of the land, the *coloni*. Although much debate has centered on the exact meaning of this term, and it is clear that the status of the *coloni* evolved, it appears that these were free men, often the original inhabitants of conquered territories, who were granted the use of the land in exchange for part of the crops and a certain amount of free labor.[14] This allowed the *conductor* to farm a portion of the land under his direct supervision, using the labor of the *coloni*. Apparently, several emperors—Hadrian in particular—tried to protect the *coloni* from excessive exploitation.[15] Still, as time went by the *coloni* became increasingly like slaves. This was possible in part because Roman tradition considered true freedom incompatible with working for hire for another person. Thus from the perspective of that tradition, there was little difference between a *colonus* and a slave, and if one slipped from one category into the other it was no great tragedy.[16]

The large latifundia normally belonged to wealthy aristocratic families of Rome, although somewhat smaller holdings were also in the hands of the wealthy citizens of other cities. These latifundia were sometimes managed directly by their owners. Columella's uncle, who held extensive lands in Spain, was personally involved in the cross-breeding of sheep.[17] On the other hand, we hear of numerous landowners who preferred to live in the cities and who visited the countryside only when the weather was favorable. In such cases, management of the property was turned over to a trusted servant, often a slave, as may be seen in the work of Columella. In the second century, Pliny the Younger, a nephew of the Elder, owned several large properties in Italy, and he entrusted these to a *procurator.*

Finally, especially during the first two centuries of the empire, there were still many small farms in the hands of free peasants, both in Italy and throughout the empire. If these were within reach of a city, their owners could make a decent living by growing vegetables and taking them to market. If not, they struggled to survive until their land, having become more valuable by the opening of new roads or the founding of new cities, was swallowed up by one of the growing latifundia.

Land that was the absolute possession of its owner—*quiritarian* property—was not subject to taxes. Originally, only the *ager romanus*—Roman soil—was thus exempt from taxation. However, during the last century of the republic this privilege was extended to all of Italy—the *ager italicus.* During the early empire, it became customary to grant certain lands and territories the "Italian law"—*jus italicum*—which meant, among other things, that the land was exempt from taxation. Since this privilege was most often granted to land held by the wealthy, it tended to shift the burden of taxes to the smaller landholders and thus to promote the growth of latifundia.

Latifundialization, which was partially counterbalanced by the practice of granting small farms to retiring legionnaires, took centuries. Although by the end of the Republic latifundism was already widespread in Italy, and there was growing concern over it, much land remained in small and medium-sized farms, even in Italy. In the provinces, the process took even longer, and at least until the second half of the second century much land remained in the hands of small farmers. Even then, however, the agricultural crisis did not reside in lack of land, for much of it was fallow. In A.D. 193 Emperor Pertinax issued a decree granting property rights and tax exemption for ten years to any who would occupy and cultivate fallow lands, including imperial lands.[18]

Industry

A second source of wealth in the Roman Empire was industry. Much of this continued, as it had throughout generations, as small-scale industry in which a shop owner, perhaps with the help of his family and a few slaves, produced the goods that he then sold. Many of the shops excavated in Pompeii appear to have been of that order; they combined production, retail, and living quarters.

At the same time, however, industry grew significantly during the first centuries of the empire. This was due both to expanding markets and to the imperial policy of creating new cities and embellishing the old. The expansion of markets provided for specialization and thus for larger workshops, even for what amounts to mass production. Tracing the seals on pottery, scholars have determined that some shops must have employed hundreds of workers, with markets extending over hundreds of miles. In Gaul, a certain Pistillus mass-produced terracotta figurines, and glassmaker Frontinus ran an enterprise that must have employed hundreds of workers as well as a vast network of shops and business representatives. The pots and pans manufactured in Italy by P. Cipius Polybus found their way down the Rhine and as far as Belgium, while the bronze pins made by the Belgian Aucissa moved just as far in the opposite direction.[19] Other industries whose products were less durable, such as the textile industry, probably also attained a similar size and market expansion. It is known, for instance, that Malta produced a particular kind of fabric known as *othonia*, and that this fabric attained wide circulation.

The increasing number and size of cities most contributed to the growth of industry. Indeed, much of the industrial activity of the Roman Empire had to do with construction. As the notion evolved that city life was the highest form of human life, the imperial government favored the founding of new cities, and the municipal governments of older cities took steps to promote public and private works. Throughout the western provinces, stone became the preferred material for construction among the well-to-do, and this in turn produced great activity in the quarries as well as along the roads and waterways that cut stones had to travel in order to reach their destination. Furthermore, not all stone was the same. If one wanted yellow marble, one might go to the quarries of Simittu in North Africa; if red, to Aïn Smara. If green porphyry was required, it could be found in some Greek localities. Egypt, on the other hand, provided red porphyry as well as red granite. And the best source for bluish violet granite was the Felsberg. Large blocks of these and other stones were used for facades and colonnades, while smaller pieces were sought for more colorful mosaics.

While the wealthy sent to distant sources for their building materials, others had to be content with whatever stone was available in the neighborhood. Thus hundreds of other less famous quarries produced various marbles, granites, and limestone and drew multitudes of stonecutters, engineers, and other workers.[20]

Most of these quarries, as well as the mines from which gold, silver, iron, copper, lead, and tin were obtained, belonged to the state. There were exceptions, however, such as the orator Herodes Atticus, who owned the marble quarries on Mt. Pentelikon.[21] Apart from such exceptions, mineral resources were managed as if they were the personal property of the emperor by his *procurator patrimonii*, the manager of his patrimony. Under him, other functionaries took charge of particular mines and quarries or of groups of them. In some cases, the actual extraction of the stone or metal was done directly under the supervision of such imperial functionaries. In others, a mine or a section of a mine was leased to an entrepreneur, who in turn supervised the extraction. In any case, most of the physical work was done by slaves. In mines under direct imperial administration, convicts—some of them Christians who would not deny their faith—were also employed as part of the labor force. Progressively, the coloni, workers who were technically free but who had little personal freedom, supplanted slave labor in the mines, just as they were doing in agriculture.

Trade

Foreign trade was not a source of wealth for the Roman Empire, although it did contribute to the luxury of the upper classes. Most trade beyond the borders of the empire dealt in luxury items. Silk was imported from China, ivory from Africa, and precious woods from Ethiopia and India.[22] Probably the most important foreign trade in necessities was the wheat imported from southern Russia, as well as some iron from Iran. The Roman Empire possessed little that these trading partners wished, and therefore most of these items had to be paid for with precious metals. The main exports to India, besides precious metals, were copper, tin, lead, and wines. These did not suffice to produce a favorable balance of trade.

Trade within the empire accounted for a much larger share of economic activity. At first, most of this trade flowed toward Rome, which was able to pay for the products of the provinces with the taxes and other resources that it had earlier taken from them. Slowly, however, trade began to grow among the provinces. Some of this was restricted in order to favor Rome. Egypt, for instance, was forbidden to export wheat anywhere but Rome. In general, however, the free movement of goods promoted trade among the provinces, and eventually much of it bypassed Rome and Italy. Africa produced wheat, oil, linen, wool, and woods. Egypt exported wheat only to Rome, but it also produced linen, papyrus, fabrics, and glassware. Syria was famous for its woods, wines, and fabrics. Asia Minor produced wine, furs, fabrics, and the famous parchment from Pergamum. Greece, although impoverished, was still famous for its marbles. Gaul sold wine, leather, sausages, and fabrics. Spain produced oil, salted meats, leather, and fabrics. Slaves—some from within the empire and some from beyond its borders—were taken to other provinces from Asia Minor, Syria, Egypt, and Africa.

Trade had become possible because the Roman Empire had built an extensive network of roads. One of these ran from Egypt along the north of Africa. Three others traversed the Pyrenees from Spain into Gaul and then took various routes to the Rhine or across southern Gaul and on to Rome. Roads leading north from Rome crossed all the major passes of the Alps. Some of these led eastward toward the Danube provinces and on to the Balkans. From there it was possible to continue to the strait of Bosporus. Having crossed it, one could travel on through Asia Minor and further east toward the Euphrates and Babylon. Another road led south from Asia Minor along the coast and all the way to Egypt. In addition to these major roads, hundreds of others connected them with each other as well as with cities, rivers, and ports.

These famous roads, however, were not as important as the waterways. Roads were intended primarily for moving armies and their supplies. They also connected areas where water transportation was difficult or impossible. In the East, roads were used by caravans carrying luxury items from the Orient. But by far the vast majority of trade took place through water transport. Indeed, it was much more expensive to carry a heavy load by oxcart for a hundred miles along a mountain road than to transport it by ship from one end of the empire to the other.

Naturally, the most important waterway was the Mediterranean itself.[23] Cleared of pirates by Pompey shortly before the end of the republic, the Mediterranean was a relatively safe means of travel and transportation. Its weather and shores were well known. Sailors preferred to sail within view of the coast and always during daytime. During fall and winter the possibility of bad weather precluded most sailing. A trip from Rome to Alexandria, hugging the coast and sailing only during daylight hours, could easily take six months. Once in Alexandria, the traveler would have to wait another six months for bad weather to pass and for sailing to resume. The return trip would take a further six months. Still, this was the least expensive means for long-distance hauling, especially of bulky or heavy materials such as wheat or lumber.

Where the sea ended, the rivers took over. Not only the Nile, the Rhine, and the Danube, but also lesser rivers such as the Rhone, the Po, and the Seine were major arteries of trade. On the shores of such rivers most new cities were founded. With the advent of the *pax romana*, many cities that formerly had perched for safety on a mountaintop moved to a nearby river. Trade with Britain took place along the fluvial systems of Gaul.

Taxation

Although trade was not restricted, it was subject to a number of taxes known as *portoria*. When an item of trade crossed a provincial border, custom duties had to be paid. These were not inordinately high, ranging from 2 to 5 percent. To these, however, were added similar fees collected by some cities along the way and tolls at bridges and mountain passes. Taxes and tolls plus the added cost of land transportation induced merchants to use the Mediterranean ports whenever possible.

Taxation was always a problem in the Roman Empire, for the ancient notion persisted that freedom was incompatible with direct taxation. In early republican times, when an emergency such as war required it, Roman citizens paid a tax, but payment was restored to them if war booty allowed it. By the first century B.C., the wealth flowing from the provinces was so great that even this tax was no longer collected.[24]

The wealthy showed their support for the state, not by paying taxes, but by making voluntary contributions. Although sometimes such contributions responded to the real needs of the state, most often they were determined by the whims of the givers. People in Rome or other cities would make a gift of a monument or a public building honoring their name. Most often, they would finance lavish banquets or spectacles.[25] This tradition of voluntary contributions to the state, known as "evergetism," became an increasing burden for the emperors. As the first citizen of Rome, the emperor was expected to make more lavish gifts than any other citizen. He was also expected to do likewise for other cities and above all for the army. This in turn required new sources of income for the state.

The need for a permanent army and a growing bureaucracy demanded new means of revenue, and Augustus imposed a number of taxes on transactions involving Roman citizens. He levied a 5 percent tax on inheritances, a sales tax whose ratio varied, and a 4 percent tax on the sale of slaves.

Such taxes, however, did not cover the expenses of the state. By far the largest sources of income were the state properties and monopolies—lands, mines, quarries—and the taxes levied in the provinces. These varied from province to province, but in general they involved both a tax on property (*tributum soli*) and a poll tax (*tributum capitis*). The very name of these taxes indicates how they were understood. They were the reward for victory on the part of the Romans. Conquered lands and conquered people must pay a tribute. Although officials made some effort at uniformity, in most cases the Romans simply continued the system of taxation previously existing in conquered territories, sometimes with adjustment. For instance, in Judea, where the Seleucids had collected a third of all cereal crops, Julius Caesar reduced this rate to a fourth.[26] But people also had to pay whatever other levies the local or municipal government and religious authorities exacted. In Judea, taxes in addition to those on land included the Temple tax of half a shekel that all Jews were to pay annually.[27] As is so often the case with taxes, Rome was always ready to continue collecting taxes even after their original purpose was no longer valid. A prime example of this is Vespasian insisting that, after the destruction of the Temple in Jerusalem, Jews must continue paying the half shekel, although now to Rome.[28]

During the republic and the early years of the empire, most of these taxes were collected by tax farmers known as "publicans."[29] Since substantial capital was required, most publican entrepreneurs were rich members of the equestrian class, who often joined in veritable holding companies. They contracted with the government to raise the taxes of a particular area and to collect a fee for this service. This fee, however, was only part of their profit. Since many agricultural taxes were collected in kind, publicans made large profits by reselling the goods collected or by hoarding them until prices rose.[30] They also served the central government as its financial agents in the provinces, employing the goods and funds that they held in order to cover such expenses as salaries and supplies for the legions. Since all this was done by means of paper transactions, it saved much of the costly and dangerous transport of goods and money.

Little government bureaucracy was in place, and therefore publicans also served as government agents in managing public works and providing some postal service. Naturally, for this also they charged a fee. When a farmer could not pay his taxes, publicans would often lend him money at annual rates that varied from 12 to 48 percent. Such loans grew rapidly as interest and new tax liabilities accumulated, and eventually the land was confiscated by the publicans. Beyond these various legal means of profit, some publicans would also take advantage of the ignorance and powerlessness of taxpayers, assessing them more than they should or undervaluing their contributions. Thus the negative image of publicans found in the Gospels was probably shared by much of the populace of the Roman provinces.

In republican times, the Senate passed a number of laws trying to prevent the abuses of tax collectors. Yet such laws had limited effect, since the government depended on the publicans for much of its income and since the publicans in many provinces shared their profits with governors and other high officials.

Augustus and the early emperors took steps to regularize the collection of taxes. In Egypt, which he acquired as an imperial province, Augustus appointed government agents to scrutinize the work of tax farmers. In other areas, he began creating a bureaucracy under government supervision to levy most direct taxes. In Asia, this resulted in an effective tax reduction of one third, without affecting the government's income. As the government's ability to collect its own taxes grew, the role of tax farmers diminished to the point that they disappeared from every province except North Africa.[31] Augustus began this process under his direct supervision with very little personnel, but fifty years later Claudius established an office to manage the finances of the state, and by the second half of the second century there was a government bureaucracy, with workers ranked in grades much like our contemporary

civil service.[32] From that point on, the bureaucracy never stopped growing, often because the corruption of the bureaucrats themselves required more bureaucrats to control them. It is estimated that between
the time of Caracalla and the fifth century, the bureaucracy increased a
hundredfold, reaching the level of thirty to thirty-five thousand employ-
ees.[33]

The government, in order to know the resources it could tax, needed records of population, livestock, and land holdings. Thus it took a
periodic census, at first every five years, and then every fifteen. Julius
Caesar began a vast project of measuring, assessing, and registering all
real estate and other assets, a process that took twenty-five years to
complete and then had to be revised constantly. It included all land
classified according to its use (pasture, woods, vineyards, cereal crops)
as well as all buildings in the country and in the cities (including the
value of their furniture), slaves, holdings in cash, and all other assets.
Taxpayers were responsible for declaring and assessing the value of
their holdings, although naturally under the supervision of government
agents.

In spite of these elaborate measures, the Roman Empire never had
a budget. The early empire customarily kept several separate treasuries,
according to the various sources of revenue and the purpose for which
funds were to be expended. To the *aerarium*, in which the Senate kept
and managed the receipts from the senatorial provinces,[34] Augustus
added the *aerarium militare*, for the army. The term *fiscus*—literally "bas-
ket"—was employed for a number of separate funds under government
administration. During the first century, there were separate *fisci* for the
provinces as well as for items such as the Jewish poll tax.[35] The emper-
or's personal *patrimonium* was kept in a different *fiscus*. Progressively,
however, the *fisci* tended to become confused, until even the emperor's
personal patrimony was considered part of the *fiscus*, and he in turn had
absolute control of the state's wealth as if it were his own.

A View from Above

What was life like in that vast empire? Who profited from the existing order, and who suffered under it? Was there need or abundance?
How were goods and power distributed? Who supported the machinery
of state? How much social mobility was possible?

In asking such questions conflicting reports begin to appear. On
the one hand, some lead us to believe that this was a golden age in
human history, an age of abundance in which most material needs were
met and in which even the subject peoples praised and loved their rulers. Indeed, long after the end of that empire the most famous historian

of its demise, Edward Gibbon, penned words of enthusiastic praise for the Roman Empire as it existed in the middle of the second century:

If a man were called to fix the period in the history of the world, during which the condition of the human race was most happy and prosperous, he would, without hesitation, name that which elapsed from the death of Domitian to the accession of Commodus. The vast extent of the Roman empire was governed by absolute power, under the guidance of virtue and wisdom. The armies were restrained by the firm but gentle hand of four successive emperors, whose characters and authority commanded involuntary respect. The forms of the civil administration were carefully preserved by Nerva, Trajan, Hadrian, and the Antonines, who delighted in the image of liberty, and were pleased with considering themselves as the accountable ministers of the laws.[36]

Many who lived at the time shared this positive picture of Rome and its rule. The person who expressed it most eloquently was Aelius Aristides in his *Oration to the Romans*. Aristides was in his midtwenties and already well on the way to fame when he delivered this oration. The occasion was a solemn one, for Rome was celebrating its 896th birthday. The place was probably the Athenaeum built by Emperor Hadrian, by then deceased.[37] Present were rich and powerful people, such as the speaker's former teachers Alexander of Cotyaeum and Herodes Atticus. Alexander carried an influential role in the emperor's household. We have already met Herodes Atticus as the wealthy owner of the marble quarries on Mt. Pentelikon. This particular year he held the exalted title of *consul ordinarius*. Who else was present, it is impossible to tell, but probably even Emperor Antoninus Pius himself. In any case, during this time the select company of cultured elites enjoyed their favorite pastime of listening to speeches, and they heaped honors and fees upon orators.

The speaker, who hailed from Smyrna, did not intend to tell his audience anything they did not already know. Entertainment and not instruction was the primary function of rhetoric by this time. Audiences expected their stars to imitate and revive the style of the famous Greek orators who had lived five or six centuries earlier. Orators spoke in Greek—even then the language of learning in Rome—and followed complex literary rules of which the audience was well aware but which baffle modern scholars.

Aristides began, as was the custom, with a preface expressing both his devotion to the gods and his humility. The task of exalting Rome, he declared, was far beyond the ability of words:

Praise of your city all men sing and will continue to sing. Yet their words accomplish less than if they had never been spoken. Their silence would not have magnified or diminished her in the least, nor changed your knowledge of her. But their encomiums accomplish quite the opposite of what they intend, for their words do not show precisely what is truly admirable. For it is she {Rome} who first proved that oratory cannot reach every goal. About her not only is it impossible to speak properly, but it is impossible to see her properly.[38]

To Rome all the goods of the world flow, as rivers to the sea, for "around it lie the great continents greatly sloping, ever offering to you in full measure something of their own."[39] From the land of the Greeks, from Arabia, India, and the farthest corners of the earth, all goods flow to Rome, "and all meet here, trade, shipping, agriculture, metallurgy, all the arts and crafts that are or ever have been, all the things that are engendered or grow from the earth. And whatever one does not see here neither did nor does exist."[40]

He then embarked on a discussion of the great powers that preceded Rome and why they were not able to produce the abundance and universal happiness with which he credited Rome. Persia's tyranny meant that people were afraid to prosper lest they draw the attention of the tyrant. "A child's beauty was a terror to its parents, a wife's beauty a terror to her husband. Not he who committed the most crimes but he who acquired the most property was doomed to destruction."[41] Alexander fared no better, for he was a conqueror rather than a ruler, "one who acquired a kingdom {rather} than one who showed himself a king."[42]

By contrast, in the Roman Empire a different order rules. Aristides expressed his awe at the vastness of the empire: "The Red Sea and the Cataracts of the Nile and Lake Maeotis, which formerly were said to lie on the boundaries of the earth, are like the courtyard walls to the house which is this city of yours."[43] Yet, what he most admired was the order existing within these vast holdings, for "your empire is much greater for its perfection than for the area which its boundaries encircle."[44]

Aristides saw a great difference between this empire and the earlier ones. Here the governed were not enslaved, "for of all who have ever gained empire you alone rule over men who are free."[45] Freedom had been made possible through the great order that existed in the empire so that governors, knowing that they in turn were governed by others, did not dare exploit their provinces as the Persian satraps did. Order resulted in a golden age of justice:

There is an abundant and beautiful equality of the humble with the great and of the obscure with the illustrious, and, above all, of the poor man with the rich and of the commoner with the noble. . . . {The emperor} as the justice of the claim may lead, like a breeze in the sails of a ship, favoring and accompanying, not the rich man more, the poor man less, but benefiting equally whomsoever it meets.[46]

Furthermore, this golden age benefits not only those who are of Roman stock but all humanity, for Roman citizenship is available to any who are worthy of it:

You have everywhere appointed to your citizenship, or even to kinship with you, the better part of the world's talent, courage, and leadership, while the rest you recognized as a league under your hegemony. . . . And as the sea, which receives from its gulfs all the many rivers, hides them and holds them all and still, with what goes in and out, is and seems ever the same, so actually this city receives those who flow in from all the earth and has even sameness in common with the sea.[47]

Thus the wonder of Roman citizenship is not that it is so highly valued; it is rather that it is so liberally shared. As a result, every city holds Roman citizens, the rich as well as the poor are served by this beneficent system,[48] and unprecedented prosperity reigns throughout the empire:

The coasts and interiors have been filled with cities, some newly founded, others increased under and by you. . . . All localities are full of gymnasia, fountains, monumental approaches, temples, workshops, schools, and one can say that the civilized world, which had been sick from the beginning, as it were, has been brought by the right knowledge to a state of health. . . . Thus like an ever-burning sacred fire the celebration never ends, but moves around from time to time and people to people, always somewhere, a demonstration justified by the way all men have fared. Thus it is right to pity those outside your hegemony, if indeed there are any, because they lose such blessings.[49]

We have no record of the audience's response, except that the *Oration* was preserved for posterity and its author enjoyed great popularity and prestige. In any case, the speech told Romans nothing they did not know—or believe—before, since it was nothing but an elegant exposition of the ideology by which the Roman Empire lived.

A Different View

Aristides apparently expressed the views of many of his contemporaries. We know from his own writings that he was a hypochondriac, but we have no indication that he was a sycophant. He truly admired the Roman system of government, and his words, flamboyant as they may seem to us late in the twentieth century, were eminently sincere. Indeed, he had the good fortune to live at the high point of the history of the Roman Empire, economically as well as politically. Still, he had correctly declared that Rome was so complex that "who could survey her adequately? And from what point of observation?"[50] Needless to say, he surveyed Rome from the point of observation of the elite who profited from Roman rule, the "better part of the world's talent," as he put it, that Rome had welcomed into its citizenship. Likewise, Gibbon's sources represented a similar point of view. Most of the literature from the time of the empire to which he had access was written from the perspective of those who, like Aristides, had every reason to be grateful for the bounty and the security of Rome. The only exceptions were a number of pieces, often religious in nature, that could be discounted as coming from radical Christians and other disgruntled groups.

Closer scrutiny, however, reveals the incompleteness of Aristides' descriptions and of Gibbon's evaluation of life in the Roman Empire, even at its high point in the middle of the second century. In relatively recent times, much material has come to light that presents a different picture of life under Roman rule. Much of this material originated in Egypt, where climactic conditions made possible the survival of thousands of papyri and ostraca (potsherds used in place of paper). Many of these fragments are tax records, receipts, accounts, and other notes illustrating the life of the lower classes in rural Egypt. As a student of this material has declared, "Such a 'view from below' is a treat that no other part of the Greek or Roman world can offer us."[51]

From these sources we know that the picture of Roman rule that Aelius Aristides drew, and Gibbon accepted, was far from the entire truth. Egyptian society was rigidly stratified along ethnic and social lines; if there was some mobility at its higher levels, there was none at the bottom.

The higher echelons of the social structure in Egypt—as throughout the empire—were occupied by Roman citizens. At the very summit were wealthy Italians who had moved to Egypt for governmental or private reasons and had remained in the area. At a similar level stood members of the old aristocracy under the Ptolomeys—mostly people of Greek descent and culture—who had been granted Roman citizenship.

Apparently, most Roman citizens in Egypt were either soldiers or veterans and their descendants. Since Rome enrolled only Roman citizens in its legions, the members of the two legions normally stationed in Egypt were already Roman citizens. As such, and as soldiers in what was in fact an army of occupation, they enjoyed a number of privileges. When they retired, after twenty-five years of service, many of them remained in Egypt, where they often acquired land. Such veterans did not normally become part of the high aristocracy, but they were fabulously rich by the standards of many of the villages where they owned land.

Auxiliary troops also lived in Egypt, in addition to the two legions normally stationed there. The rank and file of these troops were not Roman citizens but received such citizenship upon their retirement, after twenty-six years of service. Soldiers often came from a region of the empire other than that in which they served. Although they were not allowed to marry, by the time they retired, after long years of service, they had acquired common-law families, and therefore many remained in the land where they had served their last years. Thus there lived in Egypt—as in other provinces of the empire—many Roman citizens, veterans of auxiliary troops, who where natives of other provinces. All these Roman citizens, quite apart from their wealth or lack of it, enjoyed a number of privileges, among them exemption from the poll tax levied on the lower echelons of the population.

Next in status after the Romans were the Greeks. Again, most of these had never seen Greece but descended from those who had come to the country with Alexander's troops or later under the Ptolomeys. Most of them lived in the three Greek-style cities of Naucratis (dating from pharaonic times), Alexandria, and Ptolemais. Later, in A.D. 130, Hadrian founded a fourth such city, Antinoopolis, named after a friend who died at its site. Those who held citizenship in one of these urban centers enjoyed exemption from the poll tax as well as other preferential treatment. For instance, it appears that ownership of certain lands was a privilege limited to them and to Roman citizens. Many of these Greeks possessed great wealth, owning commercial enterprises as well as vast extensions of land both within the municipal boundaries and far beyond. Roman citizenship could be granted to the higher ranks of the Greek aristocracy, while poorer Greeks could achieve it by enrolling in the army, especially since, given the need to attract more recruits, it became customary to open the legions to the sons of the provincial aristocracy, who were then granted citizenship immediately upon enrolling.

In Egypt also lived a large number of Jews. Their number and status are not altogether clear. Some evidently were quite wealthy. Yet, to what degree wealth resulted in higher social or legal status is open to debate. In any case, bitter enmity ruled between Greeks and Jews in Egypt. Roughly at the same time as the advent of Christianity, a massacre of Jews took place in Alexandria. Slightly later, Emperor Claudius called on both sides to preserve the peace. The Jewish unrest, manifested during the first century throughout the empire and resulting in the destruction of the Temple in A.D. 70, was also reflected in uprisings in Egypt. A final Jewish rebellion took place in A.D. 115. This time the uprising lasted two years, after which the Jews were heavily crushed and lost most of their former privileges. During those two years, the rebellion spread throughout most of Egypt, taking the form of guerilla warfare—an indication that the Jewish population in the province was quite large and that it was not limited to Alexandria and other major cities.

The lowest echelons of the social scale in Egypt belonged to the "Egyptians," a category that comprised the descendants of the ancient Egyptians as well as any others who were technically free but who had no other citizenship. The peasants who tilled the land, the unemployed urban poor, and those—apart from slaves—who performed the lowest paid tasks all were "Egyptians." They had to pay the poll tax from which Romans and Greeks were exempt. On Egyptians also fell the heaviest burden of most other taxes. Therefore, in spite of some imperial efforts to assure that taxes were levied fairly, the tax burden of many peasants was so great that they simply fled from their homes, abandoning their land. Egyptian peasants also bore the brunt of performing various tasks for the state, a burden that became unbearable. Often a large number of the male inhabitants of a village would be transported *en masse* to work on imperial lands elsewhere. These would all be Egyptians, peasants whose poverty became greater because they could no longer till their lands.

Mobility from one of these groups to another was almost impossible, except that, as noted above, in a number of ways the local aristocracy could obtain Roman citizenship. Greeks could not inherit from Romans nor vice versa. If two people of different status married, their children belonged to the lower status. Egyptians who declared that their deceased father was a Roman were punished with confiscation of a fourth of their property, and those who enrolled their children as citizens in a Greek city were fined an amount equal to a sixth of their property. Likewise, soldiers who called themselves Roman citizens before they were such forfeited a quarter of their property.[52]

A comparison of data on food prices and wages in Roman Egypt shows that, while agricultural wages remained fairly constant from the first to the second century, the price of wheat almost doubled. At the time when Aristides delivered his *Oration* in Rome, the lowest paid agricultural workers in Egypt—not counting children, whose wages were even lower—earned 2 oboli a day. When prices were low, this could buy approximately 2.5 liters of unhulled wheat, but at high prices, it would buy seven-tenths of a liter, hardly enough to make a small loaf. Many laborers were able to survive only because they received supplements of food while working.

Low wages, however, were only one of the many burdens of the Egyptian lower classes. All male peasants between the ages of fourteen and sixty had to pay an annual poll tax that varied from 16 to 40 drachmas a year and a dike tax of 6.6 drachmas. For an agricultural laborer making 2 oboli a day (at 6 oboli per drachma) this meant the equivalent of 67 to 140 days of work. Meanwhile, the poll tax was considerably lower for the urban descendants of Greek colonists and nonexistent for the Romans.

Native Egyptians rarely owned land. When certain public lands were put up for sale, only Roman citizens and urban Greeks were allowed to purchase them. Much of the land owned by Romans and urban Greeks was free of taxes. Normally, a peasant or farmer who raised wheat had to pay a tax in kind, varying according to the nature of the land from two and a half to five bushels per acre. This tax was not considered paid until the farmer had made arrangements for its transportation from the government depository to a river port. Additional taxes on the land had to be paid in cash, as well as a head tax on domestic animals.

Given such circumstances, many Egyptians simply abandoned their land. Some moved to the cities and joined the amorphous mass of unemployed poor. Others turned to brigandage, while many simply fled to the wilderness, where they could scratch a living from the land.[53]

In spite of government efforts to keep the peasants on the land, much productive land lay fallow. The surviving records of the village of Philadelphia, which was apparently typical of the region, indicate that by the time of Nero's reign more than one out of every ten men in the area had resorted to flight. A century later two of the hamlets in the village's jurisdiction had lost all their male inhabitants. [54]

Since Rome depended on Egypt for a third of its wheat consumption, abandoning the land could not be tolerated. The only solution the authorities could find was to distribute the responsibility for working the land among those who still remained in the neighborhood. This in turn led to more flights, thus creating a vicious circle that could be broken only by ever harsher laws tying the peasant to the land.

Repeatedly these measures led to resistance, massive flights, and open rebellion. Although detailed records are not extant, texts indicate that dozens of local revolts had to be suffocated by the army. A serious riot among the Egyptians in Alexandria, in A.D. 122, may have prompted some of the relatively minor reforms attempted by Hadrian.[55] In A.D. 152— barely nine years after Aristides' glowing account of the happy state of the world—a rebellion broke out that the authorities could not quell in over a year. Similar events were repeated twenty years later and from then on throughout most of the history of Roman Egypt.

One could argue that the case of Egypt is unique, since when the Romans took it from the last descendants of the Ptolemeys they simply continued the old system that had existed under the pharaohs. That is true to a certain extent. It is also true, however, that Egypt is unique in the amount of material that has been preserved illustrating the life of the lower classes. What little information is available from other provinces generally indicates that native peasants there fared little better than their counterparts in Egypt.

As Aristides acknowledged in his speech, in the various areas they conquered the Romans recognized and drew to themselves "the better part of the world's talent, courage, and leadership." What this meant was that Romans accepted the existing elites—naturally, only as long as they supported Roman rule—and generally granted them the continuation of most of their privileges. The Roman understanding that human life at its best is city life led to a view of the empire as a conglomeration of cities, each with its surrounding territories. Each of these cities had its own municipal senate, whose members, the *decurions*, were the local aristocracy. During the early empire, before the crisis of the third century, the decurions were able to shift most of the tax burden in their municipalities to the lower classes. Thus the lot of peasants and of the urban poor throughout the provinces of the empire was quite similar to their lot in Egypt.

Just as the social and economic strata of Egypt reflected the waves of conquest, first Greek and then Roman, so did the social and economic structures in other provinces. In North Africa, Julius Caesar and Augustus promoted their project of repopulating Carthage with Roman citizens. As the city grew and its hinterlands opened to trade with the rest of the empire, a social hierarchy developed in which wealthy Roman families, owners of vast latifundia, occupied the higher ranks. Below them were other Roman citizens, the descendants of the impoverished Romans whom Caesar and Augustus sent to Carthage, bureaucrats, active or retired legionnaires, and retired auxiliaries. Then came the Punics—the ancient Carthaginians—who had become Romanized. At the bottom was the mass of Berbers whose lands had been occupied as commercial agriculture became more and more profitable and the empire expanded into Numidia and Mauritania.

This process and its results have been summarized by social historian Rostovtzeff as follows:

The process was everywhere the same. The tribes were not exterminated or driven out of the country. . . . They were first of all fixed in their original homes or transferred to other parts. A certain amount of land was assigned to them, and the rest was given either to a city inhabited by Roman immigrants (veterans and civilians) and by the native aristocracy, or transformed into estates, which were sold to wealthy members of the imperial aristocracy or reserved . . . for the emperor and members of the imperial family. As the amount of land assigned to the tribes was not large enough to support the growing population, numbers of the tribesmen were forced either to rent land from foreign or native landowners or to work on their estates as hired labourers.[56]

As in Egypt, the lower classes who tilled the land had practically no social mobility. Although there were exceptions,[57] most of those born to the land remained tillers of the land. The social and economic distance among the classes was also increased by the cultural gap between city and countryside. While in Carthage the more educated spoke Greek as well as Latin, and Latin was the language of government and trade throughout North Africa, the ancient languages remained in the countryside. Its inhabitants were considered inferior by the more sophisticated urban population.

Continuing around the Mediterranean on a clockwise tour, crossing from North Africa into Spain, we find that throughout most of the West the Roman Empire took a similar shape. Ancient cities were refurbished and new ones founded as part of the process of civilizing—that is, citifying—the provinces. These policies achieved greatest success in southern Spain and Gaul, where some cities attained great splendor. Each of these cities held an aristocracy composed of Romans and of a Romanized native elite, followed by others of lesser means who did enjoy local citizenship. In the northern reaches of Spain, Gaul, Britain, and Germania, the process of urbanization and Romanization did not advance as rapidly. In all of these areas, however, and as far east as Pannonia—now part of Hungary and Yugoslavia—Rome created as many munici-palities as possible. Thus control of a significant part of the land was wrested from the hands of the native inhabitants, many of whom were classified as *peregrini*—sojourners, noncitizens—in their own ancestral lands.[58]

Even in the most prosperous times of the Roman Empire, Greece remained an impoverished country. Its commercial and political hege-mony in the eastern Mediterranean was long past, and it could no longer profit from its former control of trade. Greek land, which had never been exceptionally fertile, was tired and in some areas depleted by ero-sion. Other provinces could produce wine and oil at lower prices. Much of Greece's former population was now scattered over the Roman Em-pire and far beyond toward the East. Therefore, except in cities such as Corinth and Athens, economic activity in Greece was limited. This tend-ed to discourage the growth of the latifundia so common to other parts of the empire, and it is significant that we hear fewer echoes of penury, misery, and unrest among the lower classes in Greece than from other supposedly richer areas.

Rome's municipal regime touched Asia Minor also, so that extensive lands belonged to ancient cities with a number of satellite towns. The cities held a highly Hellenized aristocracy, which often possessed both Roman and municipal citizenship. It was to this class that Aelius Aris-tides belonged, and the views that he expressed in his famous *Oration* were those of this particular class, which had every reason to praise Roman rule. A few of the more distinguished inhabitants of the satellite towns were granted the privileges of municipal citizenship. But in the villages and hamlets where the peasants lived, Greco-Roman culture had hardly penetrated. Even in the cities, which presented a veneer of cos-mopolitan civilization, ancestral languages and cultures persisted among the lower classes.[59]

Similar conditions existed in Syria and the neighboring provinces. The great city of Antioch, the third largest in the empire, gave an impression of far-reaching Hellenization, but the countryside retained much of its ancient culture and social structure. Edessa, for instance, had changed little from its older days when it was the seat of a local king. Even under Roman rule, these kings enjoyed much of their ancient power, as well as the quasi-divine veneration of their peasant subjects. Much of the land belonged to the kings, and they served as intermedi-aries between their subjects and the empire. Over many of these ancient kingdoms and principalities the Romans placed their own creatures, who ruled both in their name and in the name of ancient traditions. Thus a social stratification existed similar to that found in other parts of the empire: Romans at the top, followed by the local aristocracy, then by Greeks, Jews, and others whose occupation was mostly trade, by small artisans and shop owners, and finally by the peasantry who tilled the land.

The case of Judea, well known by reason of its connections with Jewish and Christian history, was typical. Even before Pompey the Great added it to the territories under Roman control, Judea had been the theater of a bitter struggle between traditional Judaism and foreign, Hellenizing influences. In that struggle, religious and theological issues mingled with economic and social ones. By and large, the higher classes profited under the Hellenistic regime whose capital was in Antioch, while the lower classes called for a restoration of the Jewish state—and temporarily won the day with the establishment of the Hasmonean dynasty.

With the advent of Rome, the struggle continued. Herod the Great was made king of Judea by the Roman Senate in an effort to bring calm to a province beset by constant revolt. He tried to claim some connection with the beloved Hasmonean dynasty by marrying into it. What historians of Judea call his "passion for building" was nothing more than a common trait of Roman rule. Following Roman policy, he rebuilt the city of Samaria, which he renamed Sebaste—a Greek translation of *Augusta*—and on the coast he founded a new city called Caesarea, also in honor of Augustus. In other cities he erected public buildings after the Greek and Roman fashion. In Jerusalem he rebuilt the Temple. To all these cities he brought Roman and Hellenistic inhabitants, many of whom enjoyed privileged positions. The gate of the Temple in Jerusalem he crowned with a Roman eagle, an act that won him increased hatred from many of his subjects, but that was part of his policy of bringing his kingdom under the aegis of what to many was "civilization."

Rome's policies resulted in a social structure much like that of other provinces. The real rulers were the Romans. Below them were local rulers and aristocrats. Some local rulers won their high positions from Rome, as had Herod. Others represented the traditional Jewish elites and were allowed to retain their status as long as they collaborated with Roman rule. This group included much of the priesthood connected with the Temple, especially the party of the Sadducees. Others did not profit directly from the existing order but felt that, given the circumstances, the best course was to steer clear of any confrontation with that order. This position, generally supported by the Pharisees, probably typified small farmers and craftsmen.

At the lowest levels of the social scale resided the masses, mostly rural but also urban. These peasants had to pay heavy taxes both to Rome and to the Temple and its hierarchy. While civil rulers spoke Latin, urban educated people spoke Greek, and Hebrew was used in the Temple ceremonies and in scholarly religious discussions, many in the lower classes spoke Aramaic, as attested by the widespread use of Targums in Palestine.

Among these masses the spirit of revolt seethed. Peasants surviving at the edge of subsistence, when hit by a poor crop or by tax bills they were unable to pay, fled to the hills to join the ranks of the Zealots, just as Egyptian peasants under similar circumstances fled to the desert. Brigands or patriots, according to who classified them, these fugitives gave the Roman authorities no peace. Others who remained in their villages often felt sympathy for them and readily revolted when an incident or a new regulation broke their restraint. Still others, despairing of this world, withdrew into communities such as Qumram, where the Dead Sea Scrolls were found.

Roman authorities remained vigilant against sedition and rebellion. Apparently they realized that religion played an important role in the reputed intractability of the Jews, and therefore the most sensitive of them refrained from vaunting their idols before their Jewish subjects. For similar reasons, the procurators normally resided in Caesarea rather than in Jerusalem. On the other hand, some quartered their legions in Jerusalem itself and plundered the treasures of the Temple. As a result of such actions, but also of the underlying social structure, riots and revolts were frequent.

Several Jewish revolts took place in the first century, even before the great rebellion of A.D. 66–70. We hear of some of these in the words of Gamaliel before the Sanhedrin: "Before these days Theudas arose, giving himself to be somebody, and a number of men, about four hundred, joined him; but he was slain and all who followed him were dispersed and came to nothing. After him Judas the Galilean arose in the days of the census and drew away some people after him; he also perished, and all who followed him were scattered."[60]

This passage is significant not only because it attests to these revolts. It also depicts a wise and respected Jewish leader of the time interpreting the preaching of the early Christians from the perspective of those earlier events. "So in the present case . . . ," Gamaliel continues his speech. Naturally, these could be words that the author of Acts is putting in Gamaliel's mouth, but at least they indicate that early Christians felt that their movement was seen in this context.

If Jews were aware of such revolts and tended to interpret Christianity in terms of them, it is not surprising that the Romans did likewise. During the trial of Jesus, as told in the Gospels, Pilate's foremost concern about Jesus is expressed in his question "Are you the King of the Jews?" Later, it is as a pretended king of the Jews that the soldiers mock him by giving him a crown and a scepter.

Given that situation, it is not surprising that the Gospels also indicate that at least some of those who heard and witnessed the teachings of Jesus were afraid that they might be charged with sedition. In the story of the passion, the chief priests and other religious leaders try to disengage themselves from any notion that they supported this sedition by joining those who mock his claim to be the king of Israel. Furthermore, it is significant that when the Gospel of John was written, clearly after the great rebellion of A.D. 70, people still had a sense that these issues played an important role in the events surrounding the life of Jesus. In that Gospel we are told that, after the raising of Lazarus from the dead, the chief priests and the Pharisees commented, "If we let him go on thus, every one will believe in him, and the Romans will come and destroy both our holy place and our nation." [61]

The Crisis of the Third Century

Aelius Aristides delivered his *Oration* at what was probably the highest moment in the history of the Roman Empire. This was the time in which, as Gibbon would later say, "the condition of the human race was most happy and prosperous." And yet, throughout its history and even at the time of Aristides, the empire had been beset by tensions that led to frequent revolts; besides the ones already mentioned, others took place in every area of the empire. While the empire was in good health, and able to contain its enemies both within and without, these revolts could be treated as local or provincial uprisings that the state could overcome by bringing to bear its vast resources. Thus were the Jewish and Egyptian revolts crushed. However, shortly after Aristides' time other concerns—especially foreign enemies and invasions—also demanded attention, and at that point rebellion and dissension come to threaten the very life of the empire. This was one of the underlying causes for the great crisis of the third century, which in truth began in the second.

The crisis sprang from yet another major source. The Roman Empire had always maintained the fiction that it was a continuation of the ancient republic. In theory, government was still in the hands of the Roman Senate and people. Theory turned to fiction during the civil wars of the first century B.C. and during the wars for the succession of Julius Caesar. When Augustus emerged as sole master of the empire, he claimed that his power came from the Senate, when in fact it came from the army. It was not as *princeps* of the Senate, but rather as *imperator*—general—of the army that Augustus held power. The Senate agreed, and for generations the fiction was kept. But the truth was otherwise.

In general, the armies of the first century were still strongly committed to Rome and to the well-being of the state. They obeyed the mandates, not only of the emperors, but also of the Senate, whom they still respected as holding the authority of the Roman people. The events of A.D. 69, the "year of the four emperors,"[62] were a sign of things to come. At that time, in the confusion following the fall of Nero, armies in various areas of the empire chose their own emperors and the Senate readily confirmed their choices. When the dust settled and Vespasian emerged as sole master of the empire, a serious precedent had been established, in that the final choice had depended almost entirely on the legions and the Senate had played only a minor role. Still, it must be remembered that at this time the legions were composed exclusively of Roman citizens, men proud of their heritage. In their view, they were privileged, not because they were soldiers, but because they were Roman citizens.

This began to change as more and more Roman citizens of ancient stock decided to avoid military service in order to enjoy the privileges of their citizenship and their wealth. There are also indications that population was decreasing in Italy, particularly among the more traditional—and richer—families, who wished to concentrate their inheritance on fewer heirs. Thus, it became increasingly necessary to extend Roman citizenship to greater numbers of people in order to have a sufficient pool from which to draw the legionnaires. Eventually, the fiction that only Roman citizens could be legionaires was maintained by granting citizenship to recruits at the time of their enlistment. In A.D. 212 Caracalla extended citizenship to virtually all free inhabitants of the empire. For the legions, this process meant that they now tended to draw their identity and pride, not from their Roman citizenship, which was becoming increasingly common, but from the military profession. What they most valued was not Roman tradition and the state that stood for it, but their own military accomplishments, and the generals who led them in such ventures. Legions with such a self-understanding stood always ready to take matters into their own hands, to proclaim their own generals as emperors, and to resolve political disputes by military might and civil war.

A further cause of unrest was the end of Roman expansion. Conquests of new provinces had brought additional wealth. This new wealth, enjoyed primarily by the higher classes of society, created the illusion that the Roman system of government made its subjects wealthier. Indeed, shortly after Italy had been conquered by Rome, the wealth of Gaul had begun to flow into Italy. Then Gaul and Spain in turn had profited from the wealth of other newly conquered provinces. The process, however, could not continue *ad infinitum*. Once it stopped, because the empire had extended its boundaries to its furthest possible limits, decline was bound to set in precisely in those areas that had most profited from the earlier expansion—Italy foremost, but also southern Gaul and Spain, as well as the many cities that the empire had built and embellished. Thus to a degree the crisis was caused by a previous economic expansion based not on improved means of production and distribution but primarily on an expansionist policy. Once that policy reached its limits, the weaknesses of the economic system began to show.

The combination of these new circumstances with the new sort of army could be destructive. Soldiers who served in the legions for a quarter of a century expected to be able to retire to a life of leisure, as others had done before them. By the end of the second century, this was becoming more and more difficult, producing dissatisfaction among the legions, where the new conditions were understood in terms of a failure in leadership.

The emperor of the happy state that Aelius Aristides described in his *Oration* was Antoninus Pius. He died in A.D. 161. Under his adoptive son and successor Marcus Aurelius the troubles of the empire first became evident. While a significant part of the army lodged on the eastern frontier, several large bodies of Germanic "barbarians" crossed the Danube and invaded the empire. One column invaded the Balkans and laid waste to the peninsula almost as far south as Athens. Another was even bolder, crossing the Alps and invading Italy itself. Collapse was averted because the victorious legions returned from the east barely on time. Even so, it took a long and costly campaign to regain control of the territory and to push most of the invaders once again to their traditional lands beyond the Danube. In order to achieve this, Marcus Aurelius resorted to two policies that would accelerate in ensuing years: first, he was forced to devote more of the financial resources of the empire to its defense; second, he authorized large-scale resettlement of Germans within the borders of the empire. Both of these measures had precedents since the time of Augustus, but with Marcus Aurelius they gained added impetus.

Commodus, the son and heir of Marcus Aurelius, was assassinated in 192, and there ensued a long period of political disorder and civil wars. His successor, Pertinax, was also killed after a reign of three months, and the next emperor, Didius Julianus, after nine weeks. In 197, Septimius Severus finally managed to gain sole and undisputed possession of the throne. By then, the Senate had been decimated, and it was clear that whoever controlled the army would rule the state. Severus obviously knew this. He enlarged the army from thirty legions to thirty-three and added to them large contingents of auxiliaries. He raised the pay of the legions, promoted more of their officers from the ranks of professional soldiers rather than the traditional aristocracy, and stationed a legion in the vicinity of Rome—a move without precedent, for until that time no legion had been stationed in Italy. Since all of this required tax increases, and since the burden of taxation continued falling on the lower and middle classes, those classes, including free landholders, continued to erode.

These policies continued under the successors of Septimus Severus. His son Caracalla granted Roman citizenship to practically all the free inhabitants of the empire. Citizenship was thus no longer a great honor and distinction, and the legions were now open to any who met the necessary physical qualifications. An empire that had been able to enrich its citizens by means of conquest, having reached the limits of conquest, was now forced to defray the expense its own defense. The army, which

in earlier years had more than paid for itself with the booty of conquered lands, now became a drain on a society that had done little to
increase its own productivity.

The militarization of the empire temporarily stopped the Germanic
invasions but did not put an end to inner disorder. The last emperor of
the dynasty of Severus, Alexander Severus, was murdered by his own
troops in 235. The soldiers then proclaimed emperor one of their own,
a Thracian peasant named Maximinus, and three years later they pro-
ceeded to murder him also. Meanwhile the Senate, which had refused
to acknowledge Maximinus, put forth its own succession of claimants to
the throne. The African legions did likewise. Thus during the single
year 238, seven different emperors reigned. From that point on, few
emperors were undisputed rulers of the empire, and then only for a few
years, until the accession of Diocletian in 284.

In the interim, large portions of the empire had fallen beyond the
effective control of Rome. In the West, under Postumus and his successors, most of Gaul, as well as Spain and Britain, constituted a separate
state—the *Imperium Gallicarum*—which for fourteen years (259–273) refused to yield to the authority of the Roman emperors. In the East,
Queen Zenobia, of the oasis city of Palmyra, proclaimed herself independent and eventually expanded her dominions to include Egypt as
well as substantial portions of Syria, Mesopotamia, and Asia Minor. Under Aurelian (270–275) these two splinter states were subdued, a feat
for which Aurelian received the title *restitutor orbis* or restorer of the
world. But the empire was forced to abandon a vast territory beyond the
Danube and retrench to more defensible borders.

In brief, from the death of Commodus to Diocletian, the empire
underwent a long crisis that was stemmed only temporarily, first under
the Severi, then under Aurelian. To stop the incursions of the barbarians from across the Rhine and the Danube, as well as to put an end to
inner dissension, the empire was militarized. At the beginning of this
period—when Aelius Aristides delivered his *Oration*, and for some time
thereafter—Roman citizenship was a thing to be coveted and the Senate
was still, in theory at least, the ruling elite. The generals of the legions,
as well as the emperors, came from its ranks, and the fiction that it
elected the emperors was still kept. By the end of the crisis, the Senate
had been decimated, and its powers, both real and symbolic, had been
greatly reduced. The military now ruled the empire. Traditionally, high
ranks of the military had been reserved for members of the Senate. But
by A.D. 260 this too had changed. Officers now rose through the ranks,
and when the throne was vacant—or even when it was not—the legions
raised their favorite generals to the purple.

These changes had a profound impact on the empire and its population that went beyond the merely political.[63] When the Severi were
able to stem the crisis momentarily, they did so by reordering the prior-
ities of society. Henceforth, an ever-increasing portion of all economic

resources was to be devoted to defense. The increase in the number of legions and of auxiliary troops, as well as the raise in pay for all the military, was not an inexpensive proposition. It was particularly burdensome at a time when military expansion had ceased and the most important source of new wealth had been shut off. Furthermore, as the military gained consciousness of their newly acquired power to create and destroy rulers, their demands became ever more pressing. It had always been customary for emperors and generals to grant financial bonuses to the troops upon accession to the throne or on the occasion of a great victory. Now the army found constant excuses to demand such bonuses as well as pay increases and other benefits.

The imperial treasury was constantly in need of money in order to survive. No rich neighbors remained to be easily despoiled. Only two solutions could be found, and the emperors had recourse to both: debasing the coin and increasing taxation.

Depreciating the coin was an easy expedient to increase the apparent wealth of the state and to make whatever payments were necessary. It worked as long as it was minor and undetected. But it was such an easy expedient, and times were so difficult, that the adulteration reached scandalous levels. Eventually, people began hoarding precious metals and refusing payment in the new debased coins. Perhaps hundreds of edicts resembled the following which was issued in Egypt in the year 260 by the governor of the district of Oxyrhyncus:

Since the public officials, meeting together, have accused the bankers of the exchange banks of having closed up shop in refusal to accept the divine coin of the Emperors, it has become necessary that proclamation be issued to all the owners of banks to open these and to accept and exchange all coin except the clearly spurious and counterfeit, and not to them alone but to all who engage in business of any kind, in the full knowledge that if they disobey this proclamation they will experience the penalties which his Excellency the governor previously ordained in their case.[64]

The very fact that the edict refers to "previously ordained" penalties shows that legislation could not force people to accept a coinage whose value they did not trust. Bankers, traders, and others of lesser importance could be temporarily forced to do so, at least until they went bankrupt or ceased doing business altogether, but military personnel were too powerful. They often insisted on payment in good coin, especially when a ruler "offered" them the bonuses that had become *de rigueur*. Eventually even the government began to refuse payment in its own debased coin, instituting new taxes to be paid in kind.

Higher and more thorough taxation was the other government resource for coping with the rising cost of the military. At first the government put forth more stringent efforts to collect the customary poll tax and the land tax. A number of new taxes were also created. These, however, did not suffice in a situation of runaway inflation. Thus the government turned to taxes in kind—the *annona militaris*. It had always been expected that in emergency situations people would help provide the foodstuffs and material necessary for the army. In ancient times, those forced to contribute in such situations were usually paid for their contributions, normally from the booty of war. Now, however, Rome possessed little or no booty, and the emergency became permanent. To make matters worse, this state of emergency also resulted in almost total unpredictability in taxation. If for some reason a military body was stationed near one's land, one's taxes suddenly became even more oppressive. If, on the other hand, one's land was inaccessible, far from the routes followed by the legions, the burden was significantly smaller.

Taxed beyond their capability to pay, the productive classes of society resented to new order, and many ceased producing. The flight of farmers from the land accelerated. This process is clearly documented in Egypt, where the flight—*anachoresis*—of farmers and peasants reached new levels. In response, the government issued a series of edicts expelling from the cities Egyptians who had no business there.[65] This, however, was not enough, for it did not address the root causes for the flight from the land. Therefore, many who were expelled from a city simply went to another or took refuge in the wilderness, where Roman authority did not reach.

A further factor increasing the tax burden on cultivated lands was the constant invasions from across the Rhine and the Danube. The old system of border defense devised by Hadrian and others when the empire reached its maximum expansion had outlasted its effectiveness. Its original purpose had been to defend the empire against incursions from the relatively small and disorganized bands of "barbarians" who lived beyond the borders. At that time, it had sufficed to build walls and to defend them and borders along rivers with a thinly and fairly evenly distributed force, supported by the legions, all of which were stationed near the borders. If a band of invaders managed to cross such fortified boundaries, it was usually small and could be disposed of before it did much damage. During the time of the civil wars of the late second and most of the third century, the various claimants to the throne had found it necessary to keep the legions near them, partially for fear of treachery. At the same time, the barbarian invaders were now better organized and their invading armies much larger than before. Border defenses could no longer detain them. When an invasion occurred, it went practically unchecked until the emperor or someone he trusted could move the necessary legions to stop the invaders. Fighting and pillage took place well inside Roman territory. The crops, flocks, and inhabitants of border regions were practically at the mercy of such sudden and unchecked raids. Therefore, border lands were abandoned and allowed to return to forests or swamps. The withdrawal of these territories from the pool of productive land further increased the tax load that had to be borne by lands still under cultivation.

Not only barbarian invaders devastated the land. The Roman legions and their auxiliary troops marching to and fro in seemingly endless civil warfare worked a similar effect even in the heartland of the empire.[66] Thus, both in the border provinces and throughout the empire, lands were being abandoned.

In order to bring these lands back under cultivation, the empire offered them to settlers from beyond the borders. Usually care was taken not to settle a particular group in lands directly facing those of their kin, for fear that they might serve as a beachhead for invasion. Still, these could only be temporary measures, since the same forces that had driven others from these lands eventually drove away the new settlers as well.

An air of calamity appeared on the land. Even in North Africa, one of the areas apparently best protected from the incursions of the Germans, inhabitants felt a sense of constant danger and impending doom. Surviving writings of Christians from that area respond to the accusation that the evils of the age are due to Rome's having abandoned the old gods. Late in the second century, pagans in Carthage were already accusing Christians of bringing disruption and destruction upon the old order. At that time, the crisis of the empire had not become acute, and Tertullian was able to argue that there had always been such calamities and that the present time was no worse than the past.[67] By the middle of the next century, after years of civil disorder and strife, Cyprian was ready to agree that conditions were indeed worse. He explained that the world was simply aging, and that as a result it was ailing.[68] It is significant that Arnobius, writing after the Diocletian restoration, returned to the view of Tertullian, that all these calamities were not new.[69]

The Reforms of Diocletian

In this context of growing calamity one must look at Diocletian and his program for restoring the Empire, a program to which Constantine would fall heir.[70] This is not the place to tell the story of Diocletian's rise to power and his total program of restoration.[71] In brief, that program involved the following elements: (1) a system of sharing power with another emperor having the title of "Augustus" (which Diocletian himself held) and later with two others known as "Caesars"; (2) a new system of defense combining heavily fortified borders with highly mobile cavalry stationed at strategic points and legions behind them to destroy invading groups that the fortifications and the cavalry could not hold; (3) an increase in the number of legions to a total of fifty-three; (4) the restructuring of government, creating an entire civil service as a hierarchy parallel to that of the military; (5) the financial machinery to support these various reforms.

Diocletian approached the task of government, as his immediate predecessors had done, from the vantage point of a military man. His first priority was the army. This he reorganized in order to stop invaders before they had the opportunity to ravage the countryside.[72] But he also tried to limit the army to its proper function and to relieve it of both the authority to create new rulers and the responsibility of collecting taxes. In order to do this, he devised a system that was supposed to guarantee the peaceful and orderly succession to the throne, and he developed a civil service to perform the nonmilitary tasks of government. He more than doubled the number of provinces into which the empire was divided, thus making them more manageable, and then grouped them into twelve dioceses. Those who would manage this system were organized into a hierarchy quite apart from the military, although with similar expectations of discipline and obedience. This new civilian bureaucracy was charged with the task of running the state in all matters except those of a military nature, including the collection of taxes.

Probably the most original achievement of Diocletian's government was not, as is often said, the development of the Tetrarchy, but rather the manner in which he reorganized the system of taxation. It had never been uniform, since in most provinces practices existing before the Roman conquest had been kept with little modification. Now, however, it had collapsed. Taxes paid in coin were practically worthless, for the effort and resources invested in collecting them often approached or even exceeded the value of the coin itself. Taxes paid in kind were irregular, grossly unfair, and often destructive of productive property.

In response to this situation, Diocletian and his government devised a new system. First he counted all the resources available, trying to assess them as fairly as possible. He set up fictitious units called the *iugum* and *caput*. Theoretically, a *iugum* was the amount of land needed for a man to support a family, and the *caput* was a person. In using these terms, Diocletian simply adhered to the old tradition that major taxes were usually either land or poll taxes. But the units and their use were much more complicated and flexible. The amount of land in a *iugum* depended on the nature of the land—mountain, plain, forest, rocky—and the type of crop produced on it. A *caput* was likewise flexible. While the head of a household usually counted as a *caput*, in some places women were counted as half a *caput*, and in others as one. Slaves, children of working age, and animals also added to the total number of *capita*—often in small and complicated fractions, so that several animals would add up to a single *caput*. Furthermore, *iuga* and *capita* were often interchangeable.

The *iuga* and *capita* were not units of taxation but units of taxable wealth. Every year the government would declare its total needs for that year, and this would be prorated among the total number of *iuga* and *capita* in the empire. Each provincial governor was then responsible for collecting the taxes apportioned to his province—again, on the basis of the *iuga* and *capita* in it—and he in turn passed this responsibility to his subalterns. If a particular region was hit by drought or other disaster, the number of its *iuga* could easily be reduced, thus shifting some of its tax burden to the more fortunate areas. This was as close as the Roman Empire ever came to having a budget.

No matter how fair it may seem to us now, the system was not received without complaint. Authorities first tried it in Egypt, where the ancient system of government-controlled economy may have provided some of the inspiration for it. The Egyptian peasants did not understand what was intended and simply thought that this was a new form of extortion on the part of the government. The elites, in particular the Greeks of Alexandria, resented the abolition of their ancestral privileges. The result was a rebellion that required both Diocletian's personal intervention and a long siege of Alexandria to subdue. Eventually, however, the system proved quite adequate and survived long after Diocletian's demise.

Diocletian faced another economic ill: inflation. Apparently he believed that the sole cause for inflation was the debasing of the coin, and he therefore set out to improve the silver content of his coinage. By decree, he cut in half the value of the older coins, made of copper with a thin silver wash.

This, however, did not end inflation. Diocletian apparently expected that simply producing better coins would automatically increase their value. What he did not realize was that increasing the number of coins in circulation, no matter what their metal content, would work in the opposite direction. Furthermore, convinced that his coins were now worth more, Diocletian encouraged his mints to produce an increasing number of them, using them to finance state expenditures that taxes did not cover.

Still prices rose. Instead of faulting the government's deficit spending Diocletian blamed merchants, who he thought must be making a fortune. He may have learned of some who had made money with insider information on his impending devaluation of the older coinage.[73] In any case, he looked upon merchants with the soldier's traditional contempt and was particularly incensed that they seemed to take advantage of the needs of the army. In the preamble to an edict issued in 301, he declared.

The evil men engaged in business actually try to predict the wind and weather by watching the movements of the stars; for they cannot endure the rains nourishing the fertile fields and promising rich future harvests, since they only reckon good weather and plenty as their own loss . . .

Who does not know that wherever the public safety requires our armies to be sent, the profiteers insolently and covertly attack the public welfare, not only in villages and towns but on every road? They extort prices for merchandise not fourfold, not eightfold, but so great that human speech cannot describe it.

Sometimes a soldier in a single purchase is stripped of both his pay and his donative. The contributions of the whole world to support the armies falls to the profits of thieves.[74]

These were the reasons given for the need to regulate prices throughout the empire. The edict listed hundreds of items and services and established a maximum price for each. Wages for a farm laborer, besides maintenance, were set at 25 denarii; for a carpenter, a baker, or a stonemason, at 50; and for a seagoing shipwright, at 60. An elementary teacher should be paid no more than 50 denarii per pupil per month, while those teaching arithmetic could charge up to 75, and professors of classical literature or geometry, 200. Passenger transportation was set at 2 denarii a mile. Wine varied, according to quality and origin, between 8 and 30 denarii a pint. The maximum price for wheat and millet was set at 100 denarii for a *modius* (approximately two gallons). Barley and rye could not be sold for more than 60, nor oats for more than 30. The price for a pair of work sandals for a farm laborer was set at 80 denarii (more than three days' wages).

Needless to say, the edict did not produce the desired effect. No matter what the emperor might say, people were not ready to sell at a loss or accept worthless money. Many items disappeared from the market. The very hoarding that the emperor blamed for inflation became more pronounced. The economy moved away from money and toward barter. Since wages, especially in large farms, were one of the most easily regulated items, farm laborers and other wage earners tended to suffer most under the disparities created by the unenforceable law. Soon the local authorities began to ignore the edict, and eventually it was forgotten.

The edict *De pretiis*, however, indicated the sort of solution that Diocletian and his successors had found to the many ills afflicting society: regulation. Their attempt to determine the price of practically every single item in the market proved unworkable, but other regulations had a much more lasting effect. The system of taxation that Diocletian devised—and that his successors continued and enlarged—required social and economic rigidity.[75] If a plot of land was valued and taxed according to the number of people living and working on it, the state had a stake in keeping those workers on that particular plot. If a city's tax roll included a certain number of tanners or of stone masons, the city and its government had a stake in maintaining that number by discouraging people from moving or from changing occupations. This, added to the tendency on the part of farmers and peasants to abandon the land, led to increasing regulations tying people and their descendants to a particular plot of land or to an occupation. Soldiers were recruited by forcing the sons of soldiers to follow their fathers' footsteps. If a particular occupation needed more personnel, steps were taken to force greater numbers into it, as, for instance, the law requiring that anyone marrying a miller's daughter had to become a miller.

For many years people engaged in particular trades had organized themselves into guilds or corporations. Now these guilds were turned into instruments of control by the state, tying people to particular occupations and allowing the state to determine the production and distribution of every item it considered important.

In this increasingly rigid structure, the emperor occupied an exceedingly exalted place. The early emperors had been Roman aristocrats, the first among a class to which Rome supposedly owed its grandeur. Later followed the military emperors, men who rose from the ranks and owed their power to their popularity with the legions. Many of these were declared divine, although normally only after their death. Diocletian himself owed his power to the army. Yet he was aware that any rival could easily claim the same right to power. Therefore, he surrounded himself—and instructed his three colleagues to surround themselves—with all the trappings of divinity. He never declared himself to be a god; such a claim had been discredited by many of his predecessors. Rather, he claimed to be a companion of the gods—of Jove, the ruler among the gods—and to embody the "genius of the Roman people." He was depicted as aloof, dignified, more than human, and the ceremonial of the court was designed to carry that impression. In short, Diocletian saved the empire by turning it into a rigid military theocracy, which is one of the reasons he felt the need to unleash the worst of the ancient persecutions against Christians.

Of all the innovations of Diocletian, the one for which he is best known, the Tetrarchy, was probably the least important in its long-term consequences. Indeed, hardly had Diocletian abdicated in 305 when civil war broke out again. Eventually, Constantine emerged as the sole emperor, and he did nothing to restore the Tetrarchy. After that time, the empire was repeatedly divided among more than one emperor. Occasionally the precedent of Diocletian's Tetrarchy was invoked, but such territorial divisions were far different from those Diocletian had envisioned.

Constantine and After

Constantine continued Diocletian's economic and social policies. He tried to restore confidence in the currency and succeeded to a limited degree by issuing a gold *solidus*.[76] Without reviving Diocletian's failed efforts to curb inflation by edict, he continued his predecessor's tendency toward regulation and rigidity. In order to manage this vast, increasingly totalitarian state, he constantly expanded the bureaucratic hierarchy.[77] This in turn required heavier taxes.[78] And, since only the wealthy could survive such heavy taxation, concentration of wealth and lands in fewer and fewer hands inevitably resulted. Under his son

Constantius II, inflation once again broke all bounds, and taxes had to keep pace.

Constantine also followed Diocletian's lead in giving his rule sacred sanction. Over the years, he shifted his allegiance slowly from *Sol Invictus,* the "unconquered Sun," to the God of Christians, but under one or another form, he always nourished the impression that his office and authority were divinely sanctioned. Increasingly throughout the fourth century, his successors encouraged and enlarged that idea.[79] The main exception was Julian, who viewed his own role as reviving the enlightened government of the mid-second century. His reforms may have gained a measure of support among the financially depressed older aristocracy, especially in the eastern portions of the empire, but they never became a viable alternative to the order that had begun to emerge since the time of Diocletian. Valentinian I (364–375) tried to mitigate some of the worst consequences of the emerging order for the poor, but with little success. By the time of Theodosius I (379–395), the empire was once again headed toward social regimentation with divine sanction.

Diocletian and Constantine managed to save the empire, but at great cost. The tendency toward centralization, militarization, and rigidity continued throughout the fourth century. Centralization required a large bureaucracy. Since bureaucrats often sought gain through fraud and extortion, more bureaucrats were required to regulate them, thus adding to the cost of government and the burden of taxation.

One solution was to make the ancient municipal authorities instruments of the central government, particularly in collecting taxes. In the centralized empire of the fourth century, the ruling municipal classes (called *curiales*) lost much of their local authority. In exchange, they were invested with the unenviable responsibility of collaborating with the bureaucratic machinery in levying imperial taxes. Those whose turn it was to discharge these duties were made responsible for any shortfall. As taxes increased, the wealthier and more powerful tended to shift the burden onto the shoulders of those of more limited means.[80] Those who succeeded eventually made it into the ranks of the senatorial class. Those who failed lost their rank and property. The system proved so oppressive to the lower echelons of the *curiales* that many simply abandoned their property along with their responsibility. Numerous edicts testify to the authorities' attempts to keep the *curiales* at their posts. Edicts classified those who evaded their responsibilities as the equals of runaway slaves or fugitive debtors and made theirs a capital crime, forbidding their flight to monastic retreat or their ordination without naming someone to discharge their responsibilities.[81] Still, no law could prevent the decline of many *curiales* into poverty.

Those *curiales* who were able to join the ranks of the senatorial class were most fortunate. Although senators were subject to a number of special taxes, those from which they were exempt were much larger. Most importantly, senators did not have to pay taxes to support municipal and other local expenses, nor did they have to participate in the burdensome and expensive task of collecting taxes. The land that lesser *curiales* and poorer farmers lost was absorbed into the ever-increasing latifundia of the senatorial class and of those who held high office.[82] The net results were higher taxes for smaller landholders and further acceleration of their decline into poverty.

The government's only recourse was further regimentation. Earlier laws had tried to prevent the depletion of the curial class by forbidding its flight. Toward the end of the fourth century, and certainly by the fifth, legislation tried to prevent the *curiales* from ascending into the ranks of the senatorial class or from avoiding their responsibilities by joining the military or the bureaucracy.[83] The tendency toward greater social rigidity that had resulted from Diocletian's reorganization of the empire and of its tax structure eventually engulfed every level of society.

Meanwhile, the ranks of the poor grew ever more numerous. Imperial edicts of the time abound in references to abuses that must be stopped and to the suffering of the less fortunate. Some unfortunates staged protests, as that of the anonymous writer who complained to the emperor that each of the governors "sends out collectors to spread ruin . . . and they drain off the resources of the taxpayers through various devices of plunder."[84] Yet, except in places such as Rome and Constantinople where the masses could threaten political stability, little was done to provide relief for the needy. The government made no attempt to stop or reverse the processes that were causing poverty. In the last analysis, legislation as well as taxation existed to protect the power of the privileged few. This is not to say that the emperors were not aware of the injustices being perpetrated or that they did nothing to correct them. Constantine, among others, bewailed the ease with which the powerful avoided paying taxes and the burden that this placed on the poor.[85]

In the fourth century the *coloni* finally were reduced to what amounted to servitude. Although they kept their free status before the law, they could no longer leave the lands to which they were assigned; their work on those lands was essential to the economy, and therefore the law tied them to the land. When a property was sold or otherwise exchanged hands, the *coloni* attached to it went with it. Eventually similar laws would be enacted—and for similar reasons—forbidding masters from selling agricultural slaves separately from the land to which they were attached.[86] Once again, the goal was to guarantee production by preventing the social and geographical mobility of the labor force.

The net result was a dismal picture:

In the voluminous enactments issued from Constantine to Majorian {who ruled until A.D. 461}, the student has before him a melancholy diagnosis of the maladies which, by a slow and inevitable process of decay, were exhausting the strength of Roman society. He will see municipal liberty and self-government dying out, the upper class cut off from the masses by sharp distinctions of wealth and

and privilege, yet forbidden to bear arms, and deprived of all practical interest in public affairs. He will find that a . . . system of caste has made every social grade and every occupation practically hereditary, from the senator to the water-man on the Tiber, or the sentinel at a frontier post . . . It will be seen that in a society in which poverty is almost branded with infamy, poverty is steadily increasing and wealth becoming more insolent and aggressive; that the disinherited, in the face of an omnipotent government, are carrying brigandage even up to the gates of Rome; that parents are selling their children into slavery . . .[87]

In the fifth century, the old order finally collapsed in the West. The divinely appointed emperors lost their power and eventually ceased to exist. But the social regimentation persisted and, through the influence of the Germanic invaders, evolved into what we now call the medieval order. In the East, the process begun by Diocletian and Constantine continued evolving into the Byzantine Empire.

NOTES

1. See W. E. Heitland, *Agricola: A Study of Agriculture and Rustic Life in the Graeco-Roman World from the Point of View of Labour* (Cambridge, Eng.: Cambridge University Press, 1927).
2. Columella, *De re rust.* 1.7, *LCL;* Pliny, *Nat. hist.* 1.18.21, *LCL.* A recent work on Roman latifundia, with detailed information on their development in Italy, is V. I. Kuziscin, *La grande proprietà agraria nell'Italia romana* (Rome: Riuniti, 1984).
3. Pliny, *Nat hist.* 1.18.13, *LCL.*
4. *De re rust.* 1.8, *LCL.*
5. In Roman law, the master of the house, or *paterfamilias*, was the rightful owner of all earnings of the family—*familia*, which included both slaves and free members of the household. A son under *patria potestas*, no matter what his age, could own no property on his own right but only as a *peculium*. The same was true of a slave. A *peculium* could be employed only within the limits defined by the *paterfamilias* and could not be disposed of by will.
6. On the connection between the supposed inferiority of slaves and the justification of slavery itself, and how it worked out in actual everyday practice, see P. Veyne, ed., *A History of Private Life: From Pagan Rome to Byzantium* (Cambridge, MA: Belknap Press, 1987), pp. 59–63.
7. *De re rust.* 1, *praef.*
8. Cato, *De agric.* 1.7, *LCL,* lists nine crops by order of profitability. Vines occupy the first place in his list, and olives the fourth. Grains are sixth. It should be noted, however, that here Cato refers to vines grown on their own trellises and as the only crop on the field—*vinea.* Vines grown with other crops, and using trees as support—*arbustum*—were much less profitable. See Richard Duncan-Jones, *The Economy of the Roman Empire: Quantitative Studies* (Cambridge, Eng.: Cambridge University Press, 1974), pp. 34-38.
9. Salvator Riccobono, ed., *Fontes Iuris Rom. Antejustiniani* (Florentiae: G. Barbèra, 1988), 2:795–96.
10. Suetonius, *Dom.* 7.2, *LCL;* Statius, *Silv.* 4.3.11–12, *LCL;* Eusebius, *Chron.* 2.160, *PG.*
11. P. A. Brunt, "The Fiscus and Its Development," *JRomSt* 56 (1966): 88. Dio Cassius, *Hist.* 53.16, 22, *LCL.*
12. It was not the custom of Rome, upon expanding its political power, to expropriate its new subjects. Normally, the former system of land tenure was continued. Rome's profit came from taxes, added trade, and lands and other properties that for one reason or another were confiscated.

13. See D. Crawford, "Imperial Estates," in *Studies in Roman Property*, ed. M. Finley (Cambridge: Cambridge University Press, 1976), pp. 45–54.
14. The classical study of this issue is M. Rostovtzef, *Studien zur Geschichte der römischen Kolonates* (Leipzig-Berlin: B. G. Tuebner, 1910). See also R. Clausing, *The Roman Colonate: The Theories of Its Origin* (New York: Columbia University Press, 1925); D. Eibach, *Untersuchungen zur spätantiken Kolonat in der kaiserlichen Gesetzgebung unter besonderer Berücksichtigung der Terminologie* (Köln: n.p., 1980); G. Giliberti, *Servis quasi colonus* (Napoli: E. Jovene, 1981); P. W. de Neeve, *Colonus: Private Farm-Tenancy in Roman Italy During the Republic and the Early Principate* (Amsterdam: Gieben, 1984). The phrase *servus quasi colonus* is taken from late Roman law: *Dig.* 15.3.16; 40.7.14, in *Corpus Juris Civilis*, ed. C. M. Galisset (Paris: Cotelle, 1867). All references to the Digest, and to the Codex Justiniani, are from this edition.
15. *CInscLat* 8:25943, 26416.
16. For instance, in *Cod. Theod.* 5.17.1 it is decreed that fleeing *coloni* are to be "enchained as slaves," so that they may be forced to do as slaves the same tasks that they would not do as free people.
17. J. M. Blázquez, *Historia económica de la Hispania romana* (Madrid: Cristianidad, 1978), p. 138.
18. Herodian, *Hist.* 2.4.6, *LCL.*
19. J. Toutain, *La economía antigua* (Mexico City, Mexico: UTEHA, 1959), p. 278; C. Jullian, *Histoire de la Gaule*, (Paris: Hachette, 1908), 5:310.
20. C. Dubois, *Etude sur l'administration et l'explotation des carrières dans le monde romain* (Paris: Hachette, 1908).
21. For other cases of private ownerhship of such mineral resources, see *Dig.* 27.9.3.6.
22. The wealth that was expended in such trade was significant. According to Pliny, in the India trade this amounted to fifty million sesterces yearly. *Nat. hist.* 6.101. Cf. 12.84, *LCL.*
23. See J. Rougé, *Recherches sur l'organisation du commerce maritime en Méditerranée sous l'empire romain* (Paris: Ecole pratique des hautes études, 1966). Chrysostom praises God for having created "the shorter route of the sea." *Ad Dem.* 2.5, *PG.*
24. C. Webber and A. Wildavsky, *A History of Taxation and Expenditure in the Western World* (New York: Simon and Schuster, 1986), p. 109.
25. Commenting on his gifts to the city of Comum, Pliny the Younger compares his purpose with that of other givers: "I was not engaging myself to endow public games or troupes of gladiators, but to defray the annual expense of maintenance for well-born youths," *Ep.* 1.8, *LCL.*
26. V. Chapot, *El mundo romano* (Mexico City, Mexico: UTEHA, 1957), p. 75.
27. In the New Testament, this is called the *didrachma*. See Matt. 22:17. For its background in ancient Israel, see Exod. 30:11–16 and Neh. 10:32–33. Josephus, *Ant.* 18.9.1, *LCL*, refers to the collection of this tax among all Jews, no matter where they resided.
28. Josephus, *De bel. Iud.* 7.6.6, *LCL.*
29. See E. Badian, *Publicans and Sinners* (Oxford: Blackwell, 1972).
30. Varro, *De re rust.* 1.57.2, *LCL*, speaks of storage bins where wheat could be kept for as long as fifty years.
31. Webber and Wildavsky, *History of Taxation* (see n.24), p. 119.
32. Ibid., p. 135.
33. R. MacMullen, *Corruption and the Decline of Rome* (New Haven: Yale University Press, 1988), p. 144.
34. Until Claudius, as part of the continuing process of centering all authority on the person of the emperor, took this privilege away from the Senate.
35. A. H. M. Jones, *Studies in Roman Government and Law* (Oxford: Basil Blackwell, 1960), p. 110.
36. Edward Gibbon, *The History of the Decline and Fall of the Roman Empire*, 2d ed. (New York: Harper & Brothers, 1850), 1:95–96. Similar views may be found in a number of modern authors. See, for instance, R. Rémendon, *La crise de l'empire romain de*

Marc-Aurèle à Anastase (Paris: Presses Universitaires de France, 1964), p. 71; C. Wells, *The Roman Empire* (London: Fontana, 1984), pp. 239–40.

37. On the chronology of Aelius Aristides, there are discrepancies among scholars, some placing his birth as early as A.D. 117, and others as late as A.D. 129. His *Roman Oration* is to be dated on either 143 or 144. See A. Boulanger, *Aelius Aristide et la sophistique dans la province d'Asie au IIe siècle de notre ère* (Paris: Boccard, 1923), pp. 461–95. Although no contemporary document indicates that the *Oration* was delivered at the Athenaeum, most modern scholars believe this to be the most likely place. J. H. Oliver, *The Ruling Power: A Study of the Roman Empire in the Second Century after Christ Through the Roman Oration of Aelius Aristides* (Philadelphia: The American Philosophical Society, 1953), p. 887, suggests that the Athenaeum, of which little is known, may have been part of the complex around the great *templum Urbis,* which had just been completed and where the ceremonies celebrating the city's birth were held.

38. *Roman Oration* 4, 6. This and all other quotations from this work are taken from the translation of Oliver, *The Ruling Power,* pp. 895–907.

39. Ibid., 11.

40. Ibid., 13.

41. Ibid., 21.

42. Ibid., 24.

43. Ibid., 28.

44. Ibid., 29.

45. Ibid., 36.

46. Ibid., 39.

47. Ibid., 59, 62.

48. Ibid., 63, 64, 66.

49. Ibid., 94, 97, 99.

50. Ibid., 6.

51. Naphtali Lewis, *Life in Egypt under Roman Rule* (Oxford: Clarendon, 1983), pp. 1–2. This excellent and readable account is the basis for much of what follows on Egypt.

52. All of these provisions come from an edict of Augustus, partially quoted in Lewis, *Life in Egypt,* pp. 32–33. Commenting on these and other rules, Lewis comes to the conclusion that the social system in Roman Egypt was "a veritable ancient apartheid" (p. 34).

53. This sort of flight, known in Greek as *anachoresis,* was a forerunner of Christian monasticism.

54. Lewis, *Life in Egypt,* pp. 164–65.

55. *Scrip. Hist. Aug.,* Adr., 12.1, *LCL.*

56. M. Rostovtzeff, *The Social and Economic History of the Roman Empire,* 2d ed. (Oxford: Clarendon, 1957), 1:323.

57. A notable case, especially since it comes from what were generally bad times in the Roman Empire (the latter half of the third century) is an epitaph from Mactar, Africa:

    Born of a poor, small family, . . . from the day of my birth I have spent my life working in the fields. . . . I reaped twelve harvests under the raging sun and then, from laborer, became contractor, and for eleven years commanded the team of harvesters. . . . This work, and a life content with little, availed to make me master of a home with a farmstead—a home that lacks no riches. Our life won the fruit of office, too: I, even I, was enrolled among the city senators . . .

    Quoted by R. MacMullen, *Roman Social Relations: 50 B.C. to A.D. 286* (New Haven: Yale University Press, 1974), p. 43.

58. For further details, as well as qualifications having to do with regional variations on this policy, see Rostovtzeff, *Social and Economic History,* 2:192–254.

59. At this point, one is reminded of the experience of Paul and Barnabas in Lystra, where we are told that the crowds were amazed by a miracle of healing, "and they lifted up their voices, saying in Lycaonian . . . " (Acts 14:11).

60. Acts 5:36–37.

61. John 11:48. A similar concern for the opinion of Roman authorities appears, in a totally different context, in Acts 19. There it is not a matter of Jewish-Christian relations. On the contrary, the followers of Artemis are upset with Paul and his companions, but also with any other Jew (11:34). In the end, the town clerk quiets the assembly, reminding them that they are in danger of being charged with rioting. Apparently, such fear puts an end to the matter.

62. See the excellent narrative of the events of that year, correcting some traditional views, of K. Wellesley, *The Long Year: A.D. 69* (Boulder: Westview Press, 1976).

63. On the reordering of society during the third century, see: P. Lambrechts, *La composition du Sénat romain de Septime Sévère à Dioclétien (183–284)* (Budapest: Magyar Nemzeti Muzeum, 1937); M. Mazza, *Lotte sociali e restaurazione autoritaria nel III secolo d.C.* (Roma-Bari: Laterza, 1973); K. Dietz, *Senatus contra principem: Untersuchungen zur senatorischen Opposition gegen Kaiser Maximinus Thrax* (München: C. H. Beck, 1980).

64. *Select Papyri* no. 230, LCL. Quoted by Naphtali Lewis, *Greek Historical Documents: The Roman Principate: 27 B.C.–285 A.D.* (Toronto: Hakkert, 1974), p. 47.

65. See, for instance, the following edict of Caracalla, quoted in Lewis, *Life in Egypt*, p. 202 (taken from, *Select Papyri*, no. 215, *LCL*): "All Egyptians who are in Alexandria, and particularly country folk who have fled thither from elsewhere and can easily be identified, are absolutely and by every means to be expelled . . . The ones to be prevented are those who flee the countryside where they belong in order to avoid farmwork, not those who converge upon Alexandria out of a desire to view the glorious city or come here in pursuit of a more cultured existence or on occasional business."

66. Synesius of Cyrene complains that, even in time of peace, the soldiers and their officers, with their rioting and greed, make war on the civilian population, and that this "peaceful war" is almost as bad as the official ones. Zosimus complains of a similar destruction in the cities. References in MacMullen, *Corruption* (n. 33 above), p. 280 n. 73.

67. "Pray, tell me how many calamities befell the world and particular cities before Tiberius reigned—before the coming, that is, of Christ? . . . But where were your gods in those days?" *Apol.* 40, *ANF.*

68. "You must in the first place know this, that the world has now grown old, and does not abide in that strength in which it formerly stood; nor has it that vigour and force which it formerly possessed." *Ad Demet.* 3, *ANF.*

69. *Adv. gent.* 1.4; *ANF:* "When was the human race destroyed by a flood? Was it not before us? When was the world set on fire, and reduced to coals and ashes? Was it not before us? When were the greatest cities engulphed by the billows of the sea? Was it not before us?"

70. On the manner in which the empire evolved from Diocletian to Constantine, and the continuity between the two in spite of their contrasting religious policies, see T. D. Barnes, *The New Empire of Diocletian and Constantine* (Cambridge, MA.: Harvard University Press, 1982).

71. For an excellent study on these matters, see Stephen Williams, *Diocletian and the Roman Recovery* (New York: Methuen, 1985).

72. R. Grosse, *Römische Militärgeschichte von Galienus bis zum Beginn der byzantinischen Themerverfassung* (Berlin: Weidmann, 1920); D. Van Berchem, *L'armée de Dioclétien et la réforme constantinienne* (Paris: Imprimerie Nationale et P. Geuthner, 1952).

73. A papyrus in the John Rylands University Library, in Manchester (#607) tells of a rich man who has heard of the impending devaluation of the older coins and instructs his steward to spend all his money before the devaluation takes effect.

74. Diocletian's edict *De pretiis*, quoted by Williams, *Diocletian* (n. 72 above), pp. 129–30.

75. S. Mazzarine, *Aspetti sociali del quarto secolo: Ricerche di storia tardoromana* (Roma: L'erma di Bretschneider, 1951); W. Goffart, *Caput and Colonate: Towards a History of Late Roman Taxation* (Toronto: University of Toronto Press, 1974).

76. See Maria R. Alföldi, *Die Constantinische Goldprägung: Untersuchungen zu ihrer Bedeutung für Kaiserpolitik und Hofkunst* (Mainz: Verlag des Römische-Germanischen

Zentralmuseums, 1963). See also A. Alföldi, *The Conversion of Constantine and Pagan Rome* (Oxford: Clarendon, 1948), where Constantine's coinage is employed as a major source to trace the development of his religious policies.

77. A. Giardina, *Aspetti della burocrazia nel basso imperio* (Roma: Edizioni dell'Ateneo & Bizzarri, 1977). See above, n. 31.

78. See T. S. Vigorita, "Nuovi indirizzi di politica fiscale nella legislatione di Constantino," in *Società romana e imperio tardantico,* ed. A. Giardina (Roma-Bari: Laterza, 1986), 2:71–80. Vigorita shows how Constantine's policies tended to concentrate property in the hands of a powerful elite.

79. See N. Q. King, *'There's such Divinity Doth Hedge a King': Studies in Ruler Cult and the Religion of Sacral Monarchy in Some Late Fourth Century Byzantine Monuments* (Edinburgh: Thomas Nelson and Sons, 1960).

80. Salvianus, *De gub. Dei* 5.28, *LCL.* The laws enacted against this practice proved of little value. Cf. *Cod. Theod.* 11.1.26.

81. *Cod. Theod.* 9.45.3; 12.1.59, 66, 108, 122.

82. J. Brissaud, *Le régime de la terre dans la société étatiste du Bas-Empire* (Paris: E. de Boccard, 1927); D. Vera, "Strutture agrarie e strutture patrimoniali nella tarda antichità," *Opus* 2 (1983): 489–533.

83. *Cod. Theod.* 12.1.171, 183, in *Theodosiani Libri xvi,* eb. Th. Mommsen (Berlin: Weidmann, 1963). All references to the *Codex Theodosianus* are from this edition. *Nov.* 8.

84. Quoted in MacMullen, *Corruption* (n. 33 above), p. 162.

85. *Cod. Theod.* 13.10.1,. On the evasion of taxes by the powerful, see MacMullen, *Corruption* (n. 33 above), p. 96.

86. *Cod. Just.* 11.48.7, (n. 14 above).

87. S. Dill, *Roman Society in the Last Century of the Western Empire* (London: Macmillan, 1899), pp. 227–28. More recent works have corrected Dill only in matters of detail and confirmed his general profile of conditions during the late fourth and early fifth centuries.

PART II

BEFORE CONSTANTINE

4/The New Testament Koinonía

Not until the second half of the first century, some twenty years after its inception, did Christianity emerge from the shadows of literary silence, first in the letters of Paul, then in the synoptic Gospels and Acts, and finally in the rest of the writings of the New Testament. Thus any attempt to reconstruct the economic life of the early community must rely on these sources and will depend on the degree to which they are considered historically accurate. While the synoptic Gospels—Mark, Matthew, and Luke—are the source in which we find most references to the earliest Christian community, even they were written years after the events they portray. Paul's first epistles, on the other hand, are slightly earlier than Mark—probably the oldest of the three synoptic Gospels. But the epistles reflect a different setting and provide little or no information about the earliest Christian community. For these reasons scholars find it difficult or even impossible to agree on which of the sayings or doings attributed to Jesus are historically true and which are not.

No matter what position one takes on those debated questions, one thing is certain: in general, the earliest portions of the synoptic Gospels, especially the materials that scholars call the "Q" source, present us with a social setting and living conditions that are very different from the urban Hellenistic situation that would soon become the setting for Christianity. With the exception of the material that can be attributed to a Hellenistic Christian origin,[1] the synoptics reflect either the very words and actions of Jesus or the words and actions that his earliest followers attributed to him. If our goal is to uncover, not necessarily the very words of Jesus, but the earliest Christian views on wealth and related matters, the synoptic Gospels, quite apart from all scholarly debates about Jesus' *ipsissima verba,* will provide us with abundant material.[2]

On the other hand, a number of other sources provide information, not directly about the earliest Jesus movement, but about conditions in

Palestine, and specifically in Galilee. The works of Josephus, the Dead Sea Scrolls, and numerous bits and pieces that can be gathered from other Jewish and Roman writers comprise such sources. From these and from the Q material in the synoptic Gospels, we draw a picture of an almost exclusively rural society, with significant urban pockets whose leadership had little contact with the peasantry, a society with practically no middle class.

The Setting

As throughout the Roman Empire, the backbone of the economy in first-century A.D. Palestine was agriculture. Here too, latifundia had increased both in size and in number, although the traditional small landholder still survived.[3] Peasants who did not own their plots lived under one of three arrangements: a fixed rent, payment of a predetermined portion of their produce to the owner, or the status of a *colonus*.[4]

The period of the Herodians (37 B.C.–A.D. 70) saw significant change in land tenure, accelerating the dispossession of the local peasantry as well as of many of the former Hasmonean nobility. Many of the latter Herod executed and then either appropriated their lands or redistributed them among his supporters. When Samaria was rebuilt and given the name of Sebaste, six thousand Roman veterans were settled in the area and given land to till.[5] In Galilee itself, most of the better land belonged to large landholders, while the small properties seem to have concentrated on the less fertile hill country. It is also likely that some of the Hasmonean nobles executed by Herod owned land in Galilee and that therefore such land was held either by the royal house itself or by its supporters.[6]

The burden of taxation was heavy, especially for the Jewish population. Foreign conquest had brought no relief from the traditional tithes and other such obligations and had added the further burden of secular taxation.[7] As elsewhere in the empire, the burden of secular taxation fell on the lower classes, and those under the protection of the authorities paid much less than their just share. Herod himself was one of Rome's richest vassals, if not the richest, and this he owed to the taxes he collected from the local inhabitants.[8] Herod's annual income, which was only a part of the royal revenue, has been estimated at 1,000 talents.[9] Eventually his exactions grew to such an extent that a delegation was sent from Palestine to Augustus.[10] The delegation complained about Herod's expropriations, implying that Herod executed people, including members of his own family, in order to disposses them. The delegation also protested against Herod's ruthless and corrupt methods of collecting taxes. Since this was a delegation of Jewish notables, and they felt so oppressed, one can only imagine how the peasantry felt. One indication may be that given the opportunity in the midst of a revolt, the Galileans killed a number of Herod's supporters by drowning them in the Sea of Gennesareth.[11] At any rate, the delegation was generally believed in Rome, where it was said that Augustus had declared that he would rather be Herod's pig than his son, presumably because Herod, being a Jew, would not kill a pig. Still, nothing was done, and Herod continued his extortions.

After the death of Herod the Great in 4 B.C., Judea was formally incorporated into the empire, but the situation did not improve. The procurators and other provincial administrators, expecting that their term of office would be short, sought to enrich themselves as quickly as possible. They found new and more ingenious ways to collect ever more revenue. To this was added the corruption of the tax collectors themselves, whose main source of profit lay precisely in gathering more taxes than they actually paid to the treasury. By the second century, a Roman official is said to have responded to a delegation of Palestinians complaining about increasing taxation: "Verily, if I had my way, I would tax your air."[12] The people made repeated appeals for tax relief, sometimes arguing that such heavy taxation simply forced inhabitants to abandon the land and resort to brigandage.[13]

The peasantry also suffered from the difficulties of competing with larger landowners. In the long run, market fluctuations favored the rich who could afford a smaller margin of profit or even some losses.[14] The peasants, on the other hand, often found that a drop in the price of their produce forced them to sell their land in order to meet expenses and especially to pay taxes. In such cases, the land would be sold to a larger landholder, and the peasant would continue to till it, although now under new conditions. To make matters worse, the three main products of the area, wheat, wine and oil, were strictly controlled by the government, which made it even more difficult for peasants to find good prices.

War, social unrest, and natural disaster also took their toll. Josephus repeatedly speaks of famine caused by drought, earthquake, or disease. As we shall see later, one of these famines occurred shortly after Pentecost, and may be related to Paul's collection for the poor in Jerusalem. Thus when Mark 13:8 says that "there will be earthquakes in various places, there will be famines," it is not speaking of unknown phenomena.[15]

Around the lake, a goodly number of Galileans made a living by fishing. Connected to fishing was a small industry of salting and preserving fish for market. Again, this appears to have been controlled by wealthy merchants, and the fisherfolk apparently had a minimum margin of profit.[16]

These conditions resulted in a social stratification in which the two extremes of wealth and poverty prevailed. It has been pointed out that the parables of Jesus speak of basically two classes, the rich landholder and the poor peasant or laborer.[17] Indeed, the relationship between creditor and debtor or between employer and day laborer or between rich master and humble servant is the subject of many parables.

The subjects of the parables must have been an important factor in people's reactions to early Christian preaching. It is not difficult to imagine how the peasantry of Galilee would respond to a parable so closely describing their situation and their feelings toward the ruling authorities in Jerusalem and in Rome as the one in Matthew 18, where the rich deal in fabulous sums such as ten thousand talents, while the poor go to jail for a mere hundred denarii:

Therefore the kingdom of heaven may be compared to a king who wished to settle accounts with his servants. When he began the reckoning, one was brought to him who owed him ten thousand talents; and as he could not pay, his lord ordered him to be sold, with his wife and children and all that he had, and payment to be made. So the servant fell on his knees, imploring him, "Lord, have patience with me, and I will pay you everything." And out of pity for him the lord of that servant released him and forgave him the debt. But that same servant, as he went out, came upon one of his fellow servants who owed him a hundred denarii; and seizing him by the throat he said, "Pay what you owe." So his fellow servant fell down and besought him, "Have patience with me, and I will pay you." He refused and went and put him in prison till he should pay the debt. When his fellow servants saw what had taken place, they were greatly distressed, and they went and reported to their lord all that had taken place. Then his lord summoned him and said to him, "You wicked servant! I forgave you all that debt because you besought me; and should you not have had mercy on your fellow servant, as I had mercy on you?" And in anger his lord delivered him to the jailers, till he should repay all his debt.[18]

Such preaching, however, was not the only response to the social tensions of the time. Revolt and rebellion waited always just below the surface, ready to explode at any time. The Zealots kept the flame of nationalism alive, feeding on the people's desire for social redress. Some sources indicate that under Roman rule Galilee fared better than Judea proper,[19] especially during and after the great rebellion against Rome. But even there the spirit of discontent and revolt seethed. Throughout Jewish territory, the memory of the Maccabees still lingered, and much opposition to the Herodians clustered around that memory. Indeed, it is possible to draw a line connecting such Maccabean memories, the many lesser revolts under early Roman rule, and the great war that ended with the fall of Masada in A.D. 72.[20] The first century A.D. clearly saw instability in Palestine, connected both with existing social conditions and with the messianic nationalism that would lead to the great war and its sequels (A.D. 66–135).

In Galilee itself, Herod had executed a certain Hezekiah whom he accused of being a brigand. In all probability Hezekiah was a Hasmonean supporter who resorted to guerrilla tactics.[21] In 4 B.C. Hezekiah's son Judas led a revolt that centered in Sepphoris and spread throughout the land.[22] Ten years later, Judas "the Galilean" led a similar revolt, and his sons and followers kept the flame of resistance alive at least until the fall of Masada.[23] If Judas the Galilean is the same as the son of Hezekiah, this would mean that there was a direct line of Galilean resistance leaders linking the Hasmoneans or Maccabees with the great revolt of A.D. 66.

From the Jesus Movement to the First Urban Churches

In this unsettled atmosphere, full of fear and resentment, of crushing poverty and messianic expectations, the Jesus movement began. It is not surprising, therefore, that Jewish leaders such as the famed rabbi Gamaliel connected it in their minds with the long tradition of revolt.[24] Nor is it surprising that the Gospels depict the early disciples as expecting the impending restoration of Israel. While such political matters and expectations are not our central concern here, it is important to keep them in mind, for they are the context of the Jesus movement's treatment of wealth.

All our sources indicate that the core of the preaching both of Jesus and of his early followers was the Kingdom of God. Such preaching had both political and economic implications. On the political side, it is clear that anyone proclaiming the coming Kingdom of God is at least by implication criticizing the present kingdom. In conditions such as those prevailing in Palestine at the time, it is not surprising that many, both among the disciples and among the authorities, interpreted the preaching of the Kingdom in the light of the long line of apocalyptic revolts and announcements of the restoration of Israel. Nor is it surprising that eventually Jesus was crucified—as many had been before him—as a pretended restorer of the throne of David.

It is the economic side of the preaching of the Kingdom that interests us here. In the Gospel narratives, the preaching of the Kingdom does indeed have a strong economic or socioeconomic component. It relates to both the justice that the Kingdom requires and the need for drastic action in view of its impending reality. Both themes appear in the preaching of John the Baptist, at least as Luke later reported it:

"Even now the axe is laid to the root of the trees; . . . He who has two coats, let him share with him who has none; and he who has food, let him do likewise." Tax collectors also came to be baptized, and said to him, "Teacher, what shall we do?" And he said to them, "Collect no more than is appointed you." Soldiers also asked him, "And we, what shall we do?" And he said to them, "Rob no one by violence or by false accusation, and be content with your wages."[25]

Themes of economic justice appear repeatedly in the preaching of Jesus and of the early movement. They show up often in the background, as in the many parables that deal with economic matters (the laborers in the vineyard, the unjust steward, the talents, and so forth). And they appear in the foreground, often in starker terms and with more radical demands than those attributed to the Baptist.

First appears the theme of the "great reversal," best summarized in the saying "the last will be first, and the first last" (Matt. 20:16). This saying, which appears in several different contexts in the Gospels (Matt. 19:30; Mark 10:31; Luke 13:30) is generally considered by scholars to have been part of the earliest Christian proclamation and to have existed quite apart from the different contexts in which it now appears. In some of these contexts, it apparently indicates that those who precede others in holiness and religiosity will not necessarily be first in the Kingdom. But in other contexts, and quite probably in its original setting, it means simply that those who are now underprivileged and oppressed will be first in the Kingdom.[26] Such is also the meaning of the parable of the rich man and Lazarus, which at least in its core is generally considered to be older than the Gospel of Luke.[27] But probably the clearest affirmation of such reversal is found in the Lukan version of the beatitudes, which is probably closer to the original proclamation of the Jesus movement than the more commonly known version in Matthew:

> Blessed are you poor, for yours is the kingdom of God.
> Blessed are you that hunger now, for you shall be satisfied.
> Blessed are you that weep now, for you shall laugh.
> But woe to you that are rich, for you have received your consolation.
> Woe to you that are full now, for you shall hunger.[28]

In this connection another of the "harsh sayings" of Jesus must be considered: his response to the "rich young ruler," and the commentary that follows regarding the camel and the eye of a needle. The story that appears in all three synoptic Gospels (Matt. 19:16–29; Mark 10:17–30; Luke 18:18–30) may be seen both as another example of the great reversal and as a call to renunciation. The reversal clearly takes place in that, barring a miracle, the rich will be excluded from the Kingdom. The call to renunciation appears both in Jesus' instructions to the rich man: "Sell what you have, and give to the poor" (which in Luke's later version becomes "sell *all* you have and distribute to the poor") and in his response to the disciples' inquiry about their own rewards: "Truly I say to you, there is no one who has left house or brothers or sisters or mother or father or children or lands, for my sake and for the gospel, who will not receive a hundred-fold now in this time, houses and brothers and sisters and mothers and children and lands, with persecutions, and in the age to come eternal life."[29]

Clearly, by the time these sayings were incorporated into the Gospel of Mark (and through it into the other Gospels) they were already presenting some difficulties for the Gospel writer. This is probably why we are told that the disciples were astonished and asked who could then be saved (Mark 10:26).[30] In any case, it is significant that the other two synoptic writers did not leave it out.

In the story of the rich ruler, a further theme has been added to that of the great reversal: the need for radical renunciation. The passage implies that, if indeed the great reversal can be expected, then what those who are first, the powerful and rich, must do is somehow to join the ranks of the last, the weak and the poor. In twentieth-century vocabulary, we would speak of "solidarity with the oppressed," but with the caveat that in these stories the solidarity that is envisioned is much more than sympathy or support, for it involves actually becoming poor.

In what context were these words actually taught? In his *Sociology of Early Palestinian Christianity*, Gerd Theissen paints a credible picture of an early Jesus movement composed both of wandering preachers and of a relatively more stable community of "sympathizers."[31] As he sees matters, the bulk of the teachings that have come down to us in the earliest material in the synoptics reflects the kind of preaching that was possible under conditions of wandering rootlessness. Jesus was not the only one who had "nowhere to lay his head" (Matt. 8:20). Those among his disciples who followed him in his wanderings and who, as Peter declared, had left everything in order to follow him continued wandering after the events of Easter. Having given up home, family, and possessions, they were able to speak and repeat the harsh sayings we find in the synoptics, and it was thanks to them that such sayings were preserved.

According to Theissen, the wandering preachers could not have survived without the active support of relatively more established communities and of individuals who had not given up all their riches. In Luke 8:1–3 we are told of a number of women who did follow Jesus, at least in part of his wanderings, but who apparently retained enough wealth to be able to support Jesus and those who followed him. Many others simply remained in their villages, at first hardly distinguishing themselves from the rest of their communities, but providing Jesus and his wandering preachers with shelter, food, and alms. As time passed and the breach between Christians and orthodox Jews became greater, these communities gained a greater sense of identity. The distinction between such communities and the preachers was not rigid. Indeed, one of the themes of the preachers was precisely calling members of the community to take up their style of life. Some did, and thus were the ranks of the wandering preachers replenished. Others did not, and the preachers did not fault them for that, for the simple reason that without the support of those who remained in their villages the preachers themselves would not have been able to continue their ministry. Thus arose ambivalent preaching on possessions as well as on other topics about which the two groups differed. While the wandering preachers and teachers recommended total renunciation, they also made room for those who were not ready to take such a step.

At this point one must take exception with Theissen's reconstruction, for he may be overstating the contrast between the "social rootlessness" of the wandering preachers and the settled life of those who remained in their villages. From what we have already seen about conditions in Galilee, it would seem that regarding material wealth and security little difference existed between the preachers and the communities of sympathizers. The poverty of the preachers, perhaps with rare exceptions, was not voluntary. It simply showed their acceptance of a condition that was quite general in their society and their rejection of the anxiety and fear that went along with such a condition. Their appeal to well-to-do sympathizers did not rest on the authority of poverty freely chosen, like Franciscans appealing to members of a tertiary order. The preachers had been born poor; they lived and wandered among others born in equal poverty, proclaiming the message that there is hope for the poor but that this hope must begin by trusting in God and giving up the anxieties that normally accompany poverty.[32] Their supposed "ambivalence" or "lack of principle," allowing for those who were not ready to adopt their way of life, was not a matter of knowing on which side their bread was buttered but simply a matter of understanding the anxieties of the desperately and hopelessly poor and knowing that such anxieties must be met, not with some dogmatic program of renunciation, but rather with a message of hope.

Returning to the passage about the rich young ruler, it should be obvious that in a way this passage is an anomaly. Most of the sayings in the Markan and Q materials are primarily addressed to poor people. What they call for is not a renunciation of goods that such people do not have but a renunciation of fear and anxiety, an affirmation of hope and solidarity. Significantly, even a passage addressed to the well-to-do, such as the story of the "rich young ruler," immediately turns the hearer's attention away from the rich and toward the anxieties of the followers of Jesus. The theme is clear: in most of the Markan and Q materials the context is a situation in which people are truly anxious and have reason to be anxious about what they will eat or wear.

The Growth of the Urban Communities

The situation is different in the material understood as Luke's. Although Luke has often been considered the "Gospel of the poor," because much is said in it about the poor, it could in fact be called the "Gospel of the prosperous," for its purpose is precisely to call to repentance an audience that was almost totally absent from the earliest preaching of the Jesus movement.[33] What we have here is an interpretation of the gospel in a setting that is mostly urban.[34] In this Christian community the "poor" are spoken of, not as present, but rather as those for whom believers ought to be concerned. In this context poverty as a voluntary choice and renunciation as a virtue become important. The disciples are depicted as leaving *everything* (Luke 5:11, 28); the rich man—now become a "ruler"—is told to "sell *all* you have" (Luke 18:22). Perfect discipleship entails renunciation of goods one could otherwise possess. For others who are not ready to go that far, Luke offers a number of examples of prosperous people whose encounter with Jesus led them to repentance and to sharing their possessions: the wealthy women who supported Jesus and his followers (Luke 8:2–3) and the chief tax collector, who upon meeting Jesus decided to give half of his wealth to the poor and to return to any whom he had defrauded four times as much as he took from them (Luke 19:8). Regarding the preaching of John the Baptist, it is Luke who gives detailed instructions as to what people making their living as tax collectors and soldiers ought to do. If, as is quite possible, the woes on the rich in Luke 6 and the last verses of the parable of the rich man and Lazarus are Lukan additions to earlier materials, they would reinforce the thesis that Luke is addressing a community that includes people for whom possessions are indeed a problem and for whom renunciation and almsgiving have therefore become a necessary sign of repentance. In short, Luke is dealing with the question that will later become a burning issue for Clement of Alexandria: how can the rich be saved?

Luke is not the only place in the New Testament addressing the question of how to deal with a church that includes both rich and poor. Apparently, the church of the Epistle of James faces a similar problem, for the text acknowledges the possibility of someone coming to the assembly with gold rings and in fine clothing and the temptation of giving that person special consideration (James 2:1–7).[35] Here one finds once again the theme of the great reversal, with an emphasis on the need to respond in the light of that coming reversal: "Let the lowly brother boast in his exaltation, and the rich in his humiliation" (James 1:9); "Come now, you rich, weep and howl for the miseries that are coming upon you . . . " (James 5:1). Here again, although indirectly, the question of the salvation of the rich is posed, and the answer appears to be a call (although not only to the rich) to works of mercy:

What does it profit, my brethren, if a man says he has faith but has no works? Can his faith save him? If a brother or a sister is ill-clad and in lack of daily food, and one of you says to them, "Go in peace, be warmed and filled," without giving them the things needed for the body, does it profit? So faith by itself, if it has no works, is dead. (James 2:14–17)

The Meaning of Koinonía

Returning to Luke/Acts, within the context of this economically mixed community we must interpret two of the most debated passages in Acts:

And all who believed were together and had all things in common; and they sold their possessions and goods and distributed them to all, as any had need. (Acts 2:44–45)

Now the company of those who believed were of one heart and soul, and no one said that any of the things which he possessed was his own, but they had everything in common . . . There was not a needy person among them, for as many as were possessors of lands or houses sold them, and brought the proceeds of what was sold and laid it at the apostles' feet; and distribution was made to each as any had need. (Acts 4:32–35)

As we look at these passages, the first obvious question is, did this actually happen? Did the early Christians practice the sort of commonality described here, or is it a fictional reconstruction of the life of the early church on the part of the author? Some scholars have held the latter, arguing that what is described here is too close to the ideal community of certain Hellenistic traditions—the Pythagorean in particular—and that it is therefore no more than an attempt to depict the early Christian church as an ideal community. Typical of this line of interpretation is Luke T. Johnson, who speaks of the passage in Acts 2 as "idyllic," and of the one in Acts 4 as a literary device to symbolize the authority of the apostles.[36] In another work Johnson points to a series of possible Hellenistic sources that have become standard in supporting this line of interpretation: Plato; a proverb quoted by Aristotle; and the lives of Pythagoras by Diogenes Laertius, Porphyry, and Iamblicus.[37] Briefly, the argument is that the author of Luke/Acts, seeking to describe the earliest Christian community, draws on Hellenistic materials extolling the value of unity and friendship, particularly as expressed in the common possession of goods.

The first difficulty with such an interpretation is that it ignores the obvious contrasts between the Pythagorean ideal and what is described here. One is an elitist association of philosophers who share things because this allows them to devote themselves to the "philosophical life"; the other is an open community that rejoices in adding thousands to its numbers and whose ability to share is the consequence of the outpouring of the Spirit and the resulting vivid eschatological expectation.

A second difficulty is the need to explain why or how the author was able to project into a fairly recent past a practice that did not exist at the time Acts was written. Indeed, one of the basic principles in the interpretation of historical texts is that writers tend to project into the past the practices and conditions of their own time. If at the time Acts was written—say in or around A.D. 80—commonality of goods was not the practice of the church, why would the author say that it had been before? Perhaps in order to present the early Christian community in ideal terms? That would be possible if Luke could be accused of presenting an ideal picture of the early church. But that is certainly not the case. Indeed, immediately after the second of the passages quoted above comes the episode of Ananias and Sapphira, a husband and wife who try to deceive the community precisely on the matter of the use of property. And soon thereafter we are told that "the Hellenists murmured against the Hebrews because their widows were neglected in the early distribution" (Acts 6:1).

A third objection to interpreting these passages as Luke's attempt to idealize the life of the early church is the high probability that these passages themselves—often called the "summaries" in Acts—are pre-Lukan material that the author of Acts incorporated at what seemed to be appropriate places in the narrative.[38] Still, one could argue that, just as Luke introduced or at least reinterpreted the theme of renunciation in the teachings of Jesus in order to shame the rich, so could the second volume of the series, Acts, introduce the theme of common property for the same purpose.

Ultimately, however, the matter of the historicity of the two accounts under discussion can be laid to rest if it can be shown that at the time Acts was written—and indeed for some time after that—what Luke has here described was still practiced. That is indeed the case, as we will show.

Before we turn to that discussion, however, another common interpretation of these passages in Acts must be mentioned. According to this interpretation, the early church did indeed have all things in common at the beginning, but this practice was soon abandoned. Usually, this interpretation includes the notion—with no basis in the texts themselves—that at least one of the reasons the Christian community in Jerusalem was poor and Paul spent so much effort on its relief was precisely the improvidence implied in this failed communistic experiment. This view is succinctly expressed in one of the biblical commentaries most commonly used today by preachers in the United States: "Whatever may have been the extent of this 'communistic' experiment at Jerusalem, it appears very soon to have broken down, first, perhaps on account of the dissension between 'Hellenists' and 'Hebrews' (6:1), and second, because the administrators who had been appointed as a result of the dispute had been driven from the city by the Jews. Probably also the eager expectation of the Parousia led to improvidence for the future, so that the Jerusalem community was always poor."[39]

The notion that the poverty of Christians in Jerusalem resulted from their improvidence in sharing all their goods and using up their capital is fairly common. Yet there is no basis for such an interpretation, either in Acts or in other contemporary records. On the contrary, Acts speaks of a great famine as the reason relief was needed (Acts 11:27–30). Josephus speaks of a famine in Judea that reached its apex around A.D. 46.[40] And Roman historians Tacitus and Suetonius mention several famines during the reign of Claudius, which is also the time at which Acts dates the famine that produced the need for a collection.[41]

In order to respond both to the "idyllic fiction" view and to the "economic disaster" interpretation, we have to begin by clarifying the commonality of goods to which Acts refers. First of all, the notion that people simply went out and sold all they had in order to share it with the rest is built on an incorrect interpretation of the Greek grammar.[42] The Greek language has two forms of the past tense. One, the imperfect, indicates a continuing past action. The other, the aorist, refers to an action completed once and for all. In the texts under discussion, all verbs appear in the imperfect. Therefore, what the text says is not exactly that "they sold their possessions and goods and distributed them to all, as any had need" (Acts 2:45), but rather that they continued doing this or, as the New American Standard Bible says, "They began selling their property and possessions, and were sharing them with all, as any might have need."

The use of the imperfect tense also points to a major difference between the community described in these texts and the Hellenistic and other communes, including that of Qumran, with which it has been compared. Here the community of goods is not the guiding principle. No matter how much Luke's Gospel has made of renunciation, what is described in Acts is a community where people relinquish their possessions, not for the sake of renunciation, but for the sake of those in need. In both passages under discussion the need of the recipients plays an important role. The goal is not an abstract or dogmatic notion of unity nor a principle of purity and renunciation but meeting the needs of others.

It is inevitable in such a community that those who are most generous, such as Barnabas, will arouse the jealousy of others such as Ananias and Sapphira. Yet the very fact that the book of Acts tells the story of both Barnabas's generosity and the deception of Ananias and Sapphira immediately after describing the community of goods indicates that this is neither an attempt to paint the early community in idyllic tones, nor to describe a dogmatically communistic commune. Peter clearly tells Ananias (Acts 5:4) that he was under no obligation to sell his property, and that having sold it he did not have to bring the proceeds to the community. Thus Acts describes an imperfect community with its share of liars and jealousy. In chapter 6 the conflict between the Hellenists and the Aramaic speakers over the distribution of relief to the widows of each group will be further proof of the imperfect nature of this community. The self-understanding of this group, however, is such that "no one said that the things which he possessed was his own." Yet, the actual working out of the sharing that this implied depended both on the needs of those who had no possessions and on the free will to share on the part of the more fortunate.

As we look further at the description of this community in Acts we must pay close attention to the word *koinonía*, by which this community is described in Acts 2:42. The Revised Standard Version and the New American Standard Bible translate it as "fellowship," and the Jerusalem Bible as "brotherhood." This is the common understanding of this word, which is usually taken to refer to the inner disposition of goodwill—"fellowship"—toward other members of the group. Thus taken, what Acts 2:42 says is simply that there were good relationships within the community.

Yet *koinonía* means much more than that. It also means partnership, as in a common business venture. In this way Luke uses the related term *koinonós*, member of a *koinonía*, for in Luke 5:10 we are told that the sons of Zebedee were *koinonoí* with Peter, meaning that they were business partners. The same usage appears outside the New Testament, sometimes in very similar contexts.[43] *Koinonía* means first of all, not fellowship in the sense of good feelings toward each other, but sharing. It is used in that sense throughout the New Testament, both in connection with material goods and in other contexts. In Philippians 3:10, what the Revised Standard Version translates as "share his sufferings" actually says "know the *koinonía* of his sufferings." In 1 Corinthians 10:16, Paul says, "The cup of blessing which we bless, is it not a participation in the blood of Christ? The bread which we break, is it not a participation in the body of Christ?" The term that the Revised Standard Version translates here as "participation," with a footnote explaining that it could also be translated as "communion," is *koinonía*. Paul's letter to the Philippians, which acknowledges receipt of a gift, begins with words in which Paul is thanking the Philippians for their partnership and sharing with him. In 1:5, he says that he is thankful for the Philippians' *koinonía*, and two verses later he declares that they are "joint *koinonoí*" of grace with him, that is, common owners or sharers. At the end of the epistle, he says that they have shared in his trouble (4:14), and the term he uses could be translated as "cokoinonized." All of this leads to the unique partnership "in giving and receiving" that he has enjoyed with the church of the Philippians (4:15), and once again the word he uses literally means "koinonized." In short, *koinonía* is much more than a feeling of fellowship; it involves sharing goods as well as feelings.

Returning to Acts 2:42, it is clear that *koinonía* there is much more than fellowship: "They devoted themselves to the apostles' teaching and *koinonía*, to the breaking of bread and prayers." The four things listed here, the apostles' teaching, *koinonía*, the breaking of bread, and prayers, are taken up in almost the same order in verses 43 to 47, where we are told (1) that fear came upon every soul, and wonders and signs were done through the apostles; (2) that all who believed had all things in common; (3) that they attended the temple and praised God; and (4) that they broke bread in their homes and partook of food with glad and generous hearts. The *koinonía* is not simply a spiritual sharing.[44] It is a total sharing that includes the material as well as the spiritual.

Having clarified the connection of the commonality of goods in Acts 2 and 4 with the idea of *koinonía*, we can now return to the question posed earlier: are there indications that such sharing of goods continued—if it ever existed—after the time that those early chapters of Acts claim to describe? Again, the question is not whether all Christians went out and sold everything at once and put it into a common treasury. As we have seen, that is not the situation that Acts describes. The question is whether we can find indications that, at other times and places in the life of the church described in the New Testament, the Christian community was a partnership that included material as well as spiritual sharing, that this sharing was to be governed by the need of the less fortunate, and that, though voluntary, this sharing and the vision behind it challenged the traditional—particularly the Roman—understanding of private property.

When the question is posed in these terms, the obvious answer is found in the collection for the poor in Jerusalem that plays such an important role in the epistles of Paul. This collection is not a responsibility added to Paul's apostleship; rather it is part and parcel of it. Indeed, as Paul himself describes his authentication by the leaders in Jerusalem, the collection for the poor was an important part of his commission (Gal. 2:10).[45] As we look at that collection and the manner in which Paul describes it in his letters, it is clear that it continues the practice of *koinonía* described in Acts 2 and 4.

Of all the churches among which Paul worked in collecting the offering for Jerusalem, the best known is that in Corinth. Paul's Corinthian correspondence provides much information both about the economic life of Christians in that city and about how Paul understood and interpreted the collection in which he was engaged. The social structure of the Corinthian church has been amply studied.[46] Probably the best conclusion is that of biblical scholar Wayne Meeks, that the prominent members of the Pauline churches, including Corinth, were people of "high status inconsistency."[47] While not all the members of a church such as that in Corinth were poor, those who had greater financial resources were people whose status was limited by other factors. In any case, it is clear that marked economic differences existed among members of the Corinthian church and that these differences created difficulties, for Paul says that when they gather for the common meal some are hungry while others are drunk (1 Cor. 11:21).

Paul is clear about the deep contradiction between such behavior, which humiliates the poor, and the very nature of the church. Those who have much to eat while others do not have enough are not only humiliating the poor but also despising the church (1 Cor. 11:22). And a case could be made that Paul is referring to them when he declares that "any one who eats and drinks without discerning the body {that is, without realizing that this community is the body of Christ} eats and drinks judgment upon himself" (1 Cor. 11:29).

In any case, as Paul speaks of the collection in Corinth, he instructs his readers to set aside a certain amount on the first day every week, so that special contributions will not have to be made upon his arrival (1 Cor. 16:1–4). The phrase that the Revised Standard Version translates "as he may prosper" is difficult to translate. It certainly does not mean that they should contribute only if they prospered. More likely it means that they should set aside as much as they could. These instructions, which Paul says that he has given also to the churches of Galatia, seem to apply to a community most of whose members are neither destitute nor rich.[48] At the same time, Paul expects the total amount he is raising to be liberal, abundant, or even lavish (2 Cor. 8:20).

Paul's theological understanding of the offering for Jerusalem is best seen in 2 Corinthians, chapters 8 and 9. Paul begins by giving the Corinthians news of the collection in Macedonia, where the response was such that "their abundance of joy and their extreme poverty have overflowed in a wealth of liberality on their part."[49] Paul makes clear throughout his argument that the gifts he is requesting should be made voluntarily. The Macedonians have given "of their own free will" (8:3). Paul stresses that his asking the Corinthians for an offering is not a command (8:8). Their offering should be "ready not as an exaction but as a willing gift" (9:5). And "each one must do as he has made up his mind, not reluctantly or under compulsion, for God loves a cheerful giver" (9:7). Thus, just as in Acts the giving was voluntary, and Peter told Ananias that he had been under no obligation to give, so here Paul makes it clear that giving must be from the heart and not out of an exterior compulsion or a dogmatic understanding of the community of goods.

The voluntary nature of the gift does not mean, however, that no goals or guidelines apply. In this text, the goal is equality: "I do not mean that others should be eased and you burdened, but that as a matter of equality your abundance at the present time should supply their want, so that their abundance may supply your want, that there may be equality. As it is written, 'He who gathered much had nothing over, and he who gathered little had no lack'" (2 Cor. 8:13–15).

The text is unclear as to how the abundance of the recipients will supply the want of the givers. Possibly it means that the Christians in Jerusalem, though materially poor, are spiritually rich, and that from this abundance the Corinthians will profit. The idea is fairly common in later patristic thought, that the prayers of the poor have greater efficacy, and that when the rich give to the poor the latter repay their benefactors by praying for them. This may be what Paul means here. Another option, however, would be to take a clue from the phrase "at the present time" and to interpret the text as meaning that when, at some future date, the Corinthians are in need, those in Jerusalem will come to their aid.

Whatever the case may be, Paul clearly says that the purpose of the offering is to promote equality. At present, the Corinthians enjoy relative abundance, at least of material wealth. It is clear from 1 Corinthians 1:26 that the church in Corinth did not include the aristocracy of that city. Still, in comparison with those in Jerusalem they lived in abundance. It is the contrast between the need in Jerusalem and the abundance in Corinth that must be overcome by the offering. The Corinthians are to give because those in Jerusalem are in need. Thus, as in the case of the original commonality of goods in Acts 2 and 4, what controls the giving is the need of the poor.

In this context, and to strengthen his argument, Paul cites the miracle of the redistribution of manna. In Exodus 16:16–18, when God provided manna the Israelites were ordered to go and collect a certain measure of it (an omer) for each member of the household. As so often happens in human societies, "some gathered much and some little." Yet, when they measured what they had gathered, they found that it had been redistributed, so that each household had the amount that God had ordered. This is the miracle of equality, which shows the will of God and which Paul is exhorting the Corinthian Christians to imitate.

The Corinthian discussion displays a remarkable similarity to what the book of Acts describes as having taken place in the early church. True, the text does not say, "They had all things in common." But the spirit and practice are certainly similar to that found in Acts, especially if we read, not only the brief account of the commonality of goods, but also the examples of how this actually worked—or did not work—in the cases of Barnabas and of Ananias and Sapphira.

Luke/Acts was written after the epistles of Paul, in a circle with strong Pauline influence. Actually, the vast majority of the book of Acts is devoted to Paul's ministry. Therefore, rather than suggesting that the description of the commonality of goods in Acts is due to Hellenistic influences and to the idealizing of the early community, it seems possible to take the opposite view: even though some of the phrases used in Acts 2 and 4 may have parallels in earlier Greek literature, what Luke was describing here was the understanding of the Christian *koinonía* that had been at the very heart of Paul's ministry. If so, Acts is not speaking about a brief idyllic moment in the early life of the church or of something limited to the Jerusalem community but of something that, fully practiced or not, was still part of the self-understanding of the church—at least of the Pauline churches—everywhere. As we shall see in future chapters, this continued to be the case for several generations.

The Later Books of the New Testament

In the later books of the New Testament we find both the continuation of themes already present in the early Christian movement and the first adumbrations of themes and situations that will become clearer in later times.

The theme of *koinonía* continues in the Johanine Epistles. Indeed, 1 John begins by declaring that the Epistle itself is written "so that you may have fellowship {*koinonía*} with us; and our fellowship {*koinonía*} is with the Father and with his Son Jesus Christ" (1 John 1:3). The writer then goes on to say that it is impossible to have *koinonía* with God unless we have it among ourselves (1:6–7). The entire Epistle leads to the conclusion that "if any one has the world's goods and sees his brother in need, yet closes his heart against him, how does God's love abide in him? Little children, let us not love in word or speech but in deed and in truth" (3:17–18).[50]

The existence of wandering preachers and the need to support them are reflected in 1 John 5–8. In the Deutero-Pauline literature (Titus 1:7–11) a problem appears that we shall find again in our next chapter, namely, preachers who are upsetting and exploiting the community "by teaching for base gain."[51]

Also in the Deutero-Pauline Epistles appear a number of references to the temptation involved in riches. The evil of the "last days" includes people who will be "lovers of self, lovers of money, proud, arrogant, abusive . . . " (2 Tim. 3:1–2). And the following passage clearly reflects a church in which some have, or at least are seeking, more than they need:

There is great gain in godliness with contentment; for we brought nothing into the world, and we cannot take anything out of the world; but if we have food and clothing, with these we shall be content. But those who desire to be rich fall into temptation, into a snare, into many senseless and hurtful desires that plunge men into ruin and destruction. For the love of money is the root of all evils; it is through this craving that some have wandered away from the faith and pierced their hearts with many pangs. (1 Tim. 6:6–10)

Along the same lines, Hebrews 10:34 praises believers who "joyfully accepted the plundering of your property, since you knew that you yourselves had a better possession and an abiding one." They are also told that Moses "considered abuse suffered for the Christ greater wealth than the treasure of Egypt, for he looked to the reward" (Heb. 11:26). And they are exhorted: "Keep your life free from love of money, and be content with what you have" (Heb. 13:5).

The theme of a reward for those who do not cling to their wealth but employ it for good deeds, sounds most clearly in 1 Timothy 6:17–19: "As for the rich in this world, charge them not to be haughty, nor to set their hopes on uncertain riches but on God who richly furnishes us with everything to enjoy. They are to do good, to be rich in good deeds, liberal and generous, thus laying up for themselves a good foundation for the future, so that they may take hold of the life which is life indeed."

Here we find, not only the notion that by making good use of treasures on earth one can acquire treasures in heaven, but also the contrast between two kinds of riches. Some are "rich in this world"; others are "rich in good deeds." While the two are not mutually exclusive, they are quite distinct. In the chapters that follow, we shall find that a fairly common theme in early Christian literature is that those who apparently are rich are in truth poor and vice versa. This theme appears already in the book of Revelation, where the words to the church in Smyrna, "I know your tribulation and your poverty (but you are rich)" (Rev. 2:9), contrast with the message to the church in Laodicea: "For you say, I am rich, I have prospered, and I need nothing; not knowing that you are wretched, pitiable, poor, blind, and naked. Therefore I counsel you to buy from me gold refined by fire, that you may be rich" (Rev. 3:17–18).

These are only a few of the many passages that should be explored in a fuller investigation of issues of faith and wealth in the New Testament. They are offered here, not in an attempt at exhaustiveness, but simply to provide the necessary background for the chapters that follow. Still, they suffice to show that the matter of the relationship between faith and wealth is not foreign to the New Testament.

NOTES

1. Much of this material consists not of long passages, but rather of changed settings or slight variations which betray a later interpretation.
2. G. Theissen, *Sociology of Early Palestinian Judaism* (Philadelphia: Fortress, 1978), pp.3–4, has expressed this point quite well:
   Thus we may leave open the question whether the traditions about Jesus are true or false. If we presuppose that a tradition is genuine, we may assume that those who handed it down shaped their lives in accordance with the tradition. If we assume that it originated within the Jesus movement in the period after Easter, we can presuppose that those who handed it down shaped the tradition in accordance with their lives. In either case the result is the same: there is a correspondence between the social groups which handed down the tradition and the tradition itself. Thus a sociology of the Jesus movement transcends the dispute of both "conservative" and "critical" exegetes over the authenticity and historicity of the tradition. It is unaffected by the dilemmas of the quest for the historical Jesus.
3. See M. Gil, "Land Ownership in Palestine under Roman Rule," *RIntDrAnt* 17 (1970): 11–53. See also R. K. Gnuse, *You Shall not Steal: Community and Property in the Biblical Tradition* (Maryknoll, N.Y.: Orbis, 1985), pp. 87–88.
4. S. Freyne, *Galilee from Alexander the Great to Hadrian (323 B.C.E. to 135 C.E.)* (Wilmington: Michael Glazier, 1980), p. 202 n. 16.
5. Josephus, *Ant.* 15.296; *De bel. Jud.* 1.403. All references to Josephus are from *LCL*.
6. Freyne, *Galilee*, p. 164.
7. A point stressed by F. C. Grant, *The Economic Background of the Gospels* (Oxford: Clarendon, 1923), p. 89.
8. Josephus, *Ant.* 17.4–5; Horace, *Epod.* 2.2.184; Strabo, *Geog.* 16.2.46.
9. S. W. Baron, *A Social and Religious History of the Jews* (Philadelphia: The Jewish Publication society of America, 1958), 1:262.
10. Josephus, *Ant.* 17.4.204; 11.2.306–7.
11. Josephus, *Ant.* 14.450.
12. Quoted in Baron, *Social and Religious History,* 1:263.
13. Josephus, *Ant.,* 18.274. Cf. Tacitus, *Ann.* ii.42, *LCL*.
14. The question of whether or not markets were actually controlled and manipulated by the wealthy is open to debate. Cf. H. Kreissig, *Die Sozialen Zusammenhänge des jüdaischen Krieges* (Berlin: Akademie-Verlag, 1970), pp. 36–51; and M. Applebaum, "Economic Life in Palestine," in *Compendia Rerum Judaicarum ad Novum Testamentum,* ed. M. Stern and S. Safrai (Assen: Van Gorcum & Co., 1974), 2:662–66.

15. Theissen, *Sociology,* (n. 2 above) p. 40. Cf. Josephus, *Ant.* 14.28; 15.299–300, 365; 16.64; 18.8; 20.101.

16. Freyne, *Galilee,* (n. 4 above) pp. 173–74. One should remember, however, that Zebedee, the father of James and John, was sufficiently wealthy to have "hired servants" working in his boat (Mark 1:20).

17. A. N. Sherwin-White, *Roman Society and Roman Law in the New Testament* (Oxford: Oxford University Press, 1963), pp. 134–36.

18. Matt. 18:23–34.

19. Freyne, *Galilee* (n. 4 above), pp. 57–91.

20. W. R. Farmer, *Maccabees, Zealots and Josephus: An Enquiry into Jewish Nationalism in the Greco-Roman Period* (New York: Columbia University Press, 1970), argues for such a connection. Freyne, *Galilee,* pp. 208–47, tends to downplay it.

21. Josephus, *Ant.* 14.159; *De bell. Jud.* 1.204. Cf. Freyne, *Galilee,* pp. 63, 67.

22. Josephus, *Ant.* 17; *De bell. Jud.* 2.43.

23. Josephus, *Ant.* 20.102; *De bell. Jud.* 2.433, 447; 7.253. Cf. J. Kenneard, "Judas of Galilee and His Clan," *JOR,* 36 (1945–46): 281–86.

24. Acts 5:35–38.

25. Luke 3:9–14. Possibly this passage in Luke reflects a slightly later time than the earliest Jesus movement, a time when there were tax collectors and soldiers in the church. Even if that is the case, the theme of the connection between justice and the Kingdom is clearly part of the earliest proclamation.

26. L. Schottroff and W. Stegemann, *Jesus and the Hope of the Poor* (Maryknoll, NY: Orbis, 1986), pp. 24–25.

27. Ibid., pp. 25–28.

28. Luke 6:20b–21, 24–25. The blessing and the woe regarding persecution have been omitted, for they are probably an addition to the earliest proclamation. Cf. Schottroff and Stegemann, *Jesus and the Hope,* p. 19. It is also possible that the entire "negative" side of woe to the rich and prosperous reflects Luke's particular interest in calling such people to repentance. In that case, this text would show that the theme of the great reversal was still central to the understanding of Christianity in Luke's urban churches.

29. Mark 10:29–30.

30. Schottroff and Stegemann, *Jesus and the Hope,* pp. 22–23:
    We must give Mark credit for transmitting this saying even though he himself and his community could not identify with it and must have found it alarming. This is clear in particular from Mk. 10:26 where the shock of the disciples is expressly mentioned. The Markan community lived in a social situation completely different from that reflected in the earliest Jesus tradition. Rich Christians too now belonged to the community.

31. Theissen, *Sociology* (n. 2 above), pp. 9–23. He calls the preachers "wandering charismatics." Since the term *charismatic* today has connotations that Theissen apparently did not intend, I have avoided the confusion that using that term could create.

32. See the critique of Theissen's depiction in Schottroff and Stegemann, *Jesus and the Hope* (n. 26 above), pp. 48–51.

33. Such is the thesis of Schottroff and Stegemann, *Jesus and the Hope,* pp. 67–120. While I have found their study helpful, and here use it extensively, I disagree with them on a number of points. The most significant is their interpretation of the "commonality of goods" as described in the early chapters of Acts.

34. For a description of such a social setting, although on the basis of the Pauline epistles rather than the Lukan material, see W. A. Meeks, *The First Urban Christians: The Social World of the Apostle Paul* (New Haven: Yale University Press, 1983).

35. On the social background and the economic teachings of James, see P. U. Maynard-Reid, *Poverty and Wealth in James* (Maryknoll, NY: Orbis, 1987). Although Maynard-Reid places the epistle at an earlier date and more primitive setting than I would, his work does show significant insight into the meaning of the social and economic texts in the epistle.

36. L. T. Johnson, *The Literary Function of Possessions in Luke-Acts* (Missoula, MT: Scholars Press, 1977), pp. 189, 198.

37. L. T. Johnson, *Sharing Possessions: Mandate and Symbol of Faith* (Philadelphia: Fortress, 1981), p. 119.

38. See, for instance, E. Trocmé, *Le "Livre des Actes" et l'histoire* (Paris: Presses Universitaires de France, 1957), pp. 195–96. On the other hand, cf. P. Benoit, "Remarques sur les 'Sommaires' de Actes 2/42 à 5," in *Aux sources de la tradition chrétienne, Mélanges offerts à M. Goguel* (Paris: Delachaux & Niestlé, 1950), pp. 1–10. A good discussion of the historical reliability of Acts, although not dealing with the issues we are investigating, is M. Hengel, *Acts and the History of Earliest Christianity* (Philadelphia: Fortress, 1980).

39. G. H. C. Macgregor, in *The Interpreter's Bible*, 9:73. R. J. Sider, *Rich Christians in an Age of Hunger* (Downers Grove, IL: Intervarsity Press, 1977), p. 101, quotes a similar view from another contemporary author, J. A. Ziesler, *Christian Asceticism* (Grand Rapids: Eerdmans, 1973), p. 110: "The trouble in Jerusalem was that they turned their capital into income, and had no cushion for hard times, and the Gentile Christians had to come to their rescue."

40. *Ant.* 20.5.

41. Tacitus, *Ann.* 12.43, *LCL* Suetonius, *Claud.* 18, *LCL*

42. Even though one finds it in the otherwise very careful book by Schottroff and Stegemann, *Jesus and the Hope*, p. 119: "The selling and distribution of proceeds are described as actions done once and for all. Thus there is no reason for assuming that they were done in case after case, whenever someone was in need."

43. In *The Amherst Papyri*, ed B. P. Grenfell and A. S. Hunt, (London: Frowde, 1900), 1: 100, No. 4, there is the case where the fisherman Hermes takes another fisherman as his *koinonós* or partner.

44. Johnson, *Literary Function* (n. 36 above), p. 185.

45. It is interesting to speculate on the relationship between Paul's "apostleship" and his commission to collect funds for Jerusalem. Apostle is the title given in a number of texts referring to people whom the Jewish patriarchs and other leaders sent to collect funds from Jews in the Diaspora. Eusebius, *In Isa.* 18.1; Epiphanius, *Pan.* 11, 30, PG; *Cod. Theod.* 16.8.14. in Theodosiani Libri xvi, ed. Th. Mommsen (Berlin: Weidmann, 1962). These descriptions of Jewish "apostles" seem very similar to what Paul was commissioned to do when he went to Damascus before his conversion. Unfortunately, all of these texts, as well as others that speak of Jewish "apostles," come from a later date. In this context, one should note that Paul speaks of his work as "my service for Jerusalem" (Rom. 15:31). Still, one wonders if this it not part of the background of Paul's insistence on his apostolate. Is he only claiming that he has been sent by the Lord, or is he also arguing for his right to collect money for Jerusalem?

46. See especially G. Theissen, *The Social Setting of Pauline Christianity: Essays on Corinth* (Philadelphia: Fortress, 1982). Particularly interesting in this study is Theissen's attempt to relate the conflicts within the Corinthian church to the contrast between rich and poor in the community: pp. 99–110, 145–74. Cf. W. A. Meeks, *First Urban Christians* (n. 34 above), pp. 51–73.

47. *First Urban Christians*, p. 73.

48. Ibid., p. 65.

49. Meeks suggests the literal translation, "abysmal poverty," but then (ibid., p. 66) suggests also that this may be hyperbole.

50. A text often quoted in modern times but much less in the patristic period, is John 12:8: "The poor you always have with you." This text must not be interpreted, as is often the case, in the sense that Christians should be reconciled to the existence of poverty and should not seek to alleviate it. In its proper context, this text means exactly the opposite. First of all, it is a quotation from Deuteronomy 15:11. The entire passage in Deuteronomy affirms that, were the people of God to obey God's law, there would be no poor among them; but that, since perfect obedience will never take place, "the poor will never cease out of the land; therefore I command

you, You shall open your hand to your brother, to the needy and to the poor, in the land." Second, in the passage in John Jesus is responding to Judas, who has commented that Mary's extravagance in anointing the feet of Jesus with costly ointment would have been better spent on the poor. In that context, Jesus' response means that, now that he is with his disciples and is preparing for death, it is proper for Mary to be extravagant in her gift to him. After he is gone, there will be ample opportunity to practice equal liberality towards the poor.

51. Cf. Phil. 1:15–18.

5/The Subapostolic Church

By the second century, the writing of the books that now form the New Testament was coming to a close. Christian literary activity, however, did not abate. On the contrary, Christians wrote letters, sermons, manuals of discipline, and, by the middle of the second century, they were also writing learned defenses of their faith. It is to these writings that we now turn.

The Didache

One of the most tantalizing historical discoveries of the nineteenth century took place in a library in Istanbul in 1875, where an ancient manuscript was found containing a document that had long been considered irretrievably lost. The *Doctrine of the Twelve Apostles,* usually known as the *Didache,* is repeatedly quoted by Christian writers from the second to the fifth centuries. After that time, most quotes seem to be secondhand, and therefore one can presume that the document was lost at some point in the early Middle Ages. It finally resurfaced in 1875 in the library of the Knights Hospitalier of the Holy Sepulchre in Istanbul. It was then added to the list of writings that are presumed to date from the subapostolic period and are usually called the "Apostolic Fathers."

Scholars disagree on the date of composition of the *Didache.*[1] Although its author had apparently read the synoptics, the setting of the *Didache* is still very similar to the early days of the Jesus movement. By this time, however, wandering "apostles" or preachers have begun to present a problem of accreditation. The same is true of "prophets," although the relationship between these two titles is not clear. How is one to know that they are legitimate? The *Didache*'s answer reveals a fear that some people might seek to profit from the preaching of the gospel. An apostle or prophet who asks for more than bread for the road—especially one who asks for money—or one who asks to be put up for more than two days is false.[2] The content of the text points to a fairly early time in the development of church structure. On the other hand, some of the members of the communities to which the *Didache* is addressed owned slaves, pointing to a time when the church is making inroads into the middle economic strata.

Since some clues in the text point toward semidesert or arid conditions,[3] it seems safe to assume that the *Didache* reflects life in a non-Pauline church, perhaps in the semidesert zones of Syria or Palestine, at a time that is impossible to determine precisely, perhaps between A.D. 70 and 140.[4] The communities to which it is addressed are not rich; yet in addition to slaves, some members own flocks, and others have grapes to press and wheat to thresh.[5]

The *Didache* includes the earliest reference outside the New Testament to the commonality of goods of which Acts speaks:

Be not a stretcher forth of the hands to receive and a drawer of them back to give. If thou hast aught, through thy hands thou shalt give ransom for thy sins. Thou shalt not hesitate to give, nor murmur when thou givest; for thou shalt know who is the good repayer of the hire. Thou shalt not turn away from him that is in want, but thou shalt share all things with thy brother, and shalt not say that they are thine own; for if ye are partakers in that which is immortal, how much more in things which are mortal?[6]

The last few lines of this quote closely parallel Acts 4:42, where we are also told that the first Christians had all things in common and that they did not claim what they had as their own. Here again, readers are commanded not to say that things are their own. They are to share (*synkoinonein*, "cokoinonize") all things with those in need. In order to support this, the writer introduces a new argument: Christians who share—literally, who are common owners, partners, *koinonoí*—in immortal things should be ready to share likewise in the less important things that are mortal.[7]

The *Didache* also agrees with Acts in that the basis for this sharing is the other's need: "Thou shalt not turn away from him who is in want." In another passage, it lists among those who follow the "way of death," besides murderers, adulterers, and thiefs, those who do not respond to the needy, "not pitying a poor man, not labouring for the afflicted, not knowing Him that made them {the afflicted}, murderers of children, destroyers of the handywork of God, turning away from him that is in want, afflicting him that is distressed, advocates of the rich, lawless judges of the poor, utter sinners."[8]

Apart from the passing reference to material goods as "mortal," there is in the *Didache* no indication that one should dispossess oneself of such goods for the sake of renunciation, nor that one should give them to the community for the sake of a principle of shared property. The reason why one should not claim the rights of private property is the need of the other. The governing principle in giving is neither a communistic ideal nor an ascetic renunciation, but the need of the other. Apparently this is the meaning of the saying which the *Didache* quotes: "Let thine alms sweat in thy hands, until thou know to whom thou shouldst give."[9] This again is very similar to what we found in the two passages in Acts referring to the commonality of goods.

As in Acts, what is envisioned here is not the abolition of property, but its subordination to the claims of those in need. The *Didache* gives instructions for the offering of first-fruits for the support of the local prophets—or, if there are no prophets, for the support of the poor.[10] Obviously, such instructions imply that those who own fields or flocks will not necessarily rid themselves of such property, but put it at the disposal of the needy.

Finally, also like Acts, the *Didache* is not speaking of an ideal community, in which love and sharing are such that all difficulties are overcome. Just as Acts knew of Ananias and Sapphira, and of the murmurings regarding the distribution of support for the widows, the *Didache* knows of those who will try to take advantage of the community and its *koinonía*. After quoting the words of Jesus to the effect that one should give to any who ask, the *Didache* continues:

Happy is he that giveth according to the commandment; for he is guiltless. Woe to him that receiveth; for if one having need receiveth, he is guiltless; but he that receiveth not having need, shall pay the penalty, why he received and for what, and coming into straits (confinement), he shall be examined concerning the things which he has done, and he shall not escape thence until he pay back the last farthing.[11]

Those who seek to take advantage of the community are warned by the text quoted above (4.5): "Be not a stretcher forth of the hands to receive and a drawer of them back to give." Likewise, the *Didache* warns against newcomers who abuse the community's hospitality, and it gives instructions for dealing with wayfarers who desire to settle in the community.

If he who cometh is a wayfarer, assist him as far as ye are able; but he shall not remain with you, except for two or three days, if need be. But if he willeth to abide with you, being an artisan, let him work and eat; but if he hath no trade, according to your understanding see to it that, as a Christian, he shall not live with you idle. But if he willeth not so to do, he is a Christ-monger.[12]

In conclusion, regardless of the date of the *Didache*, the self-understanding of the Christian *koinonía* that appears in it is similar to that found in Acts 2 and 4. The one element added—foreshadowed already in the New Testament—is that what is given serves also as a ransom for the giver's sins.[13] As we shall see, using a promise of reward as a motivation for aiding the needy will become increasingly common throughout the patristic period.

Pseudo-Barnabas

The manuscript discovered in Istanbul in 1875 contained also another document that had been lost until the nineteenth century, the so-called *Epistle of Barnabas*. Scholars already knew this text, for in 1859 in the library of the monastery of St. Catherine on Mt. Sinai Konstantin von Tischendorf had discovered another manuscript, now known as the *Codex Sinaiticus*, which also included—besides the Old and New Testaments and part of the *Shepherd of Hermas*—this so-called *Epistle of Barnabas*. Like the *Didache*, the *Epistle of Barnabas*, probably written in or near Alexandria around the year 135,[14] was frequently quoted in antiquity but was apparently lost in the Middle Ages, in this case, probably in the ninth century.

The *Epistle* interests us here because it shows the wide dissemination of the understanding of the *koinonía* of goods found in the *Didache*. The last chapters of the *Epistle* so closely parallel the early chapters of the *Didache* that a connection between the two is beyond doubt. The common material is what scholars have dubbed the "Document of the Two Ways." Whether such a document actually existed independent of the *Didache* or whether the author of the *Epistle of Barnabas* took this material from the *Didache* does not concern us. The important point is that, either quoting from a common source or repeating the words of the *Didache*, the *Epistle of Barnabas* includes the crucial text of the *Didache* on the commonality of property:

Thou shalt communicate {practice *koinonía*} in all things with thy neighbour; thou shalt not call things thine own; for if ye are partakers in common {*koinonoí*} of things which are incorruptible, how much more (should you be) of those things which are corruptible![15]

Although this text and many others in which the *Epistle of Barnabas* parallels the *Didache* add little as far as content is concerned, they prove that the view of *koinonía*—the sharing of possessions—that appears in Acts and in the *Didache* was shared by other Christians, perhaps as far away as Alexandria and as late as A.D. 135.

The Epistle to Diognetus

The final text dealing with common property in the Apostolic Fathers is the *Epistle to Diognetus*. This document, which should be classified with the apologists of the second century rather than with the Apostolic Fathers, probably dates from the time of Emperor Hadrian (A.D. 117–138).[16] Describing the life of Christians to an outsider, the *Epistle to Diognetus* declares that they "share a common table, but not a bed."[17] This is probably a brief way of contrasting the common life of the Christians with what had been advocated by Plato and others. Outsiders, acquainted as they were with the communistic utopias of antiquity, and having heard rumors of immorality among Christians, might confuse their commonality of goods with promiscuous sexual behavior. Later, and for the same reasons, Tertullian makes a similar statement. In any case, here we find once again the practice of *koinonía*, although not as explicitly as in the other texts we have studied.

A significant detail is that the author of this treatise bases this *koinonía* on the imitation of God's goodness, a theme that will appear repeatedly in later Christian writings. According to this treatise, God's majesty does not consist so much in power and riches as in love and giving, and these qualities Christians are called to imitate:

Do not wonder that a man can become an imitator of God. He can, if he is willing. For it is not by ruling over his neighbor, or by seeking to hold the supremacy over those that are weaker, or by being rich, and showing violence towards those that are inferior, that happiness is found; nor can any one by these things become an imitator of God. But these things do not at all constitute His majesty. On the contrary he who takes upon himself the burden of his neighbor; he who, in whatsoever respect he may be superior, is ready to benefit another who is deficient; he who, whatsoever things he has received from God, by distributing these to the needy, becomes a god to those who receive (his benefits): he is an imitator of God.[18]

Hermas

With the *Shepherd of Hermas,* we approach the middle of the second century. Hermas was a brother of Pius, bishop of Rome from 141 to 155, and it was probably during this time that the *Shepherd* was written.[19] Thus, just as Aelius Aristides was delivering his famous *Oration to the Romans* (in a.d. 143 or 144) Hermas may have been writing his *Shepherd.* Yet the world of Hermas is very different from that of Aelius Aristides. While Aristides speaks of a prosperous world, to which Rome had brought peace and prosperity, Hermas sees a world divided between rich and poor:

For some through the abundance of their food produce weakness in their flesh, and thus corrupt their flesh; while the flesh of others who have no food is corrupted, because they have not sufficient nourishment. And on their account their bodies waste away. This intemperance in eating is thus injurious to you who have abundance and do not distribute among those who are needy.[20]

None of the Apostolic Fathers devotes as much attention to this
problem as does Hermas. Indeed, while his central theme is the possibility of a second repentance after baptism, the question of riches and
their use is constantly interwoven with this topic. The texts that we shall
study in the following pages are just a few of many that could be cited
to show this interest and how Hermas deals with it. At the same time,
however, the *Shepherd's* main concern is not the well-being of the poor
but the salvation of the rich. The primary question is not, How can the
poor be helped? It is rather, How can the rich be saved? Naturally, this
requires helping the poor, and the rich are given some guidelines for
doing it. But in general the book addresses the rich. The poor are
spoken *about,* usually in the third person.[21] The writer's concern for a
second repentance, inasmuch as it relates to riches and their entangle-
ment, is a pastoral concern for the salvation of the rich or of those who
desire to be rich.[22] The social milieu in which Hermas is writing is very
different from that of the early Jesus movement or even of the *Didache*
or the *Epistle of Barnabas.*[23]

Hermas's pastoral concern for the rich does not mean that he simply seeks to comfort them in their riches. On the contrary, he feels
strongly that riches are an impediment to salvation. In one of the visions
he records, the church shows him a great tower that is being built—the
church itself. As a multitude of angels brings stones to the building site,
the six angels in charge of construction place some stones directly on
the wall, and cast aside others. Some of the cast-off stones are hopelessly
shattered, while others await another opportunity to be brought to the
tower. Among the latter are some white and round stones that do not
fit the construction precisely because they are round. Hermas asks his
guide,

"But who are these, Lady, that are white and round, and yet do not fit into the
building of the tower?" She answered and said, "How long will you be foolish
and stupid, and continue to put every kind of question and understand nothing?
These are those who have faith indeed, but they also have the riches of the
world. When, therefore, tribulation comes, on account of their riches and business they deny the Lord." I answered and said to her, "When, then, will they be
useful to the building, Lady?" "When the riches that now seduce them have
been circumscribed, then they will be of use to God. For as a round stone cannot
become square unless portions be cut off and cast away, so also those who are
rich cannot be useful to the Lord unless their riches be cut down."[24]

For several reasons Hermas views riches and especially the quest
after riches as impediments to salvation. First of all, concern over business keeps attention away from the faith, making it difficult for those
who are so obfuscated to understand the teachings of the church. Some
have believed and then "devote themselves to and become mixed up
with business, and wealth, and heathen friends, and many other actions
of this world." Such people do not understand the teachings of the
church, "for their minds are corrupted and become dried up," and they

"go astray in their minds, and lose all understanding in regard to righteousness."[25]

A second reason riches are dangerous has to do with the company kept by those who seek them. The reference to "heathen friends" in the previous paragraph points in this direction. In another passage, Hermas seems to distinguish between the rich and those "who are immersed in much business." Apparently the distinction is between those who are comfortably rich and the social climbers who are trying to get ahead through business ventures. In any case, the problem with both groups is that they keep the wrong sort of company. Those who are entangled in business do not "cleave to the servants of God, but wander away, being choked by their business transactions." The others, the comfortably rich, "cleave with difficulty to the servants of God, fearing lest these should ask something of them."[26] The tendency of those who are in business to avoid offending others may be what Hermas has in mind when he speaks of those who "on account of their desire of possessions they became hypocritical, and each one taught according to the desires of men who were sinners."[27]

Yet the most important reason riches are an obstacle to faith is that they involve a commitment to the present order, and in a time of persecution such commitment makes it very difficult to stand firm.

He says to me, "You know that you who are the servants of God dwell in a strange land; for your city is far away from this one. If then," he continues, "you know your city in which you are to dwell, why do you here provide lands, and make expensive preparations, and accumulate dwellings and expensive buildings? He who makes such preparations for this city cannot return again to his own . . . Dost thou not understand that all these things belong to another, and are under the power of another? For the lord of this city will say, 'I do not wish thee to dwell in my city; but depart from this city, because thou obeyest not my laws.' Thou therefore, although having fields and houses, and many other things, when cast out by him, what wilt thou do with thy land, and house, and other possessions which thou hast gathered to thyself? For the lord of this country justly says to thee, 'Either obey my laws or depart from my dominion.' . . . Thou shalt altogether deny thy law, and walk according to the law of this city. See lest it be to thy hurt to deny thy law; for if thou shalt desire to return to thy city, thou wilt not be received, because thou hast denied the law of thy city . . . Have a care, therefore: as one living in a foreign land, make no further preparations for thyself than such merely as may be sufficient; and be ready, when the master of this city shall come to cast thee out for disobeying his law, to leave his city, and to depart to thine own, and to obey thine own law without being exposed to annoyance, but to great joy."[28]

Clearly, what most concerns Hermas is the price Christians pay for social climbing. Hermas himself was a freedman. At some point he had been rich, but apparently at the time the book was written he was not wealthy. In the vision of the tower, after telling him that the wealth of the rich has to be cut away before they can be useful to God, the church reminds Hermas, "Learn this first from your own case. When you were rich, you were useless; but now you are useful and fit for life."[29] How this change in station came about is not known. Naturally, it is possible that Hermas lost his wealth through an unfortunate turn of events. But it is also possible that he gave up much of it for the sake of the gospel, as he called others to do. We know that many among the freedmen and women in the Roman Empire became wealthy. Trimalchio, the freedman in the *Satyricon,* is the successful social climber *par excellence.* It is quite possible that many among Hermas's audience are freedmen and women like himself, and that these are the people he considers unduly entangled in their business affairs and whom he calls to repentance. One can hear a note of pain as he speaks of

those that were faithful indeed; but after acquiring wealth, and becoming distinguished amongst the heathen, they clothed themselves with great pride, and became lofty-minded, and deserted the truth, and did not cleave to the righteous, but lived with the heathen, and this way of life became more agreeable to them. They did not, however, depart from God, but remained in the faith, although not working the works of faith.[30]

Hermas advises such people to share with the needy: "Do not partake of God's creatures alone, but give abundantly of them to the needy . . . Ye, therefore, who are high in position, seek out the hungry as long as the tower is not finished."[31] The passage quoted above, which compares the Christian life with living in a foreign city, leads to the following exhortation: "Instead of lands, buy afflicted souls, according as each one is able, and visit widows and orphans, and do not overlook them; and spend your wealth and all your preparations, which ye received from the Lord, upon such lands and houses. For to this end did the Master make your rich."[32]

A specific suggestion for sharing with the needy—and one that has become quite popular among antihunger activists in modern times—is that when fasting one should set aside the amount that would otherwise have been spent on food and give it to someone in need.[33] In so doing, Hermas asserts, the givers will also receive a benefit, for the poor will pray for them.

This symbiosis between the rich and the poor, so that one contributes material goods and the other contributes special prayers and piety, will become a fairly common theme in later Christian literature on almsgiving. Hermas expresses it by using the image of vines growing amid elm trees—what the Romans called the *arbustum* method of growing vines. He says that he was once walking in the countryside and thinking about how the elms and the vines helped each other, when the "Shepherd"—his guide in the later part of the book—appeared to him and told him that there was a lesson in the vines and the elms. The vine cannot yield much fruit when it trails on the ground without the support of the elm, and whatever fruit it produces rots. The elm, on the other hand, is by nature a fruitless tree, but by supporting the vine it is as if it too produced fruit. Likewise, the rich have much material wealth but are poor in matters relating to God, precisely because their wealth impedes them.

But when the rich man refreshes the poor, and assists him in his necessities, believing that what he does to the poor man will be able to find its reward with God—because the poor man is rich in intercession and confession, and his intercession has great power with God—then the rich man helps the poor in all things without hesitation; and the poor man, being helped by the rich, intercedes for him, giving thanks to God for him who bestows gifts upon him . . . Both, accordingly, accomplish their work. The poor man makes intercession; a work in which he is rich, which he received from the Lord . . . And the rich man, in like manner, unhesitatingly bestows upon the poor man the riches which he received from the Lord.[34]

Here we find two themes interwoven. The ancient theme that the poor are somehow closer to God or that God listens to their prayers in a preferential manner joins the notion that the existence of some who are poor and some who are rich produces an ideal balance. In this context Hermas uses the ancient notion of *koinonía,* for he declares that, just as the elm and the vine are partners in producing grapes, so are the rich and the poor partners—*koinonoí*—in the work of justice. Needless to say, this is a step removed from the *koinonía* of Acts, which resulted—at least as Luke describes it—in "not a needy person among them," or from the *koinonía* that Paul advocates in 2 Corinthians 8, whose result is equality.

Yet, once again, this does not mean that the rich are free to continue enjoying their riches in the midst of want, simply on the basis that the poor are a necessary part of the landscape. On the contrary, the image of the elms and the vines is addressed precisely to those among the rich who believe they can ignore the need of the poor. It may leave something to be desired as a manifesto of social justice, and it certainly implies that poverty exists because God wills it. Yet those are not the points that Hermas is trying to make. He is not addressing the poor and telling them that their poverty is willed by God. He is addressing the rich and telling them that their wealth is fruitless unless it is shared with the needy. Indeed, as he concludes his book he declares that everyone must be spared want. To be in need is a torture, and therefore to rescue another from such conditions is to earn great joy. Not to do so, on the other hand, is a great crime, for the pain of poverty sometimes leads the poor to seek their own deaths. In such cases, those who could have helped and did not are guilty of the blood of the poor.[35]

Other Apostolic Fathers

Among the Apostolic Fathers, Hermas deals most extensively with the responsibilities of the rich. However, the other Apostolic Fathers do touch on them in passing and do not contradict what has been drawn from the more explicit texts. Late in the first century Clement of Rome, writing in support of order and authority, counsels, "Let the rich man provide for the wants to the poor; and let the poor man bless God, because He hath given one by whom his need may be supplied."[36] Early in the second century, Ignatius of Antioch characterizes heretics as those who "have no regard for love; no care for the widow, or the orphan, or the oppressed; of the bond, or of the free; of the hungry, or of the thirsty."[37] He also exhorts slaves not to try to buy their freedom "at the expense of the common," lest they become slaves of greed.[38] Apparently, this is another reference to the *koinonía*, which will suffer if one slave's desire for freedom is put ahead of all the needs of the poor. Yet, the very fact that Ignatius mentions this seems to indicate that, at least in some cases, the *koinonía* was understood in terms of helping some of its members who were slaves buy their freedom. Polycarp, writing shortly after Ignatius, in passing equates greed with idolatry.[39] Finally, the so-called *Second Epistle of Clement* calls for mutual compassion[40] and declares that "almsgiving . . . is a good thing, as repentance from sin; fasting is better than prayer, but almsgiving than both."[41]

This may be the place to say a word about the doctrine of the *Pseudoclementine Homilies*. This document, although from a later date,[42] probably reflects ideas circulating in Jewish Christian gnostic circles by the beginning of the second century. Here we find a negative view of property based not on questions of the just distribution of wealth or the needs of the poor but on a radical dualism that sees the present world as belonging to evil powers. The true believers are in an alien world. Therefore what they have is not properly theirs, and those who take it away from them are not acting unjustly. "And Peter said: 'Are not those, then, who you said received injustice, themselves transgressors, inasmuch as they are in the kingdom of the other, and is it not by overreaching that they have obtained all they possess? While those who are thought to act unjustly are conferring a favour on each subject of the hostile kingdom, so far as they permit him to have property.'"[43]

The conflict between these two kingdoms is so great that one has to choose between having things of the present order and having a share in the future kingdom. Therefore, having—or desiring—anything beyond the bare minimum is sin.

Those men who choose the present have the power to be rich, to revel in luxury, to indulge in pleasures, and to do whatever they can. For they will possess none of the future goods. But those who have decided to accept the blessings of the future reign have no right to regard as their own the things that are here, since they belong to a foreign king, with the exception only of water and bread, and those things procured with sweat to maintain life (for it is not lawful for them to commit suicide), and also one garment, for they are not permitted to go naked on account of the all-seeing heaven.[44]

To all of us possessions are sins. The deprivation of these, in whatever way it may take place, is the removal of sins.[45]

Against such views, basing poverty and renunciation on a dualism that tends to deny the doctrine of creation, later Christian writers, such as Clement of Alexandria, will argue that the things that constitute wealth are not in themselves evil. They do not belong to another god or principle, these writers will say, but to the same God who has been revealed in Jesus Christ. If evil is connected with them, it resides not in the things themselves but in the greed that leads some to seek after them with an inordinate desire.

The Apologists

The only two writings of the early Apologists that deal significantly with the subject of wealth and its use are the *Apology* of Aristides and the *First Apology* of Justin.[46] Aristides, writing at approximately the same time as Hermas,[47] affirms that among Christians "the one who has gives liberally to the one who has not."[48] Also, it is interesting to note that what Hermas orders regarding the use of the proceeds of fasting, Aristides describes as the practice in his own community (although in this case those who fast are too poor to feed both themselves and the needy): "If one of them is poor or in need and they have no abundance of resources, they fast two or three days in order to supply the food that the poor need."[49]

Finally, three passages in Justin's *First Apology* deserve our attention. The briefest one is an introduction to a summary of some of the teachings of the Sermon on the Mount. Justin's words are: "We should communicate {*koinoneîn*} to the needy."[50] The second passage expresses the same idea more explicitly: "We who valued above all things the acquisition of wealth and possessions, now bring what we have into a common stock, and communicate to {share with} every one in need."[51] Thus in Justin we find once again the theme of *koinonía* as sharing that we have found repeatedly in early Christian tradition. The third passage confirms that this *koinonía* is voluntary and is carried out in a similar fashion to that of Acts. In Acts, voluntary contributions were laid at the feet of the apostles and distributed according to need:

Those of us who have assist those who are in need, and we help one another ... Those who can and will, according to their own decision, give what they consider fitting, and what is collected is given to the president who succors orphans and widows, those who are in need for reason of illness or any other cause, those who are in prison, and sojourners. In a word, it is he who provides for those who are in need.[52]

In summary, as we look at the subapostolic church through the writings of the Apostolic Fathers and the Greek Apologists, we find numerous indications that the *koinonía*, or partnership in goods, was still practiced, at least to a degree. As from the beginning, it did not require selling all and putting it into a common treasury. It did, however, require considering all members of the church as partners not only in spiritual things but in the totality of life. For this reason, while wealth as such was not condemned, wealth that was unavailable for the succor of the needy was considered a hindrance to the salvation of its owner. Among all the writings studied, the *Shepherd* of Hermas stands out as the one that, while dealing most extensively with matters of wealth and its use, says least about *koinonía* or partnership in earthly goods.

NOTES

1. J.-P. Audet, *La Didachè: Instructions des Apôtres* (Paris: J. Gabalda, 1958), argues that it is earlier than the fall of Jerusalem in A.D. 70, while J. Colson, *L'évêque dans les communautés primitives* (Paris, Editions du Cerf, 1951) argues for the third century and claims that the archaicism of the *Didache* is forged. It is also possible that the document actually includes layers from different periods, as suggested by S. Giet, *L'énigme de la Didachè* (Paris: Ophrys, 1970).

2. *Did.* 11.4–6, 9, 12. All references to the Apostolic Fathers and the Apologists are to *ANF.* The Greek text employed is from *BAC.*

3. Especially the instructions regarding baptism in cases where water is scarce. *Did.* 6.2.

4. By the mid–second century, Hermas, in Rome, quotes the *Didache*. Hermas, *Shepherd* Mand. 2.4 *Did.*1.5.

5. *Did.* 13.3.

6. *Did.* 4.5–8, *ANF* The phrase that is here translated "If thou hast aught, through thy hands thou shalt give ransom for thy sins" is probably better translated: "If thou has aught through the work of thy hands, thou shalt give of it as ransom for thy sins." In other words, that what one makes through labor is to be shared.

7. A passage that is reminiscent of Luke 16:11–12: "If then you have not been faithful in the unrighteous mammon, who will entrust to you the true riches? And if you have not been faithful in that which is another's, who will give you that which is your own?"

8. *Did.* 5.2, ANF.

9. *Did.* 1.6, ANF.

10. *Did.* 13.1–4, ANF. "But every true prophet that willeth to abide among you is worthy of his support (meaning his food). So also a true teacher is himself worthy, as the workman, of his support. Every first fruit, therefore, of the products of the wine press and threshing floor, of oven and of sheep, thou shalt take and give to the prophets, for they are your high priests. But if you have not a prophet, give it to the poor."

11. *Did.* 1.5.

12. *Did.* 12.2-5.

13. *Did.* 4.6–7, quoted above: "Give ransom for thy sins" and "thou shalt know who is the good repayer of the hire."

14. This is a matter of conjecture. There is much uncertainty about the date of composition of the "Epistle". The date 135 is based on a passage in chapter 16 that seems to refer to Hadrian's project of building a temple to Jove on the site where the Jewish temple had stood. So A. Harnack, *Die Chronologie der altchristlicher Literatur bis Eusebius* (Leipzig: J.C. Hinrichs, 1897), pp. 423–27. Others, on the basis of cryptic references in chapter 4, date the *Epistle* during the time of Nerva, in A.D. 98.

15. Barn. 19.8, *ANF* Other sections of the *Didache* we have quoted appear also, with slight variations, in the *Epistle:*
"Do not be ready to stretch forth thy hands to take, whilst thou contractest them to give ... Thou shalt not hesitate to give, nor murmur when thou givest. 'Give to everyone that asketh thee,' and thou shalt know who is the good Recompenser of the reward ... {There are} those who attend not with just judgment the widow and

the orphan, . . . pity not the needy, labour not in aid of him who is overcome with toil; . . . who turn away him that is in want, who oppress the afflicted, who are advocates of the rich, who are unjust judges of the poor" (19.9, 11; 20.2).

16. Its date, however, is much controverted. See J.L. González, *A History of Christian Thought,* 2nd. ed. (Nashville: Abingdon, 1989) 1:116 n. 83.

17. *Diog.* 5.7, *ANF.*

18. *Diog.* 10.4–6, *ANF.*

19. The unity of the *Shepherd* has been much debated, with a number of ingenious theories proposed as to the number of possible authors and their dates. I am inclined to think that the book contains a number of visions and other elements from various times, and perhaps even from different sources, all put together into approximately its present form in the dates given. As to the role of Hermas in this process, there is no reason to doubt that when the book was published it was considered his, and that therefore he is probably the author of most of it and the compiler and editor of the rest.

20. *Shepherd* Vis. 3.9.3-4, *ANF.*

21. C. Osiek, *Rich and Poor in the Shepherd of Hermas: An Exegetical-Social Investigation* (Washington, DC: Catholic Biblical Association of America, 1983), p. 47: "The poor and the needy are spoken of only as foils for elaborating on the responsibilities of the rich." While this is true, it is probably overstated on p. 133: "Economic poverty and the plight of the poor were not major concerns of Hermas." The study by Osiek is a pace-setting work on which much of the present section of this book based.

22. It may be illuminating to compare Hermas with Heb. 10:26–36, where sins committed after repentance, possessions, and the willingness to part with them are also at issue.

23. There is no doubt that Hermas knew either the *Didache* or the "Document of the Two Ways" (if such a document ever existed), for Mand. 2.4–5 is a collection of phrases from *Didache* 1.5 and 2.6–7. Significantly, Hermas does not go on to quote *Did.* 4.8, which is a sharp statement in favor of radical *koinonía.*

24. *Shepherd* Vis. 3.6.5–6, *ANF.*

25. Mand. 10.1.4, *ANF.*

26. Sim. 9.20.1–2, Also Sim. 8.8.1: "Those who are immersed in business, and do not cleave to the saints." This and all future references to the *Shepherd* are from *ANF.*

27. Sim. 9.19.3.

28. Sim. 1.1–6.

29. Vis. 3.6.7.

30. Sim. 8.9.1.

31. Vis. 3.9.2, 5.

32. Sim. 1.8–9.

33. Sim. 5.3.7.

34. Sim. 2.5–7.

35. Sim. 10.4.2–3.

36. *Clem. ad Cor.* 37.2, *ANF.*

37. *Ad Smyr.* 6.2.

38. *Ad Pol.* 4.3.

39. *Pol. ad Philip.* 11.2.

40. *2 Clem.* 4.3.

41. *2 Clem.* 16.4.

42. See González, *History* (n. 16 above), 1:62 n. 5.

43. *Clem. Hom.* 15.7, *ANF.*

44. *Clem. Hom.* 15.7, *ANF.*

45. *Clem. Hom.* 15.9, *ANF.*

46. However, on the general social background and significance of the Apologists, see R. L. Wilken, "Toward a Social Interpretation of Early Christian Apologetics," *CH* 39, no. 1 (1970): 1–22.

47. Eusebius of Caesarea (*H. E.* 4.3.3; *Chron.,* 01.226, Chr. 125, Adr. 8), *PG* affirms that the *Apology* of Aristides was addressed to Hadrian, who reigned from 117 to 138. J.

Geffcken, however, argued that it was actually addressed to Antoninus, who reigned from 138 to 161: *Zwei griechische Apologeten* (Leipzig: Teubner, 1907), pp. 28–31. Most modern critics agree with Geffcken.

48. Arist., *Apol.* 15.7. The Syriac version speaks, not of the liberality of the gift, but of its willingness.
49. Arist., *Apol.* (Syr.) 15.7.
50. *1 Apol.* 15.10, *ANF.* Clearly, better translations would be "share with the needy," "be partners with the needy," or even "have things in common with the needy."
51. *1 Apol.* 14.2, *ANF.* The same corrections apply to this translation as to the previous one.
52. *1 Apol.* 67.1, 6. In this case, the translation is mine, for the *ANF* changes the meaning by translating "those who have" as the "well to do," which gives the impression that only the wealthy are expected to contribute.

6/The Old Catholic Church

A s Christianity approached the second century, and then as it moved into the third, great changes took place in the life of the church. Historians have often referred to those changes by speaking of the birth of the "ancient catholic church." This was the time when the basic elements of the canon of the New Testament were set, when apostolic succession and episcopal authority were used against the encroachments of heresy, and when the "Old Roman Symbol," the core of our Apostles' Creed, was first formulated. In response to the challenge of heresies, especially Marcionism and gnosticism, Christianity became more rigidly organized and began establishing standards of orthodoxy. Such changes should not be overstated, for they are one more stage in a process that had begun much earlier. The pastoral Epistles—1 and 2 Timothy and Titus—represent an early move in that direction. At about the same time Ignatius of Antioch was using the term *catholic church* for the first time and arguing for the authority of bishops in order to stem the tide of heresy and division.

While historians have often studied these changes from the point of view of the development of church structure and theology, our interest here is on the parallel changes in the social composition of the church and therefore in the way Christians saw and discussed issues of faith and wealth. Again, as in the case of theology, we are not speaking of radical changes or new departures but rather of the culmination of a process whose signs were already visible at an earlier time.

In Rome, the church continued to attract an increasing number of members from the higher echelons of society, as it had since the time of Hermas. Eusebius of Caesarea describes the changing social condition of Christians in Rome: "In the reign of Commodus {A.D. 180–192} our condition became more favorable, and through the grace of God the churches throughout the entire world enjoyed peace . . . So that now at Rome many who were highly distinguished for wealth and family turned with all their household and relatives unto their salvation."[1] Similar developments were taking place elsewhere. Just before the beginning of the reign of Commodus, a number of Christians from Lyons and Vienne in Gaul suffered martyrdom. The account of their trial informs us that the authorities arrested a number of slaves belonging to Christians, who then accused their masters of gross immorality.[2] Thus even in Lyons, where Christianity had arrived at a relatively recent date, the Christian community included some who were wealthy enough to own slaves. And in North Africa, if we can take Tertullian literally, the comment was heard among pagans that even aristocrats were becoming Christians.[3] From the same area and the same time, the *Martyrdom of Saints Perpetua and Felicitas* supports Tertullian's statement, for Perpetua herself was of noble birth.[4] In Alexandria, Origen's father owned property worth being confiscated when he died as a martyr. His family thus financially ruined, a rich Christian lady supported Origen for some time.[5] Later he received financial support from a certain Ambrose, another wealthy Christian in Alexandria.[6]

This is not to say that the majority of Christians were well to do. On the contrary, Tertullian's point is that Christians of *all* ranks are joining the church. His contemporary Minucius Felix, also in North Africa, reports the complaints of a sophisticated pagan "that certain persons—and these unskilled in learning, strangers to literature, without knowledge even of sordid arts—should dare to determine on any certainty concerning the nature at large, and the (divine) majesty."[7] From his perspective, it is "a thing to be lamented" that people who are "from the lowest dregs the more unskilled" should dare criticize traditional religion.[8] And from Alexandria comes a similar complaint by Celsus: "We see, indeed, in private houses workers in wool and leather, and fullers, and persons of the most uninstructed and rustic character, not venturing to utter a word in the presence of their elders and wiser masters; but when they get hold of the children privately, and certain women as ignorant as themselves, they pour forth wonderful statements."[9]

The Christian writers who report these statements never really deny them. They probably could not have done so in all truth. What they seek to do is to show that Christianity is intellectually respectable and that even the most sophisticated can and should believe its doctrines.

Therefore, it would be wrong to depict the church of the late second and early third centuries as composed mostly of the well-to-do or of the well educated. The rank and file still belonged to the poorer urban classes—artisans, small traders, slaves. Yet the church was also spreading among the higher echelons of society and could count on a growing number of members who could hold their own in intellectual debate with pagans.

In the development of the "ancient catholic church" and its structures of authority, the changing social and economic composition of the church was no less important than the challenge of heresies. The phenomenon is well known even today in groups that are accused of abnormal behavior and lowly origins: when leadership begins to arise whose very existence refutes those charges, such leaders are rapidly given increasing authority in the group, first as those who speak for it and then as those charged with stemming deviant behavior within the group itself. Such is the process taking place in the church late in the second century and early in the third. The mass of Christians, accustomed to being not only persecuted but also mocked and despised, are beginning to find in their communities members who can provide the church with a measure of social and intellectual respectability. Such members, who tend to become the leaders of the church, are increasingly entrusted with defending the faith not only vis-à-vis its pagan adversaries but also against the inevitable centrifugal forces that arise in any community. Thus the development of the "ancient catholic church" is the result both of the challenge of heresies and of the changing social composition of the church itself.

As we study Christian views on wealth and its relationship to faith during this period, we must center our attention on the four great theologians of the time whose work has survived: Irenaeus of Lyons, Clement of Alexandria, Tertullian, and Origen.[10]

Irenaeus

The writings of Irenaeus that have survived deal primarily with the refutation of heresies—gnosticism in particular—and with the basic doctrines of the Christian faith. Therefore, in only two passages does Irenaeus touch on the subjects that interest us here, and then only briefly and in passing. This is particularly unfortunate, for in both passages we catch tantalizing glimpses of views and practices about which we would like to know more.

In the first of these passages,[11] Irenaeus is refuting the gnostics, who denied the continuity between the faith of Israel and the Christian gospel. As one of his arguments, he points to the conversation between Jesus and the rich young man who asked about life eternal. Jesus responded first by quoting the commandments of Moses, which the young man said he had always kept. Jesus knew that it was not so, and in order to show him that he had at least broken the commandment against coveting, Jesus told him to go, sell all that he had, and give it to the poor. According to Irenaeus, Jesus' injunction was simply a further clarification of the commandment of Moses, and thus the continuity between the law of Moses and the teachings of Jesus is shown.

What is most interesting about this portion of the passage is Irenaeus's comment that in inviting the young man to follow him Jesus was promising that any who sell all their goods, give them to the poor, and follow him will have "the apostles' share" (*apostolorum partem*)—whatever that might mean—and that those who have coveted can cancel out their sin by giving their goods to the poor. Within the context, the probable meaning is that those who give their possessions to the poor will share eternal life with the apostles. If such is the case, this text illustrates a theme that will become fairly common in early Christian literature, that, in a figurative sense, those who own material goods can trade them for life eternal.

Irenaeus continues his argument by citing a number of instances in which the teachings of Christ do not abrogate but continue and even extend the commandments of the Law. Here he once again touches on the use of wealth: "Instead of the law enjoining the giving of tithes, [He told us] to share all our possessions with the poor; . . . and not merely to be liberal givers and bestowers, but even that we should present a gratuitous gift to those who take away our goods."[12]

Thus Christians are to be ready to share their goods, first with the poor, but also with any who would take them away by force. In the latter case, Christians should "not grieve as those who are unwilling to be defrauded, but may rejoice as those who have given willingly."[13]

The other passage in which Irenaeus touches on economic matters is much more interesting, partly for the questions it leaves unanswered.[14] Here again the subject is the continuity between the faith of Israel and Christianity. At this point, however, Irenaeus argues against the Marcionites, who claim that the God of the Hebrews is to be rejected as a lesser being. The particular point Irenaeus discusses in this passage is the Marcionites' contention that, in telling the children of Israel on the eve of their departure from Egypt to despoil the Egyptians, the God of the Old Testament was promoting theft.

Irenaeus's answer is surprising. The Egyptians owed the Israelites their very lives, for it was Joseph who had saved them from famine. Yet they forced the Israelites to work for them as slaves, so that "with immense labor they built for them fenced cities, increasing the substance of these men throughout a long course of years, and by means of every species of slavery."[15] In exchange for this the Egyptians not only did not pay them but even planned to destroy them. As for the Israelites, had they been working for themselves, they could have been rich. Instead, they simply took "a very insignificant recompense for their heavy servitude" and went away poor. In this there is no crime. If someone forces a free person to work for many years, and then the worker finds the means to go free, the worker does not commit injustice by claiming a portion of the wealth that he or she helped create. Thus one could find support in Irenaeus for a theory of reparations, although, quite clearly, Irenaeus takes slavery for granted, and in his example the injustice for which reparation is made is the enslavement of a free person.

On the matter of taking another's wealth Irenaeus does not stop here. Indeed, he argues, all of us use wealth that we have taken from another. In a lengthy passage that must be studied in some detail, he argues that this is true first of all of Christians:

> For in some cases there follows us a small, and in others a large amount of property which we have acquired from the mammon of unrighteousness. For from what source do we derive the houses in which we dwell, the garments in which we are clothed, the vessels which we use, and everything else ministering to our every-day life, unless it be from those things which, when we were Gentiles, we acquired by avarice, or received them from our heathen parents, relations or friends who unrighteously obtained them?—not to mention that even now we acquire such things when we are in the faith. For who is there that sells, and does not wish to make a profit from him who buys? Or who purchases anything, and does not wish to obtain good value from the seller? Or who is there that carries a trade, and does not do so that he may obtain a livelihood thereby? And as to those believing ones who are in the royal palace, do they not derive the utensils they employ from the property which belongs to Caesar; and to those who have not, does not each one of these [Christians] give according to his ability? The Egyptians were debtors to the [Jewish] people, not alone as to property, but as to their very lives, because of the kindness of the patriarch Joseph in former times; but in what way are the heathen debtors to us, from whom we receive both gain and profit? Whatsoever they amass with labour, these things do we make use of without labour, although we are in the faith.[16]

A number of important points can be drawn from these words. First of all, apparently Irenaeus believes that the origin of wealth is unrighteousness. The things that Christians owned before their conversion they acquired either through their own unrighteousness or through that of their relatives. Apparently, for Irenaeus this has little or nothing to do with the amount of wealth accumulated, for it is true both of those who have brought a large amount of property from their previous life and of those whose property was small.

Second, Irenaeus's judgment that wealth is the product of unrighteousness apparently extends also to the commercial activities of Christians. Buying, selling, and trade in general are suspect. The reason for this is not clear. He may be echoing the negative view of trade that existed in some circles in antiquity and that we have found in writers such as Cicero. His words may also reflect the view, already present in Revelation 13:17, that to buy and sell in an unjust order is somehow to participate in that order. Or he may simply be rejecting the self-interest that inevitably accompanies trade.

Third, this quote shows that late in the second century there were already enough Christians in the imperial household that Irenaeus could refer to their existence as a fact known by his readers and opponents. Naturally, Caesar's household included not only what we today would call his family but all his slaves and other dependents. Irenaeus is not concerned about the status of these persons. No matter who they are, they are making use of Caesar's property, and that is his point.

Fourth, this text exhibits one more reference to the Christian custom of sharing their goods with the less fortunate. Christians give according to their ability to "those who have not." The fact that it is a passing reference makes it all the more significant, for Irenaeus simply takes for granted that this is the case and that his opponents will also know and acknowledge it.

Finally, the last sentence of the quote is intriguing. What does Irenaeus mean, that "they amass with labour" the things that Christians "make use of without labour"? Taken literally, it would seem to imply that Christians do not work. That obviously is not the case. More likely, he is referring to all the facilities that the empire offers, and of which Christians partake even though they do not contribute to them. Even if this is his meaning, it looks like Irenaeus brushes aside the degree to which Christians had to toil for the good of the empire.[17]

In any case, the point of the entire passage, particularly in the context in which it stands, is clear. Whatever we have is not our own. We are even less justified in claiming it than were the Israelites in despoiling Egypt, for Egypt owed them its very life, whereas society at large does not owe us a thing. This, however, does not mean that we should not make use of such things. In fact, continues Irenaeus after the passage quoted, the same is true of his Marcionite opponents, for only those who completely renounce society and live naked, barefoot, and homeless in the mountains can claim that they are not using anything that is another's. Therefore, if the God who told the Israelites to despoil the Egyptians is for that reason an unworthy God, the same will be true of the God who allows the Marcionites to continue using the goods of this world.

In summary, the main impression one receives in reading Irenaeus is that of a pragmatic but stern realism. He is not willing to say that whatever property one has is one's own. On the contrary, he is very suspicious of property and seems to say that it is the result of unrighteousness. At the same time, he does not advocate a sterile asceticism, renouncing all use of the goods of this world. On the contrary, he expects Christians to use these goods for righteousness even while knowing that they are not rightful belongings, and even knowing that they are the result of unrighteousness. Thus after a lengthy section that continues the argument quoted above, Irenaeus concludes: "Whatsoever we have acquired from unrighteousness when we were heathen, we are proved righteous, when we have become believers, by applying it to the Lord's advantage."[18]

Clement of Alexandria

In Clement of Alexandria appears the first attempt at a systematic discussion of the relationship between faith and wealth. Alexandria was a rich city in which a number of wealthy people had either joined the church or contemplated the possibility of doing so. How should the Christian community deal with this situation? Apparently, some insisted that there was no place for the wealthy in the church of the one who had said that it is more difficult for the rich to enter the Kingdom than for a camel to go through the eye of the needle. Others courted and flattered the wealthy, as if their wealth were proof of their goodness.

In order to deal with this situation, Clement wrote a brief treatise, *Quis dives salvetur?—Who Is the Rich to Be Saved?*—which consists primarily of a discussion of Matthew 19:16–30. This is the episode of the rich young man, followed by Jesus' comments on the camel and the eye of the needle and the disciples' response. Clement's main point in this treatise is that the way of salvation is not entirely closed to the rich, and that what really counts is one's love of God above anything else. For this reason, Clement has often been depicted as "soft" on the rich or as willing to set aside the harsher sayings of Jesus in order to accommodate as many people as possible.

Before rendering such a judgment, however, it may be well to remember what Clement himself says about those who flatter the rich:

Those who bestow laudatory addresses on the rich appear to me to be rightly judged not only flatterers and base, in vehemently pretending that things that are disagreeable give them pleasure, but also godless and treacherous; godless, . . . because they invest with divine honour men wallowing in an execrable and abominable life . . . ; and treacherous, because, although wealth is of itself sufficient to puff up and corrupt the souls of its possessors, and to turn them from the path by which salvation is to be attained, they stupefy them still more, by inflating the minds of the rich with the pleasures of extravagant praises, and by making them utterly despise all things except wealth, on account of which they are admired.[19]

On the other hand, if flattery is not the proper attitude of Christians toward the wealthy, outright condemnation is no better. Indeed, if the wealthy come to the conclusion that they cannot be saved, they will "despair of themselves as not destined to live, . . . and so diverge more from the way to the life to come."[20]

Therefore, the best course for those who wish to act out of love for both truth and the other members of the community is neither to insult nor to fawn on those who are rich but to seek their salvation by showing them, first, that it is possible and, second, that it requires a certain discipline on their part.[21] This is the purpose of Clement's treatise.[22]

Clement's usual exegetical method, quite apart from any overt social or economic agendas, is allegorical.[23] Therefore, one should not be surprised that in this particular case he interprets Jesus' injunction to the young man in a similar fashion: "He {Jesus} does not, as some conceive off-hand, bid him throw away the substance he possessed, and abandon his property; but bids him banish from his soul his notions about wealth, his excitement and morbid feeling about it, the anxieties, which are the thorns of existence, which choke the seed of life."[24]

For the young man simply to rid himself of his property would have been nothing special, for many ancient philosophers had done this. What Jesus demands of the young man is "not the outward act which others have done, but something else indicated by it, . . . the stripping off of the passions from the soul itself."[25] It is interesting to note that, while rejecting the literal interpretation because that would simply be telling the young man to do what ancient philosophers had done before, Clement's own understanding of the meaning of the passage is clearly derived from Stoic and other notions of the need to rid the soul of its passions.

If the words of Jesus were to be taken literally, argues Clement, then we could not obey his commandments about giving and sharing. Those who have nothing cannot feed the hungry or clothe the naked. Therefore, in the very commandment to feed the hungry, Jesus was telling his disciples that they should have the resources to do so. At this point, Clement may have in mind a slightly different battle, which he was waging against gnosticism and particularly against the Carpocratians. This obscure gnostic sect, about which little is known,[26] advocated a commonality of property similar to that suggested by Plato in the *Republic*, including the commonality of women. Against them, in another work, Clement employed arguments similar to those that appear here. If we are to give to any who ask, as the Lord commanded, how can we do this if nothing is our own?[27] Likewise, *koinonía* is possible only if people have something to share.[28]

Goods and possessions are not in themselves evil. Nor are they good. They are like a tool, whose goodness or evil depends on the hand that wields it. A tool that is rightly used is no better than one wrongly used. A tool is "itself destitute of blame. Such an instrument is wealth. Are you able to make right use of it? It is subservient to righteousness. Does one make wrong use of it? It is, on the other hand, a minister of wrong."[29]

Here again, Clement is likely arguing, not only against those who would condemn the rich, but also against the gnostics, many of whom considered all matter as in itself evil.

In short, the first point Clement makes is that what is important is not whether one has things or not, but one's attitude toward things. It is possible to get rid of everything one has and still continue lusting after power and riches. "Salvation does not depend on external things, whether they be many or few, small or great."[30] And ultimately it is possible for the poor to be riddled with the vices that characteristically belong to the rich and for the rich in material things to be also rich in virtue.[31]

So far, Clement appears to be simply expanding the eye of the needle so that the camel can get through it. However, this is not all he says about the rich and their possessions. On the contrary, both in this treatise and in his other works, Clement repeats and adds to the harsh words we have seen elsewhere about excessive wealth and luxury. Those who are commonly called rich may follow two every different paths. On the one hand, a rich person may approach material goods knowing their possession is more for the sake of the brothers and sisters than for the owner. This person is also "able with cheerful mind to bear their removal equally with their abundance."[32] On the other hand is the one "who carries his riches in his soul, and instead of God's Spirit bears in his heart gold or land, and is always acquiring possessions without end, and is perpetually on the outlook for more."[33] The first is truly rich, and the second is falsely so: "He then is truly and rightly rich who is rich in virtue, and is capable of making a holy and faithful use of any fortune; while he is spuriously rich who is rich, according to the flesh, and turns life into outward possession."[34]

Christians who are materially rich cannot then simply separate their financial lives from their faith. On the contrary, since love of God must be at the very heart of their lives, they must be ready to renounce their possessions if they become an obstacle in the Christian life. To a person loving wealth in such a way that it becomes a hindrance, Clement's advice is clear: "Leave it, throw it away, hate, renounce, flee."[35]

Exhortations against allowing wealth to become a hindrance are the context for Clement's strong words on luxury. As he said at the beginning of this short treatise, one should avoid both excluding the rich from the love of God and fawning on them. So far, he has told them mostly that if their attitude is right, they are not barred from the Kingdom. This by itself would give the impression that he was being lenient toward the rich in order to make them feel accepted in the community of faith. But there is another side to his teachings on the matter. The rich have the obligation to employ their wealth in a way that is consonant with their inner attitude of loving God above all things—and loving neighbor as oneself. The rich are called to use their wealth in such a way as to obtain life.[36] In truth, what the rich have is not their own, and with it they must meet the needs of others. In so doing, they must neither wait to be asked, nor should they try to determine who are the deserving poor. They should give to all in need and leave the matter of determining their merit to the final Judge.[37] Furthermore, Clement is aware that the habits of a lifetime cannot be easily changed, and that if the rich are left to determine for themselves what is their just share in giving and the proper use of their wealth, they will tend to be too lenient. Therefore, he concludes his treatise advising those among the rich who really want to take seriously the work of their salvation to find someone to help them see the proper use of their wealth:

Wherefore it is by all means necessary for thee, who art pompous, and powerful, and rich, to set over thyself some man of God as a trainer and governor. Reverence, though it be but one man; fear, though it be but one man. Give yourself to hearing, though it be but one man speaking freely, using harshness, and at the same time healing.[38]

What this harsh yet loving mentor and guide would say to the rich, we can garner from Clement's words on luxury and covetousness. To live in luxury, he says, is a sin,[39] for "it is monstrous for one to live in luxury, while many are in want."[40] It is also an irrational act that should be avoided, "lest perchance some say of us, 'His horse . . . is worth fifteen talents; but the man himself is dear at three coppers.'"[41] Clement delights in showing the senselessness of luxury and ostentation. All would agree that it would be silly to make a pickax of silver or a sickle out of gold; and yet, when it comes to household goods, many do not show the same wisdom as they do when making agricultural tools. A table knife does not cut better because it has an ivory handle, and a lamp does not give more light because it comes from the goldsmith's shop rather than the potter's. Yet the folly of luxury is such that some even have gold chamberpots, as if they could not set aside their pride even when they relieve themselves![42]

Again, this does not mean that things in themselves are evil. But there is a measure for the possession of things, and that measure is their use. The theme of the use of things appears repeatedly in the writings of Clement, precisely when dealing with the manner in which one should deal with material goods. In the passage quoted above about the senselessness of gold and silver utensils, Clement also says that the measure of such household utensils should be "use, not expense." The bowl from which the Lord ate was a common one. He told his disciples to recline on the grass, not on an ivory bed. He washed their feet in an earthen vessel, for he certainly did not bring a gold one down from heaven. In short, "He made use, not extravagance His aim."[43] There is no need to condemn the Creator for having made these things. But we must remember that, from the point of view of usefulness, that which is without ostentation is best.

The measure of proper use is necessity. Just as the size of the foot determines the size of the shoe, so should the needs of the body determine what one possesses. "All that we possess is given to us for use, and use for sufficiency."[44] Anything that goes beyond this is superfluous and is therefore a burden.[45] In short, wealth in itself is not evil, but it is very dangerous. Indeed, it is like a poisonous snake,

which will twist round the hand and bite; unless one knows how to lay hold of it without danger by the point of the tail. And riches, wriggling either in an

experienced or inexperienced grasp, are dexterous at adhering and biting; unless one, despising them, use them skillfully, so as to crush the creature by the
charm of the Word, and himself escape unscathed.[46]

Note here that riches, in order to be overcome, have to be despised.
It is not simply a matter of not allowing oneself to be ruled by them and
then continuing along one's merry way. Clement did believe that the
rich could be saved, but only by using their riches in a certain way. This
is why he suggested that rich Christians find wise mentors who could
guide them both in managing their riches and in educating their souls.
To manage wealth wisely, one must give it up knowing that one is thus
purchasing life eternal.

O excellent trading! O divine merchandise! One purchases immortality for money; and, by giving the perishing things of the world, receives in exchange for
these an eternal mansion in the heavens! Sail to this mart, if you are wise, O
rich man! If need be, sail round the whole world.[47]

Naturally, Clement does not mean that the rich literally buy their
way to heaven. He has made it plain that the mere giving up of riches
is not enough, for salvation is an inner matter. But he does mean, with
rhetorical exaggeration, that the only way the rich can enter heaven is
by sharing their possessions, and that therefore such sharing is a good
bargain. What the rich should do with the superfluous—with that which
goes beyond the necessities and is therefore a burden—is to distribute
it to those in need.[48] "He who has sold his worldly goods, and given
them to the poor, finds the imperishable treasure," for "it is not he who
has and keeps, but he who gives away, that is rich."[49] Thus the full
answer to Clement's question "who is the rich to be saved?" is that those
among the rich will be saved who measure their possessions by their real
need, consider the rest superfluous, and give it to the needy.

Behind this ethical teaching lies a theological outlook. It is first of
all an antignostic outlook. Clement rejects any notion that created things
are in themselves evil or that they are the creation or the realm of a
power that is less than God. The doctrine of creation implies the goodness of material reality. To decry all possessions seems to him very close
to rejecting the goodness of the One who made them. On the other
hand, Clement also believes that human beings are created for a higher
order and that our presence in this world is only temporary. "Things of
the world are *not our own*, not as if they were monstrous, not as if they
did not belong to God, the Lord of the universe, but because we do not
continue among them for ever."[50] Thus, as far as "possession," they are
not truly ours, but they were made for us "in respect to use."[51]

Second, this Creator had a particular order in mind:

God created our race for sharing {koinonía}, beginning by giving out what belonged to God, God's own Word, making it common {koinós} to all humans, and
creating all things for all {pánta poiésas ypér pánton}. Therefore all things are
common {koinà oûn tà pánta}; and let not the rich claim more than the rest. To
say therefore "I have more than I need, why not enjoy?" is neither human nor

proper to sharing {*ouk anthrópinon, oudè koinonikón*} . . . For I know quite well that God has given us the power to use; but only to the limit of that which is necessary; and that God also willed that the use be in common.[52]

Therefore, according to Clement, the commonality of goods—or at least of their use—is not a strange notion taught by some philosophical schools or fanatical groups. It is part of the original order of creation. At first sight, this appears to contradict Clement's statements, quoted above, to the effect that if no one had anything it would be impossible to obey the commandment of Jesus to feed the hungry and clothe the naked. One set of passages argues for private property and the other for common. To couch the matter in such terms, however, misses the central point in Clement's argument: that whatever we own we possess only for use; that any use beyond the necessary is superfluous and a burden to the Christian life; that the only way in which we can truly possess what we do not need is by giving it away; and that therefore the best management of private property is to make it available for common use.

In order to realize the import of what Clement is saying, we must place his words in the context of the understanding of private property that the Roman Empire had inherited and expanded from ancient Roman jurisprudence. Ownership entailed the right to use, enjoy, and abuse. Clement is contradicting that notion, setting two limits to the rights of property: *koinonía* and sufficiency. In the text just quoted, he literally says that the notion that ownership entails the right of enjoyment as one sees fit is against both nature and *koinonía*. As a modern interpreter of Clement has said, "The clear call is to cast aside the prevailing, absolutist, individualistic Roman law legitimation of property and embrace a new rationale of ownership, holding all things in such a way that they may be common to all."[53]

In this passage, Clement's argument has a decidedly Stoic flavor. He is basing his critique of the notion of absolute property rights on the natural created order. God created humanity for sharing and began this process by sharing the divine logos. It is our sharing in this logos that makes us human. Therefore, not to share is inhuman and goes against the very *koinonía* that is the basis of our creation {*ouk anthrópinon, oudè koinonikón*}.

On the other hand, one must remember that, when speaking of either personal property or common use, Clement is not concerned about our modern debates regarding the nature and extent of property rights. His concern is not so much for the economic order of society as for the guidance and salvation of souls. Riches he fears, not so much because of the injustice they may involve, as because they can also draw the soul away from eternal concerns. Poverty he deplores, not primarily for the suffering it causes, but because it forces the poor away from contemplation of the eternal and into concern for their physical needs.[54] He quotes with approval the Mosaic law setting aside for the poor the gleanings of the harvest and the edges of the fields, the law providing for the cancellation of debts on the jubilee, and the one that prohibits lending money on interest. He sees these measures as a way of providing a respite for the poor; above all, he sees them as a form of training for the possessors, forcing them to practice sharing and generosity.[55]

Ultimately, Clement saw the entire created world as a training ground for the soul. This was an integral part of the Platonic and Stoic traditions from which he drew so heavily. In some ways, this idea would have more impact on Christian views and attitudes on economic issues than anything Clement said directly about wealth. The importance of his treatise *Who Is the Rich to Be Saved?* is not so much in its supposed latitude toward the rich—which, as we have seen, is a false interpretation—as in the shift of focus that has taken place. That one did not have to sell everything in order to follow Christ was not new—already Peter had said that to Ananias in Acts 5:4. What was new was Clement's focusing on the soul of the giver rather than on the need of the receiver—and even in this Hermas may be seen as his forerunner.

Origen

Clement's disciple, Origen, said much less about wealth and its uses. He believed that the injunction to sell one's possessions and give to the poor should be taken quite literally, even though he normally interpreted the Bible allegorically. His most valuable possession was his library, and this he sold. However, he did not do this to give the proceeds to the poor, but on condition that the buyer would guarantee him a daily allowance of four obols, barely enough for subsistence. It is said that he also took literally the Lord's command not to have more than one cloak and to go barefooted.

All of this, however, he appears to have done more in quest of the "philosophical life" as he understood it than on behalf of the poor, as is shown by the terms on which he sold his library. Like Clement, Origen's primary concern is the salvation of the giver's soul rather than the well-being of the receiver. Riches are an obstacle for salvation, since the rich have greater difficulty controlling their passions and not being swept away by them.[56] On the other hand, in listing seven means for the remission of sins, Origen names almsgiving in the third place, immediately after baptism and martyrdom.[57] Presumably, in order to give alms, one would have to own something, as Clement had already pointed out.

One passage in Origen's *Against Celsus* bears highlighting. Origen is responding to Celsus's charges that Christians are wicked. After agreeing that they may be uneducated but not wicked, he says, "How can people with a wicked mind practice temperance and self-control, or generosity and sharing {*koinonikón*}?"[58] This passage is significant because, in spite of all the limitations of sharing among Christians by the beginning of the third century, it shows they practiced enough liberality and sharing to be used as proof against hostile pagan observes.[59]

Finally, in several passages Origen deals with the question of tribute.[60] Although these passages are not altogether clear, he seems to believe that all material property somehow belongs to Caesar and that this was what Jesus meant by the phrase "render unto Caesar what is Caesar's." To own things is to be indebted to Caesar—or, in some of the passages, to "the prince of this world"—and therefore the closer one is to being free of material possessions the less hold Caesar has on one. Christians ought to pay tribute to Caesar, because they pay out of what is his in any case. At this point, it may be well to remember that the Roman legal notion of absolute property excluded paying tribute on it and that therefore when one pays tribute on a property one is acknowledging that one does not have full ownership. In any case, Origen's assertion that the property of Christians is not theirs resembles Irenaeus's comments on the matter, although Irenaeus says only that such wealth is not rightly ours, not that it belongs to Caesar.

Tertullian

One of Tertullian's main concerns was the refutation of heresies, especially the doctrine of Marcion, who insisted on the radical discontinuity between the Old and New Testaments—between the Jehovah of Judaism and the loving Father of Christianity. Against such views, Tertullian stressed the continuity between the two testaments. In that context he quotes a long list of texts in the Old Testament in which the people of God are called to compassion and justice toward the needy and the powerless. Then he says that from the very beginning Jesus set out in his ministry "with the very attributes of the Creator, who ever in language of the same short {as that employed by Jesus in the Beatitudes} loved, consoled, protected, and avenged the beggar, and the poor, and the humble, and the widow, and the orphan."[61]

Tertullian is also writing against the detractors of the faith when he describes the finances of the community:

There is no buying and selling of any sort in the things of God. Though we have our treasure-chest, it is not made up of purchase-money, as of a religion that has its price. On a monthly day, if he likes, each puts in a small donation; but only if this be his pleasure, and only if he is able; for there is no compulsion; all is voluntary.[62]

Clearly, what Tertullian is describing here is similar to what we now call "offerings." He underscores the voluntary nature of these contributions—"if he likes," "if this be his pleasure," "there is no compulsion," "all is voluntary." He is not doing this, however, in order to reject all that we have seen so far of the early Christian understanding of *koinonía*. His purpose is rather, as the beginning of the passage shows, to underscore the contrast between Christianity, where giving is voluntary, and where the gifts of God are free, with the pagan practice of charging for the ministrations of the gods. His argument is against pagans and not against people who reject the notions of private property and voluntary giving.

It is important to keep this in mind to understand how Tertullian, just a few lines later, could speak of common possessions. He is arguing that pagans object to the Christians calling themselves brothers and sisters because among pagans such family ties have lost their meaning, and Christians put them to shame by their mutual love. At this point Tertullian comments:

> Family possessions, which generally destroy brotherhood among you, create fraternal bonds among us. One in mind and soul, we do not hesitate to share our earthly goods with one another. All things are common among us but our wives.[63]

This text and the one just quoted regarding voluntary giving appear practically back to back in Tertullian's *Apology*. It would be poorly argued indeed if Tertullian were contradicting himself within the scope of a few lines. It would also be poorly argued if he were describing practices that his pagan opponents knew not to be true. Therefore, both passages have to be seen as a whole and placed in the context of their polemical purpose. Tertullian is refuting those who criticize the way of life of Christians. From the rest of this chapter, as well as from those that follow, it is clear that Tertullian is responding to a line of argument that claims that Christians are a social evil or that they are at least useless to society. In this particular chapter, the opponents' point is that Christianity is an evil influence precisely because its members are required to be a closely knit group. Tertullian responds by affirming the closeness that exists among Christians and at the same time insisting that this is voluntary, not a demand placed on them by their leaders. That is the reason for the discussion of the meaning of the title *brothers*, which appears between the two texts quoted. That is also the reason Tertullian must emphasize both the voluntary nature and the radical character of giving in the Christian community. No one forces Christians to give. Yet, they are of a single mind to such a degree that they do not hesitate in their sharing (*communicatio-koinonía*) with each other, and that things among them are common or "undivided" (*indiscreta*).

Tertullian's argument continues. The Christian practice of love is not like that of the pagans, which is sheer debauchery. He offers a few examples of such debauchery, then comments sarcastically on pagan feasts, comparing them with the Christian love feast, about which so many evil rumors circulated. He emphasizes the importance of love feasts for the poor, and in passing he speaks of what today would be called "the preferential option for the poor":

Our feast explains itself by its name. The Greeks call it *agapè*, i.e., affection. Whatever it costs, our outlay in the name of piety is gain, since with the good things of the feast we benefit the needy; ... but as it is with God himself, a peculiar respect is shown to the lowly.[64]

A similar sentiment is found in Tertullian's treatise *On Patience*. There he is arguing that Christians should practice patience in the face of a number of ills, one of which is the loss of property. In that context Tertullian declares that "the Lord Himself is found amid no riches." Whether this means that the historic Jesus was poor or that Christians do not now find the Lord amid riches is not clear. The next sentence, however, is quite clear: "He always justifies the poor, fore-condemns the rich."[65]

This particular chapter of *On Patience* also throws further light on the question of property. Obviously, the fact that Christians must be ready to face the loss of property clearly indicates that private property has not been abolished. At the same time, Tertullian relativizes the rights of property by expanding the notion of covetousness: "Let us not interpret that covetousness as consisting merely in the concupiscence of what is another's: for even what seems ours is another's; for nothing is ours, since all things are God's, whose we are also ourselves."[66]

Christians must be ready at all times to suffer the loss of all possessions. After all, what they have is not truly theirs, and therefore to wish to possess it absolutely is to covet. Furthermore, such excessive attachment to one's property is an obstacle to sharing it. Indeed, anyone who is afraid of loss through theft or force will not be willing to "lay hand on his own property in the cause of almsgiving." Thus love of property causes both fear of losing it and unwillingness to share it. And the contrary is also true, for one "who fears not to lose, finds it not irksome to give."[67] In order to be able to dispose of one's goods, one must be ready to dispense with them.

Just before these words Tertullian declares that "patience in losses is an exercise in bestowing and communicating."[68] The use of the term *communicare* here is significant. Tertullian, the first major Latin Christian writer, describes Christian sharing with what amounts to a literal translation of the Greek *koinonein*.[69]

In these passages, as in many similar ones in Tertullian's writings, two concerns are interwoven: liberality toward the poor and the need to practice the patience and fortitude that persecution may suddenly require. About liberality toward the poor, Tertullian is ready to boast before his pagan opponents: "Our compassion spends more in the streets than yours does in the temples."[70] The second is a constant concern of Tertullian, who fears that a life too full of comforts is a poor preparation for martyrdom:

I know not whether the wrist that has been wont to be surrounded with the palmleaf-like bracelet will endure till it grow into the numb hardness of its own chain! I know not whether the leg that has rejoiced in the anklet will suffer itself to be squeezed into the gyve! I fear the neck, beset with pearl and emerald nooses, will give no room to the broadsword! Wherefore . . . let us abandon luxuries, and we shall not regret them. Let us stand ready to endure every violence, having nothing which we may fear to leave behind. It is these things which are the bonds which retard our hope. Let us cast away earthly ornaments if we desire the heavenly.[71]

That Tertullian found it necessary to write such words is ample proof that the church contained some who lived—or at least were tempted to live—in the sort of luxury that he deplored. As he stressed in the *Apology,* giving was voluntary. In such a situation, many would be tempted to retain for themselves as much as possible. In a sense, this was their right. But Tertullian was not content with that response, so he made three points to help lead rich Christians to greater largesse: (1) nothing that one has is one's own, and therefore to be overly attached to it is just as sinful as desiring what belongs to another; (2) the Lord has shown a preference for the poor, and Christians ought to do likewise; (3) excessive ease and comfort weaken believers for the many trials they may have to face, particularly the trial of martyrdom.

Clearly, the commonality of goods of which Tertullian boasts in his *Apology* did not prevent some from retaining more than Tertullian thought was justified. Yet the very fact that he could boast of it to a hostile audience, and that he could also boast of Christian charity as compared to pagan, also indicates the extent to which both sharing and charity were practiced. Again, what we have here is neither a dogmatic communalism nor a *carte blanche* for accumulating wealth. Tertullian and the church of his time, as those before them, would not force people to give, but neither would they ease the conscience of those who retained for themselves more than was necessary. As Tertullian would say, in one of those epigrammatic phrases so typical of him, "Christians always, and now more than ever, pass their time not in gold but in iron."[72]

Hippolytus

In his *Refutation of all Heresies,* Hippolytus unwittingly testifies to the degree to which Christianity had made inroads among the well-to-do in Rome. In book nine, he is attacking his arch-rival Callistus—bishop of Rome from 217 to 222—by exposing what Hippolytus says was his early career. According to this account, Callistus was a slave of a wealthy Christian named Carpophorus, who himself belonged to the "household of Caesar." Callistus began acting as a banker for other Christians, telling them that he was an agent for Carpophorus. When his business deals failed, he tried to escape, but Carpophorus captured him and forced him to work in a treadmill until the intercession of other Christians made him relent. When Callistus went into a synagogue and started a riot, hoping to be taken before the magistrates and killed as a martyr, Carpophorus went before the Roman prefect and convinced him that Callistus wished to die in order to be honored as a martyr, and should not be killed. Callistus was then sent to the mines in Sardinia and worked there until Marcia, a Christian concubine of Emperor Commodus (who reigned from 180 to 192), obtained the release of Christians condemned to the Sardinian mines.[73]

The details of this story, and certainly the innuendoes as to Callistus's motivations, may well not be true. Yet the story itself provides insight into the social composition of the church in Rome toward the end of the second century. The church has contacts with the court both through Carpophorus and through Marcia. Carpophorus may have been no more than an imperial slave; yet such slaves, in spite of their servile status, were often powerful administrators. This one had enough influence to be heard by the prefect of the city. A number of widows and other members of the church deposit their money with Callistus. We are not told the size of such deposits, but they must have been considerable enough to cause Carpophorous the distress and shame of which Hippolytus speaks.

Hippolytus's *Apostolic Tradition* confirms the presence in the church of people who owned slaves.[74] The injunction that military officers must not execute others implies that there were Christians with relatively high rank in the army. And the requirement that governors or magistrates must relinquish their office before being accepted for baptism indicates that at least some people of high rank in the civil government were seeking admission into the church.[75]

This, however, is not the entire picture of the church in Rome at the time. One may well suppose that for every person of high rank or wealth there were many of humble status and limited means. Hippolytus himself speaks of "all the poor" being buried in the Christian cemetery.[76]

Unfortunately, most of the surviving material written by Hippolytus says nothing about the subjects that interest us here. One exception is a fragment on the Lord's Prayer that interprets the petition for daily bread in a way similar to what we shall find, with more detail, in Cyprian:

For this reason we are enjoined to ask what is sufficient for the preservation of the substance of the body: not luxury, but food, which restores what the body loses, and prevents death by hunger; not tables to inflame and drive on to pleasures, nor such things as make the body wax wanton against the soul; but bread, and that, too, not for a great number of years, but what is sufficient for us to-day.[77]

Other texts, fragments of his commentary on Daniel, show that Hippolytus continues the apocalyptic expectation of Revelation that faithful

Christians who "yield no obsequious obedience to the persons of rulers"[78] will find themselves excluded from the economic order: "They shall not be able any longer to sell their own property nor to buy from strangers, unless one keeps and bears with him the name of the beast, or bears its mark upon his forehead."[79]

Cyprian

With Cyprian we reach the middle of the third century. He was approaching fifty years of age when he was converted, probably in A.D. 246. Until that time, he had been practicing rhetoric, and he possessed sufficient means to own a house and gardens. We are told that at the time of his conversion he sold his property and gave the proceeds to the poor,[80] but we are also told that, after he was a bishop, he still managed some of his patrimony.[81] He himself declares that one of the difficulties in the way to his conversion was his doubt as to his ability to lead the life of humble moderation demanded of Christians:

I used to regard it as a difficult matter, and especially as difficult in respect to my character at that time, that a man should be capable of being born again . . . When does he learn thrift who has been used to liberal banquets and sumptuous feasts? And he who has been glittering in gold and purple, and has been celebrated for his costly attire, when does he reduce himself to ordinary and simple clothing?[82]

Cyprian's career as a Christian is typical of the prominent place given in the church to wealthy or well-educated converts. Cyprian had been a Christian for less than three years when he was elected bishop of Carthage, in an election that was apparently not without opposition on the part of rival candidates with longer experience in the church. He probably was not the only North African bishop who came from the higher classes, as is attested by the Latin names of the majority of his colleagues—a sign that the conditions that would lead to the Donatist schism were beginning to develop. When persecution broke out under Decius, a few short months after Cyprian had been made a bishop, he fled the city. While this was not unheard of, and many advised it, in Cyprian's case it provoked much criticism, and after the persecution abated it led to a schism. Although a synod held shortly after the end of the persecution sustained Cyprian in his decisions, one wonders to what extent the bishops gathered in that synod were seen by the lower classes in the church—especially those of Punic and Berber stock—as aristocrats favoring one of their own. In any case, when persecution broke out again Cyprian stood firm, and in A.D. 258 he was beheaded, a form of execution befitting his rank. He marched to his death wearing the linen tunic, dalmatic, and cloak that marked him as a gentleman.[83]

Cyprian's most important work dealing with the subject of wealth and its use is his treatise *On Works and Alms* (*De opere et eleemosynis*), which may have been written in 252 at a time when a devastating epidemic swept the region. The treatise itself is an eloquent call to almsgiving on the basis of a number of arguments. His first argument—a point never before stated as explicitly—is that almsgiving is a means to atone for sins committed after baptism: "By almsgiving we may wash away whatever foulness we subsequently contract."[84] One is not saved by almsgiving, for "the blood and sanctification of Christ" are necessary to purge those sins committed before baptism. But since all sin even after baptism, none should think that they can be saved without it: "He who is pitiful teaches and warns us that pity must be shown; and because He seeks to save those whom at great cost He has redeemed, He teaches that those who, after the grace of baptism, have become foul, may once again be cleansed."[85]

A second argument, closely related to the first, is that almsgiving increases the power and efficacy of prayer and fasting. These "are of no avail, unless they are aided by almsgiving."[86] Indeed, the power of almsgiving is such that through it people can be preserved, not only from eternal death, but also from the physical or "first" death.[87]

A third point, and one on which Cyprian dwells at some length, is that those who give alms will not suffer physical want. Indeed, the treatise even implies that those who give of their wealth will become wealthier.

If you dread and fear, lest, if you begin to act thus abundantly, your patrimony being exhausted by your liberal dealing, you may perchance be reduced to poverty; be of good courage in this respect, be free from care: that cannot be exhausted whence the service of Christ is supplied . . . The merciful and those who do good works cannot want . . . By the prayer of the poor, the wealth of the doer is increased by the retribution of God.[88]

To deny this and to imagine that "he who feeds Christ is not himself fed by Christ, or that earthly things will be wanting to those to whom divine and heavenly things are given," is an "unbelieving thought" and an "impious and sacrilegious consideration."[89]

A fourth argument, and probably the basis for all the rest, is that almsgiving has been commanded by Christ, who told his followers repeatedly to devote themselves to almsgiving and not to depend on earthly possessions, but rather to lay up treasures for themselves in heaven. This commandment is so central that only "he who gives alms according to God's precept believes in God . . . Moreover, he who maintains the fear of God considers God in showing mercy to the poor."[90]

Cyprian offers also the traditional arguments regarding the folly of wealth. It is folly to be concerned about the possible depletion or failure of one's estate when life itself and salvation are failing. "While you fear, lest for the sake of yourself, you should lose your patrimony, you yourself are perishing for the sake of your patrimony."[91] "You are the captive and slave of your money; you are bound with the chains and bonds of covetousness; and you whom Christ had once loosed, are once more in chains."[92] "You are mistaken, and are deceived, whosoever you are, that think yourself rich in this world."[93]

One cannot be excused from almsgiving on the grounds that one has children for whose patrimony and inheritance one is responsible. To do so is to forsake one's real responsibility for one's children and therefore to betray them: "You are an unfair and traitorous father, unless you . . . preserve them in religion and true piety. You who are careful rather for their earthly than for their heavenly state, rather to commend your children to the devil than to Christ, are sinning twice, both in not providing for your children the aid of God their Father, and in teaching your children to love their property more than Christ."[94]

Therefore, it is a great sin to prefer oneself and one's children to Christ and not to share one's patrimony with the needy (*nec patrimonium cum indigentium paupertate communicat*).[95] This particular passage is important because in it we find that, although Cyprian focuses on almsgiving—and Christians would eventually develop a clear distinction between almsgiving and the practice of the commonality of goods (*koinonía*)—at this time Cyprian still conceives of almsgiving in terms of sharing (*communicare*).

Cyprian's other arguments for the practice of almsgiving are no less interesting. He declares that among the Gentiles donors are much more liberal when their giving is witnessed by emperors, proconsuls, and nobility, and that among Christians the same should hold true. God, Christ, and the angels are the witnesses of Christian giving, and gifts should be worthy of such an audience. On the other hand, the devil and his servants rejoice when Christians are miserly, and mock Christ saying that these people are willing to serve the devil even though he did not suffer for them. In refusing to give to the poor, Christians make themselves servants, not of Christ, but of the devil, to whom they owe nothing and who will not repay them.[96]

Finally, Cyprian bases almsgiving on the imitation of the bountifulness of God, who shares with all. After reminding his readers of the sharing that took place in the first Christian community in Jerusalem,[97] Cyprian declares that this is the true imitation of God:

For whatever is of God is common in our use; nor is any one excluded from His benefits and His gifts, so as to prevent the whole human race from enjoying equally the divine goodness and liberality. Thus the day equally enlightens, the sun gives radiance, the rain moistens, the wind blows, and the sleep is one to those that sleep, and the splendour of the stars and of the moon is common. In which example of equality, he who, as a possessor in the earth, shares his returns and his fruits with the fraternity, while he is common and just in his gratuitous bounties, is an imitator of God the Father.[98]

   This text is significant, not only for what it says, but also for what it does not say. In a number of Christian writers we shall find the notion that all things were created to be the common property of all or that all things belong to God and that humans are intended to share them equally. What this text says is different. None of the things listed as belonging to God and therefore "common in our use" can be owned privately: the day, the sun, the rain, the wind, sleep, and the splendor of the stars and the moon. On the other hand those who are "possessors in the earth"—probably meaning landowners—are to share of its produce with others. In any case, the earth is not listed among things belonging to God and therefore unsuitable for private ownership, as the Hebrew Scriptures declared it to be.[99]

   It is difficult to assess the significance of the shift in emphasis from sharing (koinonía) to almsgiving (eleemosyne). The latter term originally meant a merciful action or a gift born from kindness, and it was often used this way in classical antiquity, in the New Testament, and in early Christian writers. Only later did it come to mean small change handed to a beggar. In Cyprian's usage, it clearly means much more than this. The almsgiving of which Cyprian speaks is so great that people could object it would threaten their patrimony or their children's inheritance. Cyprian himself disposed of at least a significant portion of his estate and gave it to the poor. Therefore, it probably would be wrong to interpret his emphasis on almsgiving as an attempt to widen the eye of the needle through which the rich must pass.

   Like earlier Christians, Cyprian has harsh words for the rich who do not share their wealth with the needy, and especially for those who constantly seek greater security by augmenting their estates. Commenting on the Lord's Prayer, he declares that those who have "begun" to be disciples of Christ should ask only for their daily needs, and that this should lead one to undo all "entanglements of worldly estate."[100] And his very first epistle contains some of the harshest words penned by an early Christian writer against the acquisitiveness of the rich, "who add forests to forests, and who, excluding the poor from their neighbourhood, stretch out their fields far and wide into space without any limits." Yet, they find no peace in such enterprises, for

such a one enjoys no security either in his food or in his sleep. In the midst of the banquet he sighs, although he drinks from a jewelled goblet; and when his luxurious bed has enfolded his body, languid with feasting, he lies wakeful in the midst of the down; nor does he perceive, poor wretch, that these things are merely gilded torments, that he is held in bondage by his gold, and that he is the slave of his luxury and wealth rather than their master.[101]

   Such people, however, are to be indicted for more than their folly, which turns them into slaves of their wealth. They are also guilty of boundless greed, for their "possession amounts to this only, that they

can keep others from possessing it."[102] That is the real motivation behind the actions of those who amass large fortunes, and it is as close as
Cyprian ever comes to questioning the unlimited understanding of
property rights that prevailed in Roman law.

NOTES

1. Eusebius, *C. H.* 5.21.1 All references to this work are found in *NPNF,* 2d ser.
2. *C. H.* 5.1.14.
3. *Apol.* 1: "The outcry is that the State is filled with Christians—that they are in the
   fields, in the citadels, in the islands: they make their lamentation, as for some
   calamity, that both sexes, every age and condition, even high rank, are passing over
   to the profession of the Christian faith." *Ad. nat.* 1: 3:109: "You grieve over it as a
   calamity, that each sex, every age—in short, every rank—is passing over from you to
   us." All references to this work come from *ANF.*
4. *Passio Perp.* 2: "honeste nata." *Acta min. SS. Perp. et Felic.* 1: "de nobili genere." *PL.*
5. Eusebius, *C. H.* 6.2.13.
6. *C. H.,* 6.23.1.
7. *Oct.* 5, *ANF.*
8. *Oct.* 8, *ANF.*
9. Origen, *Contra Cel.* 3.55, *ANF.*
10. I have recently completed a study on their theology in general and the way they may
    be seen as early exponents of later theological developments: *Christian Thought
    Revisited: Three Types of Theology* (Nashville: Abingdon, 1989).
11. Irenaeus, *Adv. haer.* 4.12.5, 13.3. All references to this document are from the *ANF.*
12. *Adv. haer.* 4.13.3.
13. *Adv. haer.* 4.13.3.
14. *Adv. haer.* 4.30.1–3.
15. *Adv. haer.* 4.30.2.
16. *Adv. haer.* 4.30.1.
17. In another context, he does say that the state has been instituted by God in order to
    restrain human evil and injustice. On that basis, all that the magistrates do that is
    just is acceptable to God. Whatever they do that is unjust, tyrannical, against the
    law, or toward the destruction of the faithful will earn them condemnation. But the
    gathering of taxes is among their proper functions, and in so doing they are
    ministers of God. *Adv. haer.* 5.24.2.
18. *Adv. haer.* 4.30.3.
19. *Quis div. salv.* 1. All references to this work are from *ANF.*
20. *Quis div. salv.* 2.
21. *Quis div. salv.* 3.
22. A purpose wittingly expressed in the title of Walter H. Wagner's article, "Lubricating
    the Camel: Clement of Alexandria on Wealth and the Wealthy," in *Festschrift: A
    Tribute to Dr. William Hordern* ed., W. Freitag (Saskatoon: University of Saskatchewan,
    1985), pp. 64–77. What Wagner means is not that Clement made it easy for the rich
    to get their camels through the eye of the needle, but that he tried to show them
    how their camels could be "lubricated" by discipline and trust in God's grace.
23. See J. L. González, *A History of Christian Thought,* 2nd ed. (Nashville: Abington,
    1987), 1:194–99.
24. *Quis div. salv.* 11.
25. *Quis div. salv.* 12. Cf. 14: "The renunciation, then, and selling all possessions, is to
    be understood as spoken of the passions of the soul."
26. See González, *History,* (n. 23 above), 1:133 n. 33.
27. *Strom. 3.6, ANF.*
28. *Quis div. salv.* 13. The translation in *ANF* leaves out the theme of *koinonia,* which is
    part of the original Greek text: "For if no one had anything, what room would there

be left among men for giving?" A better translation would be: "How could sharing {*koinonía*} be possible among humans, if no one had anything?"

29. *Quis div. salv.* 14.
30. *Quis div. salv.* 17.
31. *Quis div. salv.* 14: "So also a poor and destitute man may be found intoxicated with lusts; and a man rich in worldly goods temperate, poor in {self-}indulgences, trustworthy, intelligent, pure, chastened."
32. *Quis div. salv.* 16.
33. *Quis div. salv.* 17.
34. *Quis div. salv.* 19.
35. *Quis div. salv.* 24.
36. *Quis div. salv.* 27.
37. *Quis div. salv.* 31–33.
38. *Quis div. salv.* 41.
39. *Strom.* 2.15, ANF.
40. *Paid.* 2.12. References to this work, except where noted, are from *ANF.* (At this point, the numbering of chapters in *ANF* is different from that in *PG.* Therefore, in *ANF* this is chapter 13).
41. *Paid.* 3.6.
42. *Paid.* 2.3.
43. *Paid.* 2.3.
44. *Paid.* 2.3.
45. *Paid.* 3.7. Cf. *Paid.* 2.3. "On the whole, gold and silver, both publicly and privately, are an invidious possession when they exceed what is necessary, seldom to be acquired, difficult to keep, and not adapted for use."
46. *Paid.* 3.6.
47. *Quis div. salv.* 32.
48. *Paid.* 3.7.
49. *Paid.* 3.6.
50. *Strom.* 4.13.
51. *Strom.* 4.13, ANF.
52. *Paid.* 2.13, PG.
53. C. Avila, *Ownership: Early Christian Teaching* (Maryknoll, NY: Orbis, 1983), p. 41.
54. *Strom.* 4.5, *ANF:* "For it {poverty} compels the soul to desist from necessary things, I mean contemplation and from pure sinlessness, forcing him, who has not wholly dedicated himself to God in love, to occupy himself about provisions; as, again, health and abundance of necessaries keep the soul free and unimpeded, and capable of making a good use of what is at hand."
55. *Strom.* 2.18, *ANF.* On the issue of loans on interest, Clement has been variously interpreted. He quotes the ancient Jewish prohibition against taking usury from a "brother" and then clarifies that a brother is "not only him who is born of the same parents, but also one of the same race and sentiments, and a participator in the same word." Does participating in the same "logos" mean being a fellow Christian? Or does it mean simply participating in the same principle of all rationality? If the former, Clement rejects usury only when one Christian lends to another. If the latter, he holds that no Christian should collect an interest, no matter who the borrower might be.
56. *Comm. in Matt.* 15.20, PG.
57. *Hom. in Lev.* 2.4, PG.
58. *Contra Cel.* 3.78. References to this text are from *ANF.*
59. On the other hand, there is a negative side to this, as Celsus is quick to point out, namely, that people of limited means may become Christians seeking to benefit from the wealth of others who are already members of the church. Origen concedes the possibility that this may be true in his time, when "not only rich men, but persons of high rank, and delicate and high born ladies" are joining the church. *Contra Cel.* 3.9.
60. *Comm. in Mat.* 17.28; *Hom. in Luc.* 23, PG; *Comm. in Rom.* 9.25, PG.

61. *Adv. Marc.* 4.14. All references to this work are from *ANF.* Shortly after this quote, Tertullian goes on to speak of "a wealth of good works."

62. *Apol.* 39. References to this text are from *ANF.*

63. *Apol.* 39. The last two sentences read, *Itaque qui animo animaque miscemur, nihil de rei communicatione dubitamus. Omnia indiscreta sunt apud nos, praeter uxores.*

64. *Apol.* 39.

65. *De pat.* 7. The Latin: *Semper pauperes justificat, divites praedamnat* (*PL*). On the hermeneutical advantage of the poor, see Minucius Felix, *Oct.* 16, *ANF:* "Rich men, attached to their means, have been accustomed to gaze more upon their gold than upon heaven, while our sort of people, though poor, have both discovered wisdom, and have delivered their teachings to others." References to this text, except as noted, are from *ANF.*

66. *De pat.* 7.

67. *De pat.* 7.

68. *De pat.* 7, *PL*, reads, *Patientia in detrimentis exercitatio est largiendi et communicandi.*

69. In another passage in the same treatise, Tertullian translates another use of the same verb, "to make common" in the sense of defiling, with the same Latin word: *De pat.* 8, *PL.*

70. *Apol.* 42, *ANF.*

71. *De cult. fem.* 2.13, *ANF.*

72. *De cult. fem.* 2.13., *ANF.* Or: "For Christians, the time is always, and particularly now, a time of iron, and not of gold."

73. *Philos.* 9.7, *ANF.*

74. *Trad.* 16.4, *The Apostolic Tradition of Hippolytus,* ed. B.S. Easton (Cambridge, Eng.: University Press, 1934).

75. *Trad.* 16.17–18.

76. *Trad.* 34.1.

77. *Frag. in Matt., ANF.*

78. *Susan.* 41, *ANF.*

79. *Frag. in Dan.* 12.1, *ANF.*

80. Jerome, *De vir. ill.* 67.

81. *Ep.* 7.81.

82. *Ep.* 1.3.

83. *Acta Procons.* 5.

84. *De op. et eleem.* 1. This document is taken from *ANF.*

85. *De op. et eleem.* 2. In *Christian Thought Revisited,* I have pointed out that this concern for postbaptismal sins is characteristic of the theology that was developing in the West and is intimately connected with an entire theological outlook.

86. *De op. et eleem.* 5.

87. *De op. et eleem.* 6.

88. *De op. et eleem.* 9.

89. *De op. et eleem.* 12. It is interesting to note that Cyprian does not ask how it is then that some Christians are in need of almsgiving.

90. *De op. et eleem.* 7. Again, the central role of the very notion of commandment characterizes this particular type of theology developing in North Africa and will eventually dominate the entire Christian West.

91. *De op. et eleem.* 10.

92. *De op. et eleem.* 12.

93. *De op. et eleem.* 14.

94. *De op. et eleem.* 18.

95. *De op. et eleem.* 17.

96. *De op. et eleem.* 21–22.

97. See also *De unit. ecc.* 26, *ANF,* where Cyprian compares the sharing of that early community with what exists in his time. Such "nostalgic remembrance" of the early *koinonia* has in Cyprian one of its first exponents.

98. *De unit. ecc.* 25.

99. T. G. Fogliani, *T. C. Cipriano: Contributo alla ricerca di referimenti legali in testi extragiuridici del IIIo sec. d. C.* (Modena: E. Brassi e Nipoti, 1928), devotes an entire chapter (the third) to the subject of Cyprian's understanding of property and its proper use.

100. *De dom. orat.* 19–20, *ANF.*

101. *Ep.* 1.12.

102. *Ep.* 1.12.

7/Preparing the Way for Constantine

An astounding event awaited Christians who lived at the end of the third century and the beginning of the fourth. Almost immediately after the worst persecution Christians had ever experienced, the Roman Empire made an about face and became officially Christian. To those living at the time, both pagan and Christian, the change was as unexpected as a bolt from heaven. Nothing—not even in their wildest dreams—had prepared them for this eventuality. And yet, as we now look at the last years of the third century from a perspective of almost two millennia, we can detect signs that, quite unwittingly, the church was preparing itself for the accommodations that Constantine's conversion would require.

An Evolving Situation

As Christianity approached the fateful events of the fourth century, its social and economic profile continued to change. In the cities and even in a number of secondary towns, it continued making inroads into the middle classes. Increasingly throughout the latter half of the third century, some of the well-to-do are listed as Christians or buried in their cemeteries. Yet the high aristocracy remained virtually untouched by the new faith. Very few senators, perhaps no more than one, embraced it. As the *Apostolic Tradition* of Hippolytus shows, conflicts between the church and the empire made it difficult for high officers of the state to become Christians and retain their posts. Therefore, Christianity made little headway among the higher ranks of civil service. The well-to-do among Christians tended to be wealthy matrons who could stay aloof from imperial functions and successful business people—often freedmen and freedwomen or their descendants—who had no political ambitions.

The first possessions that the church could legally own were cemeteries, for the state recognized the existence of churches only as funeral associations. The cemeteries of the latter half of the third century, particularly the catacombs of the Via Latina, show evidence of a community that is not mired in poverty, but rather is composed mostly of middle class and lower middle class artisans and traders, with a fair number of members in relatively comfortable circumstances. In Carthage, certainly by the early fourth century, and probably by the second half of the third, the church had a body of lay *seniores* whose responsibilities were similar to those of today's trustees.[1] Their very presence and their function reveal a community with a certain amount of material resources. In North Africa, even in the second-rate town of Abitine, the Christian community counted among its members a man whom the records call "senator" and a woman whom they call "clarissima."[2]

Naturally, this is not the whole story, for each of these cities included also large numbers of Christians belonging to the lower classes. In the "acts" of the martyrs, for every Christian whose high status or prestigious occupation is listed, there are dozens for whom nothing but the name is given. Presumably many or most of these belonged to the lower classes. In A.D. 251, the church in Rome was supporting fifteen hundred widows and poor people. Needless to say, the Christian community in Rome was large, for Bishop Cornelius was aided by forty six presbyters, seven deacons, seven subdeacons, and ninety four others in minor orders—acolytes, exorcists, readers, and doorkeepers. The church, composed as it was of people of diverse economic levels, was gaining a reputation for its charitable work.

Such work required, not only masses of poor people to feed and clothe, but also the resources of Christians of more abundant means. In most of the major cities of the empire, Christians now numbered thousands. The face-to-face sharing that had taken place in earlier times was no longer possible. The church found it necessary to promote giving on the part of those who had means and to organize the distribution of what was received. This led to two parallel developments whose early stages we saw in the last chapter, developments that would continue long after Constantine's conversion. On the one hand, the power and authority of bishops grew, as attested by the 155 members of Cornelius's clergy. It was the bishop's responsibility to administer the funds and properties of the church and to oversee the just distribution of available resources among those in need. In an operation the size of that in Rome—and probably in most large cities of the empire—this was a major administrative task, requiring able assistants, keen powers of discernment, and unquestionable authority. The increasing authority of bishops resulted, therefore, not only from theological developments requiring greater care for orthodoxy, but also from economic developments requiring greater care in managing the church's resources. Significantly, although an increasing number of bishops came from the upper classes, and many of them made large contributions to the church and its poor—some to the point of selling all their possessions—the roles of benefactor and leader were kept separate, at least until the fourth century.[3] This was partly because the tradition persisted that riches were not objects of pride, and that their best use was to give them away. Thus those who had enough wealth to use it as a source of power in the church lost some of their prestige precisely because they had retained such wealth.

On the other hand, a number of able intellectual leaders produced the sermons and writings necessary to promote giving. Some of these people were bishops and some were not. All belonged to the intellectual elites, for only so would they be able to reach and convince those whom they were calling to greater liberality. In that context arose the literature that deals with issues of faith and wealth. It is literature produced by the well educated and addressed to the well heeled. In the second century, the treatise *Who Is the Rich to Be Saved?* by Clement of Alexandria provides an early sample of this sort of literature. In the middle of the third century, Cyprian's *On Works and Alms* illustrates its further development. In the period just before Constantine, the most notable of these calls to Christian giving and compassion appears in the *Institutes* of Lactantius.

Lactantius

Lucius Caelius Firmianus Lactantius was a native of North Africa who continued the tradition established in that area by Christian writers such as Tertullian, Cyprian, and Arnobius—his own teacher of rhetoric, whom we have not had occasion to discuss here. For a time, apparently having been summoned there by Emperor Diocletian,[4] Lactantius taught in Nicomedia, the summer residence of the emperor and his court. When persecution broke out in A.D. 303, he resigned his post and lived in obscurity for the next fourteen years, until Emperor Constantine appointed him as tutor to his son Crispus. The work that most interests us here, the *Divine Institutes* (*Divinae institutiones*), was written for the most part before the end of persecution, although book seven was apparently written after the edict of Milan in A.D. 313. The *Institutes* are a veritable summa of theology, in which the author both refutes the pagan philosophers and shows the beauty and rationality of the Christian faith.

Much of what Lactantius says about wealth and its use had been said in earlier writings. The traditional Christian theme of compassion is not absent from his arguments, for after chiding those who waste their wealth in vain pursuits and those who simply rid themselves of it as an evil thing, he sets out to explain what would be a better use of one's wealth. At this point he brings in the value of care for the needy:

If you have so great a contempt for money, employ it in acts of kindness and humanity, bestow it upon the poor; this, which you are about to throw away, may be a succour to many, so that they may not die through famine, or thirst, or nakedness . . . You have it in your power to escape the possession of money, and yet to lay it out to advantage; for whatever has been profitable to many is securely laid out.[5]

The exact meaning of the last words in this quote is not clear. To "lay out" money to advantage (*bene collocare*) knowing that it is secure (*salvus*) implies that Lactantius is proposing an investment, as if he were saying, "You can both escape the power of money and invest it securely, for whatever profits many is safely invested." If so, this is another instance of a theme found in earlier writers, that will become common in the following century: that giving to the poor is an investment in eternity. In a different context, he says that by giving to the poor one can "make a frail and perishable good everlasting," and then calls his readers to "bestow your riches upon the altar {or, according to another reading, coffer} of God, in order that you may provide for yourself firmer possessions than these frail ones."[6]

Like other authors before him, Lactantius believes that liberality atones for sins, as long as one does not rely on it in order to continue sinning. Repentance is still necessary, and it would be a grievous error to think that mere liberality without repentance will atone for sin. On the other hand, it would also be a serious mistake to claim that, since one has no sin to blot out, liberality is not necessary. On the contrary, if anyone is just, that person must continue practicing liberality, if not in order to atone for sin, then simply out of virtue.

Nor, however, because offences are removed by bounty {*peccata largitione tolluntur*}, think that a license is given you for sinning. For they are done away with {*abolentur*} if you are bountiful to God because you have sinned; for if you sin through reliance on your bounty, they are not done away with {*si fiducia largiendi pecces, non abolentur*}. For God especially desires that men shall be cleansed from their sins, and therefore He commands them to repent. But to repent is nothing else than to profess and to affirm that one will sin no more . . . Nor, however, if any one shall have been purified from all stain of sin, let him think that he may abstain from the work of bounty because he has no faults to blot out. Nay, in truth, he is then more bound to exercise justice when he is become just, so that that which he had before done for the healing of his wounds he may afterwards do for the praise and glory of virtue.[7]

Sins consist not only of deeds but also of words and thoughts. While someone might abstain from sinful deeds and words, to abstain from sinful thoughts is almost impossible. Thus "if the condition of mortality does not suffer a man to be pure from every stain, the faults of the flesh ought therefore to be done away with by continual bounty."[8] Clearly, what is taking place here is the absorption of the practice of almsgiving into the emerging penitential system, a practice that would become so important in the development of Western theology.[9]

Such liberality, in order to be virtuous, must exclude any desire of financial gain. For this reason Lactantius agrees with the traditional Christian prohibition on lending money at interest. To charge interest is no longer to act out of mercy. Furthermore, it is tantamount to robbery, for the result is that one takes the other's property by taking advantage of the other's need.[10]

Like Cyprian before him, Lactantius also had to face those who objected that if they helped all the needy, they themselves would soon join their ranks.

Some one will perhaps say: If I shall do all these things, I shall have no possessions. For what if a great number of men shall be in want, suffer cold, shall be taken captive, shall die, since one who acts thus must deprive himself of his property even in a single day, shall I throw away the estate acquired by my own labour and by that of my ancestors, so that after this I myself must live by the pity of others?[11]

His reply to this objection is twofold. First, he argues that to take such a position is to "pusillanimously fear poverty." At this point he draws on the classical tradition of long standing, that wealth is a source of anxiety and unhappiness and poverty a value to be sought. Riches are not only a burden but even a temptation to others, including one's family. Therefore, "it is part of a great and lofty mind to despise and trample upon mortal affairs."[12]

On the other hand, Lactantius is aware that such complete dedication is not common, and therefore he offers another alternative. Those who are also called to share what they have, and to be as one person, are many. If all these people take responsibility for the needy, the burden of each donor will not be heavy. So Lactantius's readers, exhorted to excel in giving, are also told that this will not lead to a diminution of their wealth. Thus in the end the call to great sacrifice is reduced to a call to forego superfluous pleasures and to use those resources to help the needy:

And do not think that you are advised to lessen or exhaust your property; but that which you would have expended in superfluities, turn to better uses. Devote to the ransoming of captives that from which you purchase beasts; maintain the poor with that from which you feed wild beasts . . . Transfer things about to be miserably thrown away to the great sacrifice, that in return for these true gifts you may have an everlasting gift from God.[13]

Finally, Lactantius continues and strengthens an earlier tradition that affirms one is responsible for whatever happens to those whom one fails to help. Responsibility extends to the point of being guilty of homicide: "He who is able to succour one on the point of perishing, if he fails to do so, kills him."[14]

In book three of the *Institutes* Lactantius offers his most interesting comments on the subject of the economic ordering of society. This book is devoted to refuting the errors of the philosophers, and in this context Lactantius writes what some interpreters have taken to be one of the clearest early Christian defenses of private property.[15] On Plato's communistic proposal, he comments, "This is capable of being endured, as long as it appears to be spoken only of money." What most disturbs him is Plato's advocacy of common marriage among all citizens, which gives him the opportunity to declare with some sarcasm, "If you were to give the sovereignty to this man of such justice and equity, who had deprived some of their property, and given to some the property of others, he would prostitute the modesty of women."[16]

Thus in defending private property Lactantius employs arguments having to do primarily with the preservation of family, marriage, and chastity. Yet, others of his arguments deal more directly with the issues of private over against communal property, and some of these have a modern ring. Lactantius argues, for instance, that if nothing were to belong to anyone all motivation for frugality would be lost. In other words, private ownership is the reason people take care of things, and in a communistic society this incentive would disappear. It is true, he says, that private property can lead to many evils, but it can also lead to good. The same cannot be said of a system in which there is no private property: "The ownership of property contains the material both of vices and of virtues, but a community of goods contains nothing else than the licentiousness of vices."[17]

Plato's error, according to Lactantius, is that he did not understand that what matters is the inner life and not the outward:

He {Plato} did not find the concord which he sought, because he did not see whence it arises. For justice has no weight in outward circumstances, not even in the body, but is altogether employed on the mind of man. He, therefore, who wishes to place men on an equality, ought not to take away marriage and wealth, but arrogance, pride, and haughtiness, that those who are powerful and lifted up on high may know that they are on a level even with the most needy. For insolence and injustice being taken from the rich, it will make no difference whether some are rich and others poor, since they will be equal in spirit, and nothing but reverence towards God can produce this result. He thought, therefore, that he had found justice, whereas he had altogether removed it, because it ought not to be a community of perishable things, but of minds.[18]

The most interesting feature about this entire argument is that Lactantius "out-Platos" Plato. Ignoring all of Plato's philosophical system, even the manner in which he had moderated his proposal in *The Laws,* Lactantius accuses Plato of being preoccupied too much with material things and not enough with the inner life of the soul. Lactantius here clearly states a view that would eventually become common in Christian circles, namely, that riches or poverty matter little as long as one's attitude is right. As we have seen, however, this is not the last word of

Lactantius on the matter, for he is quite concerned with the proper use of riches, liberality in giving, and avoidance of usury.

Furthermore, in another passage Lactantius discusses common property. Here he deals with the notion widespread in the ancient world that there was a primal "golden age" without war or enmity, and in which all things were held in common. In general, he accepts this notion,[19] but he corrects it by indicating that what existed, rather than joint ownership, was a spirit of liberality in sharing. The description of the golden age by the poets:

Ought so to be taken, not as suggesting the idea that individuals at that time had no private property, but it must be regarded as a poetical figure; that we may understand that men were so liberal, that they did not shut up the fruits of the earth produced for them, nor did they in solitude brood over the things stored up, but admitted the poor to share the fruits of their labour . . . Nor did avarice intercept the divine bounty, and thus cause hunger and thirst in common; but all alike had abundance, since they who had possessions gave liberally and bountifully to those who had not.[20]

In order to understand the import of these words, we must see them in their proper historical context. It is clear that Lactantius is rejecting any plan for social reform based on legislation, such as Plato and many others had proposed. Yet he is not simply sanctifying and endorsing the existing situation. What he is saying is rather than humankind was created for sharing, not as a matter of obligation, but as a matter of compassion—the result of our sharing of common human nature. This was destroyed, he tells us, by the fall, when the true worship of God was lost and with it the knowledge of good and evil. The present situation of greed and injustice leading to hunger and suffering must not remain. Yet, as the original situation was based on the worship of God and the love of neighbor consequent on that worship, so its restoration must be based on that worship and that love.

For this reason the passage just quoted is so reminiscent of what the book of Acts tells us about the commonality of goods in the earliest Christian community, and of the understanding and practice of *koinonía* at a later time. Lactantius is arguing that justice must be reestablished and that this can be done only through the true worship of God. Elsewhere he declares, "You long for justice on the earth, while the worship of false gods continues, which cannot possibly come to pass."[20] Justice has two parts, "piety" and "equity." Piety is the knowledge and service of God; equity consists in making oneself equal to others. The latter is based on the former, for all human beings are created after the divine image. "The worshippers of gods adore senseless images, and bestow upon them whatever they have which is precious." Even more so should Christians "reverence the living images of God," that is, other human beings.[22] Furthermore, since God is bountiful, this bounty is to be shared equally by all, and "in His sight no one is a slave, no one a

master; for if all have the same Father, by an equal right we are all
children. No one is poor in the sight of God, but he who is without
justice; no one is rich, but he who is full of virtues." This is why it is it
impossible for pagans to practice justice.

Therefore neither the Romans nor the Greeks could possess justice, because
they had men differing from one another by many degrees, from the poor to
the rich, from the humble to the powerful; in short, from private persons to the
highest authorities of kings. For where all are not equally matched, there is not
equity; and inequality of itself excludes justice.[23]

By contrast, in the Christian community justice can be done and
the primal order of sharing restored, because it upholds both the worship of the one God before whom all are equal and the practice of
making all equal.

Some one will say, Are there not among you some poor, and others rich; some
servants, and others masters? Is there not some difference between individuals?
There is none; nor is there any other cause why we mutually bestow upon each
other the name of brethren, except that we believe ourselves to be equal . . . For
it is justice for a man to put himself on a level with those of lower rank.[24]

It is impossible to know exactly what this affirmation of what we
would now call "solidarity with the oppressed" meant in concrete terms
for Lactantius and his community. It clearly did not mean that the rich
gave all that they had and became as needy as the poor. On the other
hand, since it was something of which Lactantius felt he could boast as
distinguishing Christians from pagans, it must have meant much more
than that they spoke of the poor as their brothers and sisters. Most
probably, it meant liberal almsgiving of the sort that Cyprian had advocated.

In any case, in the next chapter, after criticizing Plato, Lactantius
shifts his emphasis and attacks the philosophers who say that wealth
ought to be despised. These people "abandon the property handed
down to them from their parents." To dispose of one's property simply
because wealth can be dangerous, he declares, is like committing suicide
in order to avoid death. At this point, Lactantius shows his thorough
Romanity (*romanitas*), for he says that these people "throw away the
means by which they might have acquired the glory of liberality without
losing honor and grace."[25] So would a Roman of the classical age have
spoken, for to them one of the uses of wealth was to acquire glory by
dispensing it liberally in public works and celebrations—the typical Roman practice called "evergetism." Yet, in another section of his work
Lactantius decries the folly of those "who by building of public works
seek a lasting memory for their name."[26] As we have seen, he is convinced that the wisest use of wealth is to invest it in eternity through
liberality towards those in need.

His argument against the philosophers leads Lactantius to the
theme of sympathy or mercy—*misericordia* or, in other passages, *huma-*

nitas. At this point he turns against the Stoics and their claim that sympathy is to be avoided as a weakness or a vice, countering with an argument that he will repeat elsewhere: Providence (or God, in another passage) has bestowed upon each animal its own means of protection both against its enemies and against the weather. Humans, by contrast, are weak and have no other protection than their mutual support. Such mutual support and the sympathy that makes it possible are the Creator's gifts to humans for their protection.

> For God, who has not given wisdom to other animals, has made them more safe from attack in danger by natural defences. But because He made man naked and defenceless, that He might rather furnish him with wisdom, He gave him, besides other things, this feeling of kindness {*hunc pietatis affectum*}; so that man should protect, love, and cherish man, and both receive and afford assistance against all dangers. Therefore kindness {*humanitas*} is the greatest bond of human society; and he who has broken this is to be deemed impious.[27]

Our common humanity stems from our common ancestry, for Lactantius insists that God created a single human being from whom all the rest are descended.[28] Since we are all kindred, we owe each other aid in times of distress or difficulty. To stand aside and do nothing is to descend to the level of beasts, which are incapable of kindness (*humanitas*). Not to have seen this is the error of all classical philosophy, for according to Lactantius the philosophers had nothing to say on kindness, which is not only the basis for social existence but also the very means for human survival in a hostile world.

By making it a virtue not to feel, the Stoics make it a virtue not to be moved by the distress of others, and they therefore glorify inhumanity. "And though they generally admit that the mutual participation of human society is to be retained, they entirely separate themselves from it by the harshness of their inhuman virtue."[29] This passage is interesting and even ironic, for Lactantius is accusing the most respected pagan philosophers, those whose wisdom had most influenced the best pagans in the Roman Empire, of precisely the same thing of which Christians had been accused earlier: they refuse to participate in the full life of society but insist on drawing on its benefits. Now the argument is turned around by centering attention, not on outward signs of civility such as civic ceremonies, but on works of mercy. Those who refuse to do works of mercy are not really human and have no right to the benefits of human society. "He who withdraws himself from affording assistance must also of necessity withdraw himself from receiving it."[30]

This type of assistance must be determined by the need one encounters; Lactantius argues for material help for the needy. Few people, if they see another perishing in a fire, attacked by a beast, or being carried away by a river, and having the means to save the one in distress, would refuse to come to their aid. Yet, some see others suffering from hunger, thirst, or cold and ignore their need. The reason is that such people are ready to help only those who can help them. Someone saved from a fire will try to find a way to repay such a debt of gratitude. But "in the case of the needy, they think that whatever they bestow on men of this kind is thrown away."[31] They believe some are "suitable" and some are "unsuitable" to be helped—or, as some would say today, that one must distinguish between the "worthy poor" and those who are not, giving only to the former.

In response to such views Lactantius develops the argument that one should give to the most needy and the most incapable of repaying what one gives. In a phrase reminiscent of the paradoxical style of Tertullian, who was one of his literary models, Lactantius declares, "We must not bestow our bounty on suitable objects, but as much as possible on unsuitable objects." What this means is that so-called suitable recipients are those who are able to repay the donor in some way. From that perspective "those who are worn out with nakedness, thirst, and hunger" are the least suitable, for there is small possibility that they will be able to repay the donor in any way. Thus Lactantius advises to "give especially to him from whom you expect nothing in return." "Be bountiful to the blind, the feeble, the lame, the destitute, who must die unless you bestow your bounty upon them."[32]

Lactantius is the last Christian writer to discuss these issues before the time of Constantine. As we shall see, with Constantine and his successors great changes took place in the life of the church. There is no indication that Christians expected or even suspected the surprising turn of events of the fourth century, with emperors declaring themselves Christian and the church receiving increasing support from the state. Lactantius, like every other Christian before him, was writing from within a community of Christians who knew themselves to be marginal to society, always in danger of persecution, and not counting among their ranks the vast majority of those in power.

Yet as one reads the *Institutes* one cannot help but feel that one is witnessing a further stage in a long process extending from the early preachers of the Jesus movement to Luke, then to Hermas, to Clement of Alexandria, Cyprian, and now to Lactantius. It is a process whereby the church continues to penetrate ever-higher echelons of society. Lactantius wrote a good part of his *Institutes* during a time of persecution. As a Christian, he had to abandon his teaching post in Nicomedia, the emperor's summer residence, and live long years in exile and obscurity. Still, he greatly appreciated pagan culture, and to a great extent he partook of it. With just cause he has been called "the Christian Cicero," for his style is refined and his language elegant. Indeed, he is so much at home addressing the better parts of pagan society that in his major work it is not always altogether clear whom he is addressing. At one point, his call to liberality is based on what "your philosophers" praise.

At another, it is based on the Christian conviction that humans are created after the divine image.

Perhaps the most significant twist in the dialogue between Christian and pagan just before the time of Constantine is Lactantius's argument that the Stoics, while seeking to abstain from the feelings on which society is based, continue benefiting from the life of society. This was very similar to what pagans had earlier said about Christians: they undermine society by abstaining from its constituent practices and ceremonies, and therefore they have no right to claim the benefits of that society. Now, with Lactantius, Christians are claiming that the love they practice (*humanitas*) is the very heart of social existence, and that those who abstain from it should also abstain from society. The stage is set for Constantine.

Other Currents

Not all Christians, however, were joining the mainstream of culture and society. Much of the ancient apocalyptic expectation remained, with its hope for a cataclysmic reversal of fortunes. W.H.C. Frend, a modern church historian, comments on this period, "Christianity had been slow to make an impact on the rural populations of the empire. When it began to do so, however, it was the literal message of the New Testament that appealed, combined with hopes for the reversal of fortunes between rich and poor that apocalyptic literature sustained."[33] Given the nature of the surviving materials, it is impossible to gain a complete picture of Christianity's inroads into poorer rural areas, or even among the urban poor. It is even more difficult to discover how these converts from the lower classes viewed the relationship between their faith and the economic order of society. By definition, the illiterate do not write, and by force of circumstances what the poor do write is seldom preserved for posterity.

We do know, however, that by the end of the third century Christianity had spread into the villages of several provinces of the Empire. In Egypt, to the flight of the poor from taxes and other obligations—the old *anachoresis* that for centuries had been the last resort of the poor—was now added the flight of Christians from persecutions or simply from the temptations of "the world." Sometimes it was difficult to distinguish the motives of these two flights,[34] and eventually the term *anchorite* came to mean a solitary Christian recluse. In North Africa, the rapidly increasing lists of bishops present at synods point to an accelerated penetration into ever more remote areas.

While it is impossible to discover what these converts from small villages and from remote rural areas thought regarding the social and economic order, one may surmise, as does Frend, that they were attracted by the apocalyptic promises of a reversal of fortunes. We have already spoken of how such promises were kept alive even among relatively well educated writers such as Hippolytus. Those whose theology was more influenced by the Platonic tradition tended to either ignore or reinterpret those eschatological promises that from their point of view seemed crass or materialistic.[35] Yet, some sources indicate that the more "materialistic" and radical views were common among the lower classes and the less educated.

One such text is the *Canonical Epistle* of Gregory the Wonderworker. Early in the second half of the third century—some five or six years after Cyprian's death—a horde of barbarians invaded Pontus, where Gregory was bishop. Some of the residents of the area took the opportunity to enrich themselves. At least a number of these were Christians. Gregory complains that "some {Christians} should have been audacious enough to consider the crisis which brought destruction to all the very period for their own private aggrandizement."[36] "Forgetting that they were from Pontus, and Christians, {they} have become such thorough barbarians, as even to put those of their own race to death."[37] Significantly, Gregory takes for granted that these people should have behaved otherwise, not only because they were Christians, but also because they were from Pontus, that is, because they were part of the empire that the barbarians had invaded. Their Christianity and their Romanity should have worked together, opposing them to the barbarians. Instead, they have become barbarians to others whom they despoiled and to captives whom they held for ransom. Their crime, for which Gregory's letter excommunicates them, is that they did not behave as Christians nor as civilized people. "It is not lawful," argues Gregory on the basis of Deuteronomy, "to aggrandize oneself at the expense of another, whether he be brother or enemy."[38]

As one reads this letter, one wonders, is this merely a case of generalized looting, which some unscrupulous Christian looters joined? Or is it rather a case of some Christians becoming convinced that the incursion by the barbarians was a sign of the last times, when the reversal of fortunes would take place? Frend suggests the latter and sees in the events of the third century in Pontus a parallel to what would take place in North Africa in the following century with the rebellion of the Circumcellions.[39]

Thus was the church preparing itself for the momentous events of the fourth century. Some of its intellectual leaders—people like Lactantius and Gregory the Wonderworker—saw Christianity and Romanity as perfectly compatible. For Lactantius, the *humanitas* at the heart of Christian *koinonía* was the only solid foundation for society. At the same time, as the church expanded among the marginalized both in urban society and in remote rural areas, it came to include significant numbers who perceived a vast and irreconcilable difference between the empire in which they lived and the Kingdom that they awaited. All of these forces would be at play during the fourth century.

NOTES

1. See M. Caron, "Les *seniores laici* de l'église africaine," *RIntDrAnt* 6 (1951):7–22; W. H. C. Frend, "The *Seniores Laici* and the Origins of the Church in North Africa," *JTS*, n.s. 12 (1961):280–84.
2. The *Acta* call Dativus "senator," but it is not clear whether he was a Roman senator or one of the curiales who formed part of a town senate. Victoria is called "clarissima" and "of noble birth." *Acta sanct. Saturn. et al. in Africa*, 1, 3, 7, 16, published in *PL*. The fact that the edict of Valerian referred specifically to senators and equestrians indicates that some members of those higher classes must have been Christians. Cf. Cyprian, *Ep*. 81, *ANF*.
3. L.W. Countryman, *The Rich Christian in the Church of the Early Empire* (New York: Edwin Mellen, 1980), pp. 162–73. Countryman analyzes the conflict that arose between clergy and rich Christians who hoped to have in the church the same status that their pagan counterparts enjoyed in the clubs and societies of the time.
4. Jerome, *De vir. ill.* 80, *NPNF*, 2nd ser.
5. Lactantius, *Inst.* 3.23, *ANF*. All references to *Inst.* are from *ANF*.
6. *Inst.* 6. 12, Cf. *Inst.* 6.12, *ANF*: "Those who refuse a small gift to the wretched, who wish to preserve humanity without any loss to themselves, squander their property, for they either acquire for themselves frail and perishable things or ... " This passage, and several others in the same chapter, imply that those who have money can invest it for eternity by giving to the needy, and that using it for other purposes is squandering it.
7. *Inst.* 6.13.
8. *Inst.* 6.13.
9. See J.L. González, *Christian Thought Revisited: Three Types of Theology* (Nashville: Abingdon, 1989).
10. *Inst.* 6.18:
    If he {the true worshipper of God} shall have lent any money, he will not receive interest, that the benefit may be unimpaired which succours necessity, and that he may entirely abstain from the property of another. For in this kind of duty he ought to be content with that which is his own; since it is his duty in other respects not to be sparing of his property, in order that he may do good; but to receive more than he has given is unjust. And he who does this lies in wait in some manner, that he may gain booty from the necessity of the owner.
11. *Inst.* 6.12.
12. *Inst.* 6.12.
13. *Inst.* 6.12.
14. *Inst.* 6.11.
15. G. Barbero, quoted by R. Sierra Bravo, *Doctrina social y económica de los padres de la Iglesia* (Madrid: COMPI, 1976) p. 617.
16. *Inst.* 3.21.
17. *Inst.* 3.22.
18. *Inst.* 3.22.
19. *Inst.* 5.6: "Since God had given the earth in common to all, that they might pass their life in common, not that mad and raging avarice might claim all things for itself, and that that which was produced for all might not be wanting to any."
20. *Inst.* 5.6.
21. *Inst.* 5.9.
22. *Inst.* 6.13.
23. *Inst.* 5.15.
24. *Inst.* 5.17.

25. *Inst.* 3.23, *PL.*
26. *Inst.* 6.11, *ANF.*
27. *Inst.* 6.10. Cf. 3.23;7.4.
28. *Inst.* 6.10.
29. *Inst.* 6.10.
30. *Inst.* 6.10.
31. *Inst.* 6.11.
32. *Inst.* 6.11.
33. W. H. C. Frend, *The Rise of Christianity* (Philadelphia: Fortress, 1984), p. 421.
34. Athanasius, when praising life in the desert in times of Anthony, declares that "there was neither the evil-doer, nor the injured, nor the reproaches of the tax-gatherer." *Vita S. Ant.* 42, *NPNF,* 2nd ser.
35. In *Christian Thought Revisited* (n. 9 above), I have shown how the traditions to which Hippolytus belonged, and which included also Irenaeus and the book of Revelation, differed from the Platonizing tradition of Origen and his followers on this point among others, and what were some of the social agendas involved in this difference. Gregory the Wonderworker, an admirer and disciple of Origen, belonged to a very different tradition from that of Hippolytus.
36. Gregory the Wonderworker, *Ep. can.* 2, *ANF.*
37. *Ep. can.* 7.
38. *Ep. can.* 7.
39. Frend, *Rise of Christianity* (n. 33 above), p. 422.

PART III

CONSTANTINE AND BEYOND

8/The Church Under the New Order

L actantius may well have been putting the finishing touches on book six of his *Institutes* when unexpected events took place that would change the course both of his life and of the life of the Church.

The New Order

It was late October of 312. Constantine, then on his way to power, had invaded Italy and was preparing to do battle with his rival Maxentius when he ordered his soldiers to fight under a strange symbol. Constantine won that day. In the press of his fleeing troops, Maxentius fell into the Tiber and drowned. Constantine entered the city in triumph, and the Senate proclaimed him Augustus. Thus began a revolution that would change the religious face of Europe—and eventually of much of the world—for centuries to come.

From the beginning, Constantine attributed his successes to a divine protector. What was not entirely clear was exactly who that protector was. Was it the *Sol Invictus,* the unconquered Sun? Was it the Christ, whom the Christians worshiped? Most likely, Constantine himself did not know, and it was only through the passing of years that he progressively clarified his own beliefs. In the end, shortly before his death, he was finally baptized a Christian, most likely by the Arian Eusebius of Nicomedia. To this day, the debate continues as to the motives of his conversion, his sincerity, and his understanding of the Christian faith.[1]

What is most important from our point of view is the impact of Constantine's conversion—whatever that may mean—on the social and economic life of the church. One point is obvious: under Constantine and his successors Christianity rapidly passed from the status of a persecuted "superstition" to that of the official religion of the empire. The change was not immediate, nor did it proceed without interruption. The pagan reaction under Julian (361–363) and unsuccessful attempts to regain the throne for paganism, such as that of Eugenius (392–394),[2] reminded Christians that their victory was not yet complete. Yet in general it is true that the Christian church enjoyed ever-increasing favors and privileges throughout most of the fourth century.

Constantine himself was the first to grant such privileges. As early as 313, and for reasons that are not altogether clear, he wrote to his officials in North Africa ordering them to make a substantial contribution to the church there, and he wrote also to bishop Caecilian of Carthage letting him know what he had commanded.[3] At about the same time, he also ordered that the catholic clergy of North Africa—that is, not the Donatists—be exempt from personal taxes.[4] Later he extended this privilege to the catholic clergy throughout the empire.[5] In the city of Rome, he donated the Lateran Palace to the bishop and built a number of churches, including the first Basilica of Saint Peter. These were endowed, at government expense, with rich ornaments, vases, and chandeliers. Most significantly, he set out to build an entirely new city, named Constantinople in his own honor, where he restored and enlarged the cathedral of Saint Irene (Holy Peace) and built a magnificent Church of the Apostles to serve as his own tomb. Meanwhile, his mother Helena took particular interest in Palestine, where she donated sumptuous basilicas to mark the Holy Sepulcher in Jerusalem, the site of the nativity in Bethlehem, and the tombs of the patriarchs in Hebron. Although these cases are outstanding, they are part of a general policy, for Eusebius has preserved a copy of a letter that Constantine apparently sent to all bishops, at least to those of metropolitan cities:

With respect, therefore, to the churches over which you yourself preside, as well as the bishops, presbyters, and deacons of other churches with whom you are acquainted, do you admonish all to be zealous in their attention to the building of the churches, and either to repair or enlarge those which at present exist, or, in cases of necessity, erect new ones.

We also empower you, and the others through you, to demand all that is needful for the work, both from the provincial governors and from the Praetorian Praefect. For they have received instructions to be most diligent in obedience to your Holiness's orders. God preserve you, beloved brother.[6]

While these policies simply granted direct financial benefits to the church and its leaders, Constantine also saw himself as "bishop of those outside" the church,[7] and he therefore enacted laws by which he apparently sought to apply Christian principles to the ordering of society. Many of these concerned sexual customs and morality[8] or keeping Sunday as a day of rest, at least for certain officers of the empire.[9] Others, however, apparently had a deeper social motivation, as well as concern for the powerless. One such law punished masters who mistreated their slaves, and another prohibited the breaking up of slave families through the sale of some of their members.[10] Another law simplified the process for the manumission of slaves, which could now be performed by a simple declaration in a church and with priests as witnesses.[11] Still other laws protected prisoners from police brutality,[12] peasants from the expropriation of their work animals, and motherless children whose fathers ignored their needs.[13] Finally, in a law reminiscent of similar injunctions in the Old Testament, the state became the defender of widows and orphans.[14] While some historians have pointed to these laws as signs of Constantine's Christian convictions and their impact on his policies, others can point to an equal number of laws prescribing cruel punishment for criminals, runaway slaves, and others. Thus, while some of his laws may reflect the influence of Christian advisors, it is clear that Constantine's main concern was for the welfare and order of the state.[15]

Constantine issued no edicts against the traditional religion of Rome and clearly affirmed that it could continue to be practiced in complete freedom.[16] What edicts he issued forbidding practices such as private divination simply continued the policies of his predecessors, seeking to maintain the purity of ancient religion, and probably trying to interdict the possible subversive uses of private divination.[17] He himself, as well as his immediate successors, continued using the title *pontifex maximus* of traditional religion. However, as time went by, with the brief respites of Julian and—in a section of the Empire—Eugenius, paganism continued to exist under ever-increasing political and legal pressures.

The greatest of these pressures was the sacking and destruction of temples. Constantine had set the example by raiding the works of art of the entire empire in order to embellish Constantinople. Under his sons, and in particular under Constantius, pagan temples in Syria, Egypt, Cappadocia, and other parts of the empire were destroyed, often by mobs instigated by Christian clergy. Jovian (363–364) began the practice of seizing the property of pagan temples and using it to his own ends. Valentinian I (364–375) and Valens (364–378) apparently followed a more impartial policy, except that Valens, like Constantius before him, supported the Arians against the catholics.

Under Gratian (375–383) and Theodosius (379–395) laws began to be enacted against paganism. Until then all that had been prescribed, as in the time of Constantine, was private divination and secret sacrifices. In 381, Theodosius issued a law declaring that former Christians who converted to paganism had no right to receive an inheritance nor to dispose of their property by will.[18] Since this was one of the ancient rights on which Roman law was based, it amounted to a significant restriction of the civil rights of apostates. Much more damaging, however, was the severing of the traditional connection between the ancient gods of Rome and the state. Until Gratian, no emperor had rejected the title of *pontifex maximus*. This Gratian did, openly rejecting the priestly vestments when they were offered to him in a traditional ceremony. In 382,

Good Summary of Church & State.

he issued an edict depriving the pagan priesthood of the exemptions from taxes and other public obligations that they had traditionally enjoyed—privileges now given to the Christian clergy. The same edict also confiscated much of the endowment of pagan worship and ordered that the resources of the state until then employed for such worship be diverted to other uses.[19] At about the same time he ordered that the altar of victory be removed from the Senate-House.[20] Earlier, Constantius had removed it. Julian, as part of his pagan revival, had restored it to its traditional place. For these reasons, its presence in the Senate-House had become a symbol of the traditional aristocratic religiosity of the Senate. When a delegation of pagan senators (probably the majority were still pagan) sought an audience with the emperor to request the restoration of the altar, they were not even granted an audience, apparently due to interference from St. Ambrose.[21] Thus at long last was the Roman Empire completely disengaged from its ancient religion.

From disengagement to prohibition the transition was rapid. In 391 Emperor Theodosius issued two decrees, one canceling all civil and political rights of Christians who reverted to paganism, and another forbidding most pagan practices in the city of Rome.[22] These were followed late in the next year by a further edict extending that prohibition and others to the entire empire.[23] The date was November 8, 392. Paganism was officially abolished.

The very name *paganism* is significant. Originally, the term *paganus* meant "rustic," "villager," "peasant." It also had the meaning of "civilian." Tertullian was the first to use it to refer to those who were not Christian, although probably in the sense that they were not part of the "militia Christi."[24] Not until the latter half of the fourth century did it become generally associated with the traditional religion of Rome.[25] Pagan was both a pejorative name and a statement of fact. As pejorative, it implied that the true heirs of ancient civilization were not those who continued worshiping the gods, but the Christians; note the contrast between "civilized" or "citified" and "pagan" or "rural." The reason, however, that such a *tour de force* was possible was that in fact some of the remotest places of the countryside served as a last refuge for the worship of the ancient gods.[26]

On the other hand, throughout most of the fourth century the high aristocracy and the intellectual elite were the other strongholds of traditional religion. At least until well into the second half of the century, the majority of Roman senators clung to paganism. The same was true of many professors of rhetoric, who were convinced that the beauty of language and expression that they sought was indissolubly connected with the religion from which it had sprung. Thus many among the noblest families and the ablest rhetoricians of the fourth century retained the religion of their ancestors.[27]

At some points, the conservatism of the peasantry and that of the aristocracy sought each other's support. The famous rhetorician Libanius of Antioch, arguing that the abandonment of traditional religions would result in economic disaster, declared that in a countryside where the temples no longer stand "the courage of the workers disappears jointly with their hope. They are convinced that they labor in vain if they are deprived of the gods that crown their labors with prosperity."[28]

When Constantine came to power Christianity was mostly a religion of the middle and lower classes among the urban population. Except in North Africa and Egypt, it had made little progress in the countryside and much less among the high aristocracy. With the founding of Constantinople and the creation of a new Senate that did not have the ancient roots of the Roman Senate a new aristocracy began developing that did not have the ties to tradition of the older aristocracy, and many of whom were Christian. Also, it was the practice of the emperors of the fourth century to raise to the highest positions in the empire people of humble origin whose service had been valuable. This caused consternation and even opposition among the older aristocracy. Libanius of Antioch, who was also John Chrysostom's teacher, complained of an age when mere stenographers could rise to the position of praetorian prefect.[29]

Although all positions were open to pagans until late in the fourth century, and there are countless instances of pagans in places of high prestige and responsibility, it soon became obvious to some that professing Christian faith would not hinder and might even help in career and social advancement. Eusebius of Caesarea, who seldom saw anything negative in the consequences of Constantine's conversion, deplored "the scandalous hypocrisy of those who crept into the Church, and assumed the name and character of Christians" in order to gain advancement.[30] Some people changed their religious allegiance repeatedly according to the wind that blew.[31] Yet one should not conclude from this that the great numerical gains of the church in the fourth century were all due to conscious hypocrisy. Most likely, the old paganism, for a number of reasons, was losing power and Christianity, suddenly come to light and enjoying the prestige of imperial favor, filled the vacuum left by the old religion.

As could have been expected, the sudden influx of wealth and power affected the life of the church. One of its most obvious consequences was an enormous increase in the resources now available to the church for charitable work.

The Christians received and redistributed huge donations, some from Constantine himself. Whereas the corn doles of pagan cities had been confined to citizens, usually to those who were quite well-off, the Christians' charity claimed to be for those who were most in need. Swollen by the Emperor's gifts, it helped the sick and the old, the infirm and the destitute. By the later fourth century, it had led to great hostels and charitable centers.[32]

On the other hand, this sudden influx of wealth and influence also brought other changes that were not as positive. Since joining the ranks of the clergy was one of the few ways in which the *curiales* (the minor aristocracy of provincial towns) could avoid the heavy burden of their responsibilities,[33] ordination became a commodity that some were willing to buy and others to sell. John Chrysostom complained about the priesthood being up for sale.[34] Palladius writes of a bishop of Ephesus who apparently sold bishoprics almost wholesale. When he and his clients were discovered and brought before the authorities, their punishment was little more than a slap on the wrist.[35] Basil the Great himself was not above suggesting that a protegé pay a bribe in order to get a post that would free him from some of his tax obligations.[36] And Augustine was ready to be lenient toward bishops who had pretended that their personal property belonged to the church in order to gain tax exemption.[37]

The new conditions also resulted in an increased number of wealthy people entering the church. Some were fabulously rich, such as a certain Melania, who freed eight thousand slaves in a single day.[38] And Chrysostom's preaching clearly indicates the presence in his congregation of some who were rich enough to be able to afford beds of ivory, silver, and gold.[39]

In spite of this, it would be wrong to suppose that the social configuration of the Christian church changed radically overnight. It is clear that well into the fourth century, and in many cases long after that, the church was particularly strong among the urban working classes in both East and West;[40] that is lagged far behind in its penetration of the older aristocracy, particularly in the West;[41] and that, except in North Africa, Egypt, and probably a few other areas in the East, the majority of the rural population continued practicing the ancient religion that by now was called "pagan."[42] Indeed, it has been estimated that as late as A.D. 400, that is, toward the end of the period we are studying, the majority of people in the empire remained non-Christian.[43]

One interesting point in this entire process in the absence of indications that the aristocracy, the army, or the peasantry showed any signs of rebellion as laws were enacted against their traditional religion. The aristocracy protested but never rebelled. The closest they came to an outward revolt was when the usurper Eugenius, who was nominally Christian, promised them the restoration of their ancient faith, and many of the ancient Roman aristocracy flocked to his banner. Yet that aristocracy was never able or willing to organize any resistance other than literary. The army, accustomed as it was to obeying orders, and mostly composed of recruits who had been uprooted from their ancestral traditions, generally followed the religion of its superiors. As for the peasants, apart from a few riots and the murder of an occasional Christian missionary zealot, they too remained quiescent. Quietly, in some cases apparently for centuries, they continued their ancient religious practices, their incantations and sacrifices in order to ensure a good crop. But they too did not rebel. The only peasants who offered serious resistance to imperial policy on religious grounds were Christians who disagreed with the sort of Christianity being promoted by the empire—the Donatists. Pagan peasants quietly acquiesced, or if they revolted, as many did in Gaul and Spain, they did this for reasons other than loyalty to paganism; by contrast, Christian peasants in North Africa who disagreed with imperial religious policies organized resistance and eventually took arms in open rebellion. Clearly, centuries of persecution had taught Christians that the authority of the empire was not ultimate.

Yet most Christian leaders did not take that position. The emperor's conversion and support were so unexpected and represented such a great reversal of the situation that had existed at the time of the Great Persecution under Diocletian that most bishops had nothing but gratitude for the man who had brought it about. Eusebius of Caesarea, a respected leader of the church and the foremost Christian scholar of his time, wrote a *Life of Constantine* and a *Panegyric on Constantine*. In the *Life,* he states that he would "select from the facts which have come to my knowledge, such as are most suitable, and worthy of lasting record."[44] This clearly implies that he was aware of other "less suitable" facts and chose to ignore them. His purpose was to write a life of "this thrice-blessed prince" that would inspire others. He did not attempt or achieve a balanced account, for he omitted anything that would make Constantine appear less than a saint and even an apostle. In the *Panegyric,* Eusebius overflows with boundless praise: "His reason he derives from the great source of all reason: he is wise, and good, and just, as having fellowhip with perfect Wisdom, Goodness, and Righteousness: virtuous, as following the pattern of perfect virtue: valiant, as partaking of heavenly strength."[45]

Such praise is far more than mere adulation. It is the outcome both of boundless gratitude for the end of persecution and of Eusebius's theological understanding of the nature of the empire at its best.[46] His Platonic outlook allows him to see the earthly kingdom headed by the emperor as the temporal image of the heavenly Kingdom.[47] The corollary is that the emperor reflects the very image of God and that God is most like the emperor.[48] Eusebius is simply expressing in more sophisticated terms what many must have felt and believed. His significance lies, not in his uniqueness or originality, but in his expressing commonly held views. Eusebius himself declares that "the divine qualities of the emperor's character continued to be the theme of universal praise," and that on occasion such praise became so extravagant that the emperor himself rebuked those who offered it.[49] At the great council of Nicea, Bishop Eustathius of Antioch spoke for most of the bishops assembled as he "crowned the emperor's head with the flowers of a panegyric, and commended the diligent attention he had manifested in the regulation of ecclesiastical affairs."[50] This attitude of praise and respect for the person of the emperor—sometimes seen as God's representative on earth—continued to be the opinion of the majority for a long time. Late in the fourth century, Optatus of Milevis, in refuting the Donatists, declared that Donatus was wrong in acting as if he were above the emperor. Only God is above the emperor, and therefore any who claim to be above the emperor are claiming divinity for themselves.[51] Even the great Athanasius, who would later have strong things to say about the unwarranted intervention of imperial power in theological matters, at first shared the enthusiasm of his older contemporaries for a new order in which the empire would protect the church without limiting its freedom.[52]

Donatist Resistance

One region that did not share this view of imperial power and its place in God's order was North Africa. Since the beginning of the third century, Christianity there had been characterized by its rigor and its strong countercultural stance. Tertullian's "what indeed has Athens to do with Jerusalem? What concord is there between the Academy and the Church?"[53] was more than a catchy phrase. It epitomized an attitude of opposition, not only to philosophy, but to society at large and to culture—in short, to "the world"—that was typical of many Christians in the region. Although martyrs and confessors enjoyed great respect and even veneration in other parts of the empire, nowhere was this as marked as in North Africa. The church at large condemned the practice of offering oneself spontaneously for martyrdom, yet this practice was common—and admired—in North Africa. There the church since the time of Tertullian had vehemently condemned the practice of fleeing from persecution, although in other regions the church condoned and even commended it.[54] In the middle of the third century, Cyprian's authority as bishop had been undermined because he had fled from persecution. The prestige of the confessors—those who had remained and suffered for their faith—rose higher than the bishop's, and to them rather than the bishop the fallen turned for restoration. If, in the time after Constantine, Cyprian and his theology enjoyed great prestige in North Africa, it was because later Cyprian too had suffered as a martyr. The North African church venerated martyrs and confessors, not only for their valor and fortitude, but also for their firm stance against the power of the state and of society. Martyrs often openly criticized the Roman Empire and its social and economic order. Minucius Felix, at approximately the same time as Tertullian, had condemned both the hypocrisy and the greed of the Romans:

Thus, whatever the Romans hold, cultivate, possess, is the spoil of their audacity. All their temples are built from the spoils of violence, that is, from the ruins of cities, from the spoils of the gods, from the murders of priests. This is to insult and scorn, to yield to conquered religions, to adore them when captive, after having vanquished them. For to adore what you have taken by force, is to consecrate sacrilege, not divinities. As often, therefore, as the Romans triumphed, so often they were polluted; and as many trophies as they gained from the nations, so many spoils did they take from the gods. Therefore the Romans were not so great because they were religious, but because they were sacrilegious with impunity.[55]

Also, during the last century before the conversion of Constantine, Christianity had made great gains among the rural population in North Africa. It is impossible to follow this process in detail, for we lack contemporary documents to describe it and the archeological evidence is fragmentary and disorganized. But it is clear that Christianity, which at first had been an urban faith confined to Carthage and other major cities near the coast, rapidly penetrated the interior during the third century, so that by the time of the conversion of Constantine it was strong, not only in the more Romanized province of Proconsular Africa, but also in the hinterlands of Numidia and Mauritania, the two other provinces of the region.

By spreading into rural North Africa, Christianity had also moved beyond the confines of Greco-Roman culture, into the Berber and Punic-speaking lower strata of society. Throughout the region, older Berber and Punic elements had been suppressed by the Latin-speaking colonizers after Rome defeated Carthage in the Punic wars (third and second centuries B.C.). The older cultural elements, however, had not disappeared, and many even in the city of Carthage spoke Punic. Rural people apparently shared resentment against the conquerors, their culture, and the order they had imposed. It is quite likely that such resentment contributed to the widespread acceptance of Christianity by these sectors of the population at a time when it was persecuted by the empire and when it openly contradicted "the world" and its values.

Christianity's growth in the rural areas of North Africa took place at a time when significant social and economic changes were spreading throughout the region. The crisis of the third century, with its civil war and economic disruption, was deeply felt in North Africa. Its cities never recovered, nor did the owners of small to medium farms, which were the backbone of the economy. Yet the reforms of Diocletian and later of Constantine required that the area pay substantial taxes. The region's only option was to transfer the burden of those taxes to the only sector of society still productive: the rural areas. In Proconsular Africa, much of the land was in the hands of wealthy landowners who could minimize their taxes by several of the various means always available to the powerful. Still, taxes had to be collected, and therefore the peasants of the hinterland experienced increased pressures and extortion.[56] Since collecting taxes fell to the urban lower aristocracy—the *curiales*—masses in the countryside viewed *curiales* as their oppressors. The *curiales* them-

selves were caught in an increasingly untenable position, having to supply from their own resources any shortfall in the taxes they were able to
collect. Thus social tension was great, with the lower, especially rural,
classes seeing both the rich landowners and the less fortunate *curiales* as
their oppressors, and the latter caught in a vise from which they could
not escape.

After the time of Constantine many Christians in that region did
not accept the new religious arrangement. The main theological issue
in dispute was whether sacraments offered by unworthy ministers—specifically, those who had surrendered the Scriptures to government officials during the recent persecution—were valid. However, other
underlying social and economic issues fueled the tension. As Constantine and most of his successors supported the party that maintained
communion with the rest of the church—called here "catholics" for the
sake of convenience, although both parties claimed that title—the other
party, known by its opponents as "Donatists,"[57] became the rallying point
for much social unrest and anti government feeling. Eventually a party
developed—the Circumcellions—who took up arms in defense of
Donatism and also in revolt against the economic oppression of the
peasantry.

This is not the place to follow the controversy or the Donatist movement through its various stages.[58] What is important from our point of
view is to underline the social and economic agenda of Donatism, and
its opposition to the Constantinian settlement. Unfortunately, little remains of the writings of the Donatists themselves, and practically nothing from the Circumcellions beyond inscriptions and other archeological
evidence. This makes it impossible to draw a detailed picture of their
views or of the actual steps in the controversy. For our purposes, however, the records are quite clear, and there is no reason to doubt the
main lines of what the catholics said of the Donatists, namely that they
tended to disregard imperial authority and that they represented a
movement of social unrest and revolt.

Regarding imperial authority, it is clear that at first the Donatists
saw nothing wrong in appealing to the emperor. When Constantine
sided with the catholics at the very beginning of the controversy, they
wrote to him bringing charges against their main opponent. Constantine, apparently loath to intervene directly in the matter, ordered that
the leaders of both parties travel to Rome, there to be judged by a group
of bishops headed by Miltiades, the bishop of Rome. When that decision
went against them, the Donatists appealed to the emperor once more,
with the result that the Council of Arles was charged to decide on the
matter. When the council also decided against them, the Donatists continued importuning Constantine with constant petitions and appeals; at
least, so says Augustine, who was anything but an impartial reporter.[59]
Finally, by the year 316, the Donatists apparently reached the conclusion
that they would receive no justice from the emperor, and they began

drawing more consistently on the ancient North African view of the church as irreconcilable with the world and therefore with the empire.

After 316, the Donatists insisted on the independence of the church to decide its own matters. In phrases reminiscent of Tertullian, Donatus is said to have asked, "What do Christians have to do with kings? What do the bishops have to do with the palace?"[60] And, "What does the Emperor have to do with the church?"[61] Still, we are told that during the reign of Julian, when the government followed an impartial policy toward both sides of the dispute, the Donatists recovered much of their church property by bringing suit before imperial authorities against the catholics who had dispossessed them.[62] In 372, when the Mauritanian leader Firmus rebelled against the empire and took the title of king, the Donatists supported him, and they followed the same path later in the century when Firmus's brother, Gildo, led another rebellion. Thus, while the Donatists' theology supported the separation of church and state, that separation was ignored—as is so often the case—when the power of the state favored them.

On their social stance, the Donatists were much more consistent, at least, so their opponents tell us. From the beginning, they represented the lower peasant and rural classes of Numidia and Mauritania as well as elements allied to them in Carthage and other major cities. At the height of their power, they did include members from all classes of the population. Still, their strength resided in the strata of society that suffered most from the existing economic order. Their opponents repeatedly chided them both for their low social origins and for their revolutionary stance. In Rome, their enemies spoke of the small contingent of Donatists in the city as "mountain people" and as "rock dwellers."[63]

Economic times were hard in North Africa, particularly for the lower classes,[64] and the masses believed—probably with justification—that the church possessed more than its share of goods and that clergy were among the exploiters. Since the official church was the one in communion with Christians in the rest of the empire, all the advantages of state support went to the catholics in North Africa and none to the Donatists. Thus, at a time when the taxation of the poor and the middle classes grew to an extortionate rate, the catholic clergy, through the concessions of Constantine and his successors, received ever-greater exemptions. A biographer of Augustine says in so many words that the lands it possessed were the reason why many hated the church.[65] Augustine himself faced the accusation of avarice, for the estates that as a bishop he had to administer were extensive.[66] Nor were the accusers entirely out of line, for some clergy did allow avarice to guide their actions. A council gathered at Carthage, probably in 348, had to take action against bishops trying to supplant others whose churches possessed greater financial resources.[67] The same council decreed that clergy should abstain from money lending, a particularly offensive practice in light of the church's attitude toward loans on interest, and especially given the precarious conditions in which the masses in Africa lived at the time.[68] To make matters worse, apparently the catholic bishops had little idea of the economic distress of the masses and felt that, as long as there was no Circumcellion activity, all was peaceful and prosperous.[69]

Given such circumstances, it is not surprising that the Donatists took the opportunity to attack their rivals for their greed and economic success. A Donatist document declares that as a reward for their sin the devil gave those who had lapsed during persecution—that is, the catholics—the restoration of all their honors, the friendship of the emperor, and worldly riches.[70] Those who followed the catholic way, they declared, were simply preferring riches to their souls.[71] In contrast, the more radical Donatists insisted on the value of poverty, and apparently many practiced it, either by abandoning their (usually limited) wealth or by giving it to the poor.

We have no description of the revolutionary activity of the Donatists except from the pens of their enemies. Often they blame all Donatists for the acts of the radical Circumcellions, even though Donatist leaders showed ambivalence toward that branch of their church. In any case, catholic opponents of Donatism saw the Donatists as social reformers, usually by violent means—and themselves as the defenders of law and order.

Typical of the catholic reaction to the Donatists and Circumcellions are the following words from Augustine:

Unity is shunned, and the peasants are emboldened to rise against their landlords; runaway slaves, in defiance of apostolic discipline, are not only encouraged to desert their masters but even to threaten their masters, and not only to threaten but to plunder them by violent raids. All this they do at the suggestion and instigation, and with the authorization to commit crime, of those prize-winning confessors of yours, who magnify your rank "for the glory of God," and shed the blood of others "for the glory of God."[72]

And, in another epistle:

Among them {the Donatists} unbridled bands of abandoned men disturbed the peace of the innocent in various cases. What master was not forced to fear his own slave if once he fled for refuge to their patronage? Who would even dare to threaten a destructive servant or his instigator? Who could dismiss a wasteful warehouseman, or any debtor, if he sought their help and protection? Under fear of clubs and fires and instant death, the records of worthless slaves were torn up so that they could go free. Receipts extorted from debtors were returned . . . Some land-owners of honorable birth and gentlemanly breeding were dragged off half-dead after scourging, or were tied to a mill-stone and forced by blows to turn it as if they were beasts of burden.[73]

We have no indication that Augustine exaggerated here, although clearly he was describing the most extreme incidents. What is certain is that social unrest in North Africa was so great that for a time the Donatists were in the majority.[74] When Augustine was writing, is spite of decades of suppression and persecution, Donatists were still numerous, especially in the provinces of Numidia and Mauritania. It took the invasions, first of the Vandals, then of the Byzantines, and finally of the Moslems, to make them disappear, along with the rest of the church. Of their social and economic teachings, practically nothing remains, for they were quoted by their opponents only in order to make them appear in the worst possible light. Yet, as the two passages from Augustine just cited indicate, and as we shall see in another part of this book, their most important legacy to the history of the Christian church was the reaction they provoked, aligning the church ever more closely with the powerful in society.

The Flight to the Desert

Just before the time of Constantine, Christianity had grown significantly in Egypt. As we have seen, Egypt was a land of profound and fixed social and economic contrasts between Romans and Greeks, on the one hand, and the native Egyptian or Coptic population on the other. It was also a land where many of the poorer Copts, unable to pay their taxes or simply disgusted with the existing order, fled to the desert, a practice that had long received the name of *anachoresis*. In Egypt the people quietly and bitterly resisted the established order. During the third century, as persecution of Christians increased, the number of Christians among the Copts also increased, apparently, at least in part, because many Copts felt more at home in this religion than in that officially espoused by the state. At the same time, economic conditions became intolerable. Many who had fled to the desert organized into brigand bands that terrorized the countryside.

Already in the second century, in A.D. 152 and then again in A.D. 172 and 173, riots had broken out that had developed into full-scale revolts. Armies of Egyptian peasants, apparently moved both by economic grievances and by nationalistic zeal, had defeated Roman armies, and authorities had called troops from Syria and elsewhere to put down the rebellion.

These revolts, however, paled by comparison with the one that took place late in the third century. Uneven inflation meant that the peasants had to pay much more for their purchases and received relatively less for their products. In March of 295, Diocletian's edict on tax reform was promulgated in Egypt. Many among the privileged Greeks saw that it meant the loss of some of their privileges. The peasants, however, knew only that there was to be a new system of taxation, and past experience convinced them that this could only mean higher taxes. In an apparent coalition between some of the Greek leadership in the cities and the Copts in the countryside, all of Egypt revolted. A rival emperor was proclaimed. Diocletian himself marched to Egypt, and in a campaign that lasted almost three years he finally subdued the rebels. His vengeance was frightful.[75] The tax edict was enforced. In order to ensure against further revolts Roman garrisons were increased, and soldiers were deployed into the countryside. One may surmise that the traditional resentment of the native Egyptians against the occupying Romans increased further.

As Diocletian undertook systematic persecution of Christians, it was natural that many Egyptians would view Christianity as opposed to the empire and therefore aligned with Coptic nationalism. Significantly, from that point on, whenever there was religious strife, Egyptian masses tended to side with those opposed by the structures of power. We are told that when Arius was perceived as the victim of powerful Bishop Alexander, the crowds took to the streets chanting his slogans. Were these crowds composed only of relatively sophisticated Greeks, or were there also among them Copts who took the opportunity to protest established authority? Significantly, Arianism began to lose its hold in Egypt when it gained political ascendancy in Constantinople, after A.D. 328. Athanasius, its great opponent, was probably himself a Copt,[76] and his main source of support was among the populace in Egypt and among the monks of the desert, many of whom were also Copts. In the fifth century, when the official church of the empire rejected Monophysitism, the Copts embraced it, and they retained it, at least nominally, to this day.

Such was the matrix in which Egyptian monasticism took shape. Antony, usually reputed as its founder—although it is doubtful that the movement, spontaneous in nature as it was, had a founder in the usual sense—fled to the desert just as the revolt against Diocletian was about to begin. And Pachomius, the reputed founder of the system of communal life among the monks of the desert, abandoned his military career and became a monk at the height of Diocletian's persecution. These two are important, for they represent the two basic forms that monasticism took in Egypt and later in other parts of the empire.[77]

Antony did not belong to the poorer classes. Although a Copt, he was the son and heir of a small farmer in the village of Coma, on the left bank of the middle Nile. Yet among anchorites he was an exception, for the early monastic movement drew most of its recruits from the impoverished Coptic masses.[78] Few knew Greek, and many were illiterate in both Greek and Coptic. It is significant that these people received the title of anchorites, that is, practitioners of the flight that for a long time had been the only recourse of the poor in Egypt. *Anachoresis* had also come to mean the ancient equivalent of a strike, when people absconded as a means of protest or simply because their situation had become untenable. To authorities of the existing order, *anachoresis* was a crime, and those who had recourse to it were no better than brigands, which they often became by force of circumstances. Thus, the early Egyptian monastics continued an ancient movement born of economic desperation and social protest. This is one reason the origins of Christian monasticism lie hidden in the mists of history: they hark back to pre-Christian times and are not to be found solely in religious ascetic practices.

Pachomius came from a background similar to Antony's, although his village of Esna lay further up the river. While he is credited with founding "cenobitic" or communal monasticism, what he most likely did was organize and give a measure of stability to a style of life that had evolved naturally out of the earlier forms of anachoresis, just as much later, in the western hemisphere, slaves who fled singly into the jungle eventually created their own communities.

In any case, the question of wealth and its use was from the beginning an important subject among the monastics of Egypt. Some of their leaders and founders had given up wealth in order to follow the monastic life, among them, both Antony and Pachomius. Others, the majority, had never possessed wealth, and their flight to the desert represented a rejection of the larger society, in which wealth had been used to oppress and exploit them.

In consequence, the monastics held a view of wealth that had two facets. Carried to an extreme, the ideas were mutually contradictory, but they usually were kept in tension. On the one hand, monastics disparaged wealth and all material possessions. On the other, they valued the ideal of communal property, believing all things should belong to all in the community.

Early monastic piety included a strong ascetic component. Many of the heroes of early monasticism were those who could survive on a few beans—which they counted—and no more than three or four hours of sleep. Excessive fasting and lack of sleep became such a problem that most of the teachers of monasticism had to commend moderation. Likewise, for many the monastic ideal was absolute poverty,[79] often spoken of as "nakedness." The monastic was to leave for the desert in symbolic—and sometimes literal—nakedness, taking no more than absolutely necessary. This usually included little more than a mat, a tunic, and a jug or container for water and food. Those who could read sometimes had a Bible or a portion of it, but others combined their asceticism with a profound mistrust for reading and learning and therefore declared that even a book was too much to own. As one of them asserted, monastics should own nothing that they will have to leave behind at death.[80] From this perspective, poverty itself, even to the point of deprivation, was a virtue.

This attitude toward wealth, although with some moderation, characterizes Antony, at least as he is depicted by Athanasius. He considered renunciation of wealth a good bargain, since heaven is much more valuable than all earthly possessions, and in any case one cannot take such possessions through the passage of death:

Nor let us think, as we look at the world, that we have renounced anything of much consequence, for the whole earth is very small compared with all the heaven. Wherefore if it even chanced that we were lords of all the earth and gave it up, it would be nought worthy of comparison with the kingdom of heaven. For as if a man were to despise a copper drachma to gain a hundred drachmas of gold; so if a man were lord of all the earth and were to renounce it, that which he gives up is little, and he receives a hundredfold. But if not even the whole earth is equal in value to the heavens, then he who has given up a few acres leaves as it were nothing . . . Further, we should consider that even if we do not relinquish them for virtue's sake, still afterwards when we die we shall leave them behind . . . Why then should we not give them up for virtue's sake, that we may inherit even a kingdom?[81]

On the other hand, some monastics held that what was to be avoided was not so much things themselves as private ownership. This was the basis of cenobitic monasticism, at least as understood by the biographers of Pachomius. They tell us that at first a group of anchorites gathered around Pachomius, and that he told them that each should seek to be self-sufficient and contribute to the needs of all. Unsatisfied with such an arrangement, Pachomius decided to follow a stricter course of communal property and establish a "perfect partnership" like that described in the book of Acts. The first experiment failed, but Pachomius insisted on perfect partnership and began anew.[82] When he finally developed the rule for his communities, the common possession of all goods was an essential part of it. This went far beyond what we have found in the book of Acts and in the Christian literature of the first three centuries. In his rule, all things were to be held in common, not only in the sense that they must be at the disposal of the needy in the community, but even more in the sense that no one would be able to dispose of them. Since monks could own nothing, they could not engage in any of the other activities that usually go with owning: lending, borrowing, exchanging, giving, or receiving. Only the community, or the abbot in its name, could dispose of such common property. The motivation behind the rule of Pachomius lay not so much in asceticism of poverty as in a high regard for communal life, indeed, the word *cenobitic,* which describes this form of monasticism, means "common life," or "life in *koinonía.*" In this community, where none could own anything, the only thing one could give to another was service and obedience—two other pillars of Pachomian cenobitism. Slightly later, Theodore, Pachomius's third successor, would declare that the community is so significant that anything that might belong to it in truth does not belong to the monks but to Jesus himself.[83]

From a very early time, and throughout its entire history, monasticism had to deal with the tension between these two attitudes toward material wealth. We are told that the tension arose at least as early as the time of Theodore, who was greatly saddened by seeing the monastic communities growing rich.[84]

It is difficult for us today to envisage the attraction of monasticism in its early days. After the conversion of Constantine the numbers of those fleeing to the desert to follow the monastic way increased dramatically, especially among the Copts.[85] As always, people's motives for joining the movement were mixed. We read, for instance, that many who were not even Christians arrived at the gates of Pachomian monasteries seeking admission, and that it was necessary to catechize and baptize them. This is not so surprising if we remember that in those early days of the movement the line was not clearly drawn between Christian and traditional *anachoresis*, between those who became fugitives from the world in search of Christ and those who became fugitives from creditors, tax collectors, and the like.

Fugitive peasants who joined monastic communities probably enjoyed greater economic security than those living on small plots of land constantly threatened by the extortions of the powerful. Above all, monasteries granted human dignity to many who were treated like beasts of burden, and they even exemplified the apocalyptic reversal of fortunes that so often is the only hope of the oppressed. Stories abound of anchorites and monasteries that would receive the poor and the fugitive with open arms but close their doors to the rich and powerful or treat them harshly.[86] Little wonder then that many slaves decided to flee the master's home for the monastery.

Before long monasteries began losing this radical character. The manner in which they and the church dealt with runaway slaves clearly indicates this process. We have no record of monastic leaders in the early days refusing to accept proselytes simply because they were runaway slaves. On the contrary, we are told that a number of the early monastics were "servants," with no further indication as to how or whether they were released from their obligations. Yet three generations later Theodore is spoken of with respect and admiration, for he had the power to tie down slaves with mysterious bonds so that they could not flee. It was also said that after his death, a master looking for a runaway slave only had to sleep on Theodore's tomb and the slave's hiding place would be revealed to him. At about the same time, Eustathius of Sebaste and his disciples were accused of inciting slaves to flee into the monastic life.[87] The Council of Gangra in Asia Minor condemned Eustathius and his followers.[88] The stories about Theodore supported the view that slavery could not be avoided by taking up the monastic style of life. At the same time, the government issued laws forbidding monasteries from granting asylum to runaway slaves.

As the monastic movement progressively returned to the life of the larger society and of the institutional church, many of its original radical traits and sharp edges were either modified or abandoned. As a result, the commonality of goods now became an option alongside the more "normal" option of those who wished to "remain in the world," retaining their possessions and limiting their sharing of goods to almsgiving. Theologically, this developed into the distinction between the precepts or commandments of Jesus, which all must obey, and the "counsels of perfection," intended only for those who desire to follow the monastic life. One of these counsels of perfection was selling all of one's property and giving to the poor.

Two different ways of being Christian were now open: one the more radical way of the monastics, including voluntary poverty and the commonality of goods; the other the common way of the majority of Christians, for whom the connection between faith and wealth receded into the background. Still, throughout the Middle Ages the monastic community, with its attempt at radical obedience on economic matters, remained a constant challenge to the entire church, reminding it of its early call and ultimate vocation to *koinonía*. Therefore, when the Protestant Reformation did away with monasticism, rejecting what it took to be an attempt to gain heaven by works, it also did away with what had long been monasticism's reminder to the entire church of the need for obedience in economic matters. However, such developments, important as they are, fall beyond the scope of the present volume.

The Disillusionment of Athanasius

The first of the great leaders of the church in the generation immediately after Constantine was Athanasius. Still a young boy when persecutions ceased, Athanasius did not have opportunity to experience the positive side of the contrast between the times before and after the conversion of Constantine. Perhaps for that reason he was freer than an older man like Eusebius of Caesarea to see the dangers in the new situation. Still, for almost half a century after the Edict of Milan, Athanasius continued viewing Constantine and his successors with a reverence similar to that of Eusebius. Like Eusebius—although, as we shall see later, with a different theological slant—he continued to compare God with the emperor.[89]

His relations with imperial authority were by no means easy or entirely happy. Soon after the first flush of enthusiasm over the Council of Nicea had passed, Athanasius was accused of threatening to cut off the grain supplies from Egypt, and he had to go into the first of his many exiles. Later, under Constantine's three sons, he was forced into exile once again. By A.D. 353, it was clear that Constantius, who had become sole emperor, was ready to throw the entire weight of imperial power in support of the Arian cause. In A.D. 356, Athanasius went into exile for a third time, on this occasion hiding among the monks in the

Egyptian desert. Here he composed his "Speeches Against the Arians" (*Orationes contra Arianos*), mentioned above as still using the image of the similarity between God and emperor. Shortly thereafter he wrote an appeal to Constantius (*Apologia ad Constantium Imperatorem*) which is most deferential both to the person and the office of Constantius.[90]

A year later, however, still from his hiding place among the monks, Athanasius wrote and published anonymously a blistering attack on Constantius, the *History of the Arians (Historia Arianorum)*. There he calls Constantius "patron of impiety and Emperor of heresy," "this modern Ahab, this second Belshazzar," the "enemy of Christ, leader of impiety, and as it were antichrist himself."[91] Thus, driven by circumstances, Athanasius came to question the role that the emperor had played in the life of the church, at least since Constantine convened the Council of Nicea:

When was such a thing heard of before from the beginning of the world? When did a judgment of the Church receive its validity from the Emperor? or rather when was his decree ever recognized by the Church? There have been many councils held heretofore; and many judgments passed by the Church; but the Fathers never sought the consent of the Emperor thereto, nor did the Emperor busy himself with the affairs of the Church.[92]

For this reason historian K. M. Setton concludes that "Athanasius seems to have been the first to perceive the new danger which confronted the Church, and the contrast between his earlier and later attitudes towards the Emperor clearly reveals the extent of this reaction."[93] This is true if we leave aside the Donatists and probably some of the early monastics. In any case, what is significant is that Athanasius was the first among the great leaders of the church in the fourth century to call attention to the need for the church to retain its independence from imperial authority, a need that would become clear to others as Julian attempted to restore paganism, and even more so as Valens and others continued lending their support to Arianism.

These matters were not entirely disconnected with the economic issues we have been following. Indeed, Athanasius claimed that one of the most disgraceful things that the Arians had done was to join the powerful in their disregard for the poor, the widows, and the orphans. He tells the story of the collaboration in Alexandria between Duke Sebastian, a Manichee, and the Arians. Among other incidents, he declares that when the duke gave the churches to the Arians, the latter expelled the poor and the widows who used to receive sustenance from the church. The orthodox clergy in charge of these services assigned places where these people in need could meet in order to receive their ministrations. The Arians retaliated by beating the widows and accusing their benefactors before the authorities. Athanasius comments,

Here then was a novel subject of complaint; and a new kind of court now first invented by the Arians. Persons were brought to trial for acts of kindness which

they had performed; he who shewed mercy was accused, and he who had received a benefit was beaten; and they wished rather that a poor man should
suffer hunger, than that he who was willing to shew mercy should give to him.[94]

Athanasius himself, at least in his surviving works, did not have as
much to say on economic justice and the care of the poor. His main
concern was the Arian controversy, and that is the subject of most of his
surviving works. Apart from his anger against the Arians for their ill
treatment of the poor and the widows, and apart from the words on
poverty and care for the needy that he puts in Antony's mouth, Athanasius refers to these issues primarily in letters, where he repeatedly
reminds his readers of the need to care for the poor.[95] Therefore, the
significance of Athanasius for our inquiry is not in what he says regarding the issues, but rather in his being the first example of a critical
attitude toward the empire and toward society in general. This critical
stance will characterize the next generation of Christian leaders and will
allow them to take a more radical stance vis-à-vis the economic order of
their time.

NOTES

1. The bibliography on the subject of Constantine's conversion and its significance is
   enormous. Some of the most important books, and those that may lead the reader
   to further bibliographical information, are: A. Alföldi, *The Conversion of Constantine
   and Pagan Rome*, 2d ed. (Oxford: Clarendon, 1969); N. H. Baynes, *Constantine the
   Great and the Christian Church*, 2d ed. (Oxford: Oxford University Press, 1972); J.
   Burckhardt, *The Age of Constantine the Great* (London: Routledge & Kegan Paul,
   1949); S. Calderone, *Costantino e il cattolicesimo* (Firenze: Le Monnier, 1962); H.
   Dörries, *Das Selbszeugnis Kaiser Konstantins* (Göttingen: Vandenhoek & Ruprecht,
   1954); A. H. M. Jones, *Constantine and the Conversion of Europe* (London: English
   Universities Press, 1949); P. Keresztes, *Constantine: A Great Christian Monarch and
   Apostle* (Amsterdam: J. C. Gieben, 1981); A. Piganiol, *L'empereur Constantin* (Paris:
   Rieder, 1932); L. Voelkl, *Die Kirchenstiftungen des Kaiser Konstantine im Lichte des
   römischen Sakralrechts* (Köln: Westdeutscher Verlag, 1964). Probably the best brief
   introduction to the development of Constantine's religious policies is still Alföldi's
   The Conversion.
2. Although Eugenius was, at least nominally, a Christian, the power behind his
   rebellion, Arbogast, was not. In any case, his party made promises and concessions
   to the pagan aristocratic party in Rome and won their enthusiastic support.
3. Eusebius, *Hist. Eccl.* 10.6. All references to this text are from *NPNF*, 2d ser.
4. *Hist. Eccl.* 10.7.
5. *Cod. Theod.* 16.2.2 All references to this text are from *Theodosiani Libri xvi*, ed. Th.
   Mommsen (Berlin: Weidmann, 1962).
6. Eusebius, *Vita Const.* 2.46, All references to this text are from *NPNF*, 2d ser.
7. *Vita Const.* 4.24.
8. *Cod. Theod.* 3.16.1; 9.7.1, 8.1, 9.1, 24.1, The ancient laws requiring marriage were
   also abolished, perhaps in deference to the high regard in which Christians held
   celibacy: *Cod. Theod.* 8.16.1.
9. *Cod. Theod.* 2.8.1. Cf. *Cod. Just.* 3.12.2, in *Corpus Juris Civilis,* ed. M. Galisset (Paris:
   Cotelle, 1987)
10. *Cod. Theod.* 2.25.1; 9.12.1.
11. *Const. Sirm.* 1. See F. Fabbrini, *La manumissio in ecclesia* (Roma: Istituto di Diritto
    Romano, 1965).
12. *Cod. Theod.* 9.3.1–2. Another law ordered that criminals' faces should not be marred,
    for they bear the divine image: *Ibid.,* 9.1.1.

13. *Cod. Theod.* 9.40.2. Cf. 11.27.1–2, where children are protected from cruel treatment by their parents. See M. Sargenti, *Il diritto privato nella legislatione di Costantino: Persone e famiglia* (Roma: Istituto di Diritto Romano, 1938).

14. *Cod. Theod.* 1.22.2. On the entire question of the economic order that Constantine sought and the result of his legislation in this regard, see C. Dupont, *La réglementation économique dans les constitutions de Constantin* (Lille: Morel & Corduant, 1963).

15. On the relationship and interaction between Roman law and Christianity, particularly canon law, see C. von Hohenlohe, *Einfluss des Christentums auf das Corpus juris civilis: Eine rechtshistorische Studie zum Verständnisse der sozialen Frage* (Wien: Hölder-Pichler-Tempsky, 1937), and J. Gaudemet, ed., *Droit romain et droit canonique en Occident aux IVe et Ve siècles* (Paris: Letouzey et Ainé, 1950).

16. Eusebius, *Vita Const.* 2.48–60.

17. See, for instance, *Cod. Theod.* 11.16-1–3 and 16.10.1.

18. *Cod. Theod.* 16.7.1–2. On this entire period, see N. Q. King, *The Emperor Theodosius and the Establishment of Christianity* (London: SCM, 1961).

19. See Ambrose, *Ep.* 17.5, *PL.*

20. Symmachus, *Relat.* 3.3–4, in J. Wytzes, *Der letzte Kampf des Heidentum in Rum* (Leiden: Brill 1977).

21. *Relat.* 3.1, 20, in Wytzes, *Der letzte Kampf.* Cf. Ambrose, *Ep.* 17.10, *PL.*

22. *Cod. Theod.* 16.10.10.

23. *Cod. Theod.* 16.10.12. Further decrees by Arcadius and Honorius along similar lines: *Cod. Theod.* 16.10.13–20.

24. Tertullian, *De cor.* 11, *ANF.*

25. J. Zeiller, *Paganus: étude de terminologie historique* (Fribourg and Paris: Librairie de l'Université, 1917). B. Altaner, "Paganus: Eine bedeutungsgeschichtliche Untersuchung," *ZKgesch* 58 (1939): 130–41, argues that the origin of the term *pagan* as a religion is not to be found in its rural connotation but in its civilian meaning. A non-Christian, one who was not a member of the "army of Christ," was a "civilian" or a "pagan."

26. The antipagan legislation of Theodosius II, in the fifth century, gives clear indications that such was the case. Cf. *Cod. Theod.* 16.10.22–25.

27. The classical work on the intellectual resistance to Christianity is P. de Labriolle, *La réaction païenne: Etude sur la polemique antichrétienne du Ier au IVe siècle,* 2d ed. (Paris: L'Artisan du Livre, 1948). See also R. L. Wilken, *The Christians as the Romans Saw Them* (New Haven: Yale University Press, 1984). On the aristocracy that refused to yield to Christianity, see S. Dill, *Roman Society in the Last Century of the Western Empire* (New York: Meridian, 1958).

28. *Pro templis* 8, *LCL.*

29. *Orat.* 2. 46, 58, etc., *LCL.* This was a favorite grudge of Libanius, who repeated it whenever he had opportunity. On occasion he even listed the names of those who had thus risen from what he thought were the lowest echelons of society.

30. *Vita Const.* 4. 54, *PG.* Cf. Libanius, *Orat.* 2.31; 30.28–29, *LCL.*

31. For instance, the sophist Hecebolius. See C. Baur, *John Chrysostom and His Time* (London: Sands & Co., 1959), 1:47.

32. R.L. Fox, *Pagans and Christians* (New York: Knopf, 1987), p. 668.

33. Which was one reason why laws were enacted trying to stem the practice. *Cod. Theod* 12.1.49.1.

34. John Chrysostom, *De virg.* 24, *PG.*

35. *Dial.* 48–51, *PG.*

36. Basil, *Ep.* 190, *PG.*

37. Augustine, *Ep.* 96.2, *PL.*

38. Palladius, *Hist. Laus.* 61, *PG.*

39. See a summary of some of the luxuries that Chrysostom mentions among Antiochene Christians of his time in Baur, *Chrysostom* (n. 31 above), 1:377.

40. Sozomen, *Hist Eccl.* 4.15, *PG,* tells of an incident that is illuminating. During the reign of Julian, the city of Cyzicus—by which is meant its leading citizens—sent an

embassy to the emperor requesting the restoration of the pagan temples. This Julian granted, also expelling the bishop. In describing the incident, Sozomen says that Julian feared sedition, for there were among the Christians in Cyzicus many who practiced the manufacture of wool or who coined money, that is, who worked in the local mint. In short, leading citizens wanted the temples to be restored, but among the working classes were enough Christians for the emperor to fear a riot.

41. See the events narrated by Paulinus, *Vita Ambrosii* 31, *PL.*

42. The persistence of paganism among the rural population, even in those areas least disturbed by the Germanic invasions, is easily documented. For fourth-century Gaul: Sulpitius Severus, *Vita Mart.* 12–15. For the area near Constantinople at the same time: John Chrysostom, *Hom. in Act.* 18.4, *PG.* For Sardinia, late in the sixth century, Gregory the Great, *Ep.* 4.23–29, *PL.*

43. R. MacMullen, *Christianizing the Roman Empire (a.d. 100–400)* (New Haven: Yale University Press, 1984), p. 83.

44. *Vita Const.* 1.10.

45. Eusebius, *Paneg.* 5. All references to this text are from *NPNF,* 2d ser.

46. See R. Farina, *L'impero e l'imperatore cristiano in Eusebio di Cesarea: La prima teologia politica del Cristianesimo* (Zürich: Pas Verlag, 1966); H. Berkhof, *Die Theologie des Eusebius von Caesarea* (Amsterdam:Uitgeversmaatschappij Holland, 1939).

47. *Paneg.* 3: "Invested as he {Constantine} is with a semblance of heavenly sovereignty, he directs his gaze above, and frames his earthly government according to the pattern of that Divine original, feeling strength in its conformity to the monarchy of God." *Ibid.,* 4: "And by an indescribable power he {Constantine} filled the world in every part with his doctrine, expressing by the similitude of an earthly kingdom that heavenly one to which he earnestly invites all mankind, and presents it to them as a worthy object of their hope."

48. A further corollary, which need not detain us here, is that monarchy is to democracy as monotheism is to polytheism, and that therefore, just as monarchy leads to an order that reflects the Kingdom of God, democracy leads to anarchy and disorder. *Paneg.* 3.

49. *Vita Const.* 4.44. In this case, the one whom Constantine rebuked was a bishop who declared that Constantine was "blessed, as having been counted worthy to hold absolute and universal empire in this life, and as being destined to share the empire of the Son of God in the world to come."

50. Theodoret, *Hist. Eccl.* 1.6, *NPNF,* 2d ser.

51. Optatus, *De schis. Donat.* 3.3, *CSEL.* All subsequent references to this text are from *CSEL.*

52. K. M. Setton, *Christian Attitude towards the Emperor in the Fourth Century, Especially as Shown in Addresses to the Emperor* (New York: Columbia University Press, 1941), pp. 71–77.

53. *Praesc.* 7, *ANF.*

54. A subject to which Tertullian devoted an entire treatise: *De fuga in persecutione.* Cf. his *Ad uxorem* 1.3; *De pat.* 13. All in *ANF.*

55. *Octavius* 25, *ANF.*

56. Some insight into the plight of poor rural residents may be gained from a rate of expected payments for legal action, published in Numidia around A.D. 362. At that time the going rate was five bushels of wheat if no official had to travel more than a mile, with an added charge of two bushels per additional mile. Needless to say, such a system tipped the balance of civil justice against peasants and poor rural dwellers. See R. MacMullen, *Corruption and the Decline of Rome* (New Haven: Yale University Press, 1988), pp. 154–55.

57. A name that the Donatists eventually adopted. See Optatus, *De schis. Donat.* 3.3.

58. The best study on the subject is W. H. C. Frend, *The Donatist Church: A Movement of Protest in Roman North Africa* (Oxford: Clarendon, 1952). Much of the material in this section has been derived from that work, which has become a classic in its field.

59. Augustine, *Contra Cresc.* 3.56.67, *PL.*

60. Optatus, *De schis. Donat.* 1.22: *quid christianis cum regibus? aut quid episcopis cum palatio?*
61. *De schis. Donat.* 3.3: *quid est imperatori cum ecclesia?*
62. *De schis. Donat.* 3.3.
63. Optatus, *De schis. Donat.* 2.4.
64. The relationships and contrasts between the rich and the poor in North Africa during the fourth and fifth century have been ably researched and summarized, quite apart from the question of Donatism, by P. V. Chiappa, *Il tema della povertà nella predicazione di Sant'Agostino* (Milano: A. Giuffrè, 1975), pp. 97–118.
65. Possidius, *Vita Aug.* 23, *PL*.
66. Augustine, *Ep.* 126.8. All references to Augustine's epistles are from *FOTC*.
67. Canon 10 of the council presided by Gratus.
68. Canon 13.
69. See, for instance, Victor of Vita, *Hist. persec.* 1.1.3, *PL*.. In this regard, he and others seem to illustrate what Salvian declared of the attitude of the clergy in many of the provinces of the empire, that many of the clergy either said nothing on such issues or spoke ineffective words. *De gub. Dei* 5.5.20, *PL*.
70. *Passio Donati*, PL.
71. Augustine, *Contra litt. Pet.* 2.99.225, *PL*.
72. Augustine, *Ep.* 108.18.
73. Augustine, *Ep.* 185.15.
74. Optatus, *De schis. Donat.* 7.1, affirms that toward the end of the fourth century there were "few" catholics in North Africa.
75. It is said that in Alexandria he declared that the slaughter of captured rebels should continue until their blood reached his horse's knees. When his horse slipped and fell on his knees, Diocletian took this to be an omen and ordered that the killing be stopped. As a result, the Alexandrians built a statue to the emperor's horse. References in Williams, *Diocletian and the Roman Recovery* (London: B. T. Batsford, 1985), p. 246 n. 10.
76. His enemies referred to him as "the black dwarf," mocking both his short stature and his low, probably Coptic, breeding. Apparently he spoke Coptic and may well have been born in one of the small Coptic villages along the Nile. Some scholars doubt Athanasius's knowledge of Coptic on the basis of a passage in the *Life of Pachomius* in which it is said that the letters of Athanasius were translated into Coptic in the Pachomian monasteries. Athanasius may well have known Coptic and still written his festal letters, intended for a wider audience, in Greek.
77. While the general outlines of the *Life of Anthony* by Athanasius are probably historically accurate, there is no doubt that this *Life* has been written with agendas that have greatly affected it. See R. C. Gregg and D. E. Groh, *Early Arianism: A View of Salvation* (Philadelphia: Fortress, 1981), pp. 131–59. Much earlier, and breaking the ground on this subject, was H. Dörries, *Die Vita Antonii als Geschichtsquelle* (Göttingen: Vandenhoeck und Ruprecht, 1949). Also: L. Bouyer, *La vie de Saint Antoine: Essai sur la spiritualité du monachisme primitif* (Paris: Editions de Fontanelle, 1950) and B. Steidle, *Antonius Magnus Eremita: Studia ad antiquum monachismum spectantia* (Roma: Orbis Catholicus, 1956). On Pachomius, see L. Th. Lefort, *Les vies coptes de saint Pachôme et ses premiers successeurs* (Louvain: Bureaux du Muséon, 1943).
78. The previous occupations of most of the anchorites of the desert are not known. Also, one would expect that those whose occupations are given would represent the exception rather than the rule, and that those whose occupations are not given would represent lower echelons of society. Still, even the occupations listed are by no means distinguished. Macarius of Alexandria was a small merchant, perhaps a peddler; Macarius the Great, a camel driver; Moses had been a servant and a thief; Alexandra, a servant. Of a number of others we are told that they were peasants. Those who belonged to the higher classes were few, and they were not Copts. See G. M. Colombas, *El monacato primitivo* (Madrid: Biblioteca de Autores Cristianos, 1974–1975), 1:65, where these individuals and occupations are listed and discussed.

79. On the early monastic ideal of poverty, see P. Resch, *La doctrine ascétique des premiers maîtres egyptiens du quatrième siècle* (Paris: Gabriel Beauchesne, 1931); B. Steidle, "Die Armut in der frühen Kirche und im alten Mönchtum," *EuA* 41 (1965): 460–81.

80. G. Morin, "Un curieux inédit du IVe–Ve siècle," *RevBened* 47 (1935): 103.

81. *Vita Ant.* 18, *NPNF*, 2d ser.

82. Pachomius's emphasis on perfect sharing may be seen in Lefort, *Vies* (n. 77 above), p. 3.

83. Quoted in Resch, *La doctrine* (n. 79 above), p. 74.

84. Lefort, *Vies*, p. 21.

85. According to Palladius, in Oxyrhynchus there were twenty thousand women and ten thousand men following the monastic life (*Hist. Laus.* 5, *PG*), and in the region of Antinoe were twelve monastic residences for women (*Hist. Laus.* 58). In Nitria lived five thousand monks, some alone and some in communities. (*Hist. Laus.* 7).

86. For instance, the story of Arsenius, the tutor of Emperor Theodosius's sons, who was ordered by John the Lesser, an Egyptian monk, to eat bread on the floor like a beast.

87. Some scholars have doubted that the person condemned at Gangra was the same Eustathius of Sebaste who had been a friend of Basil the Great and who figured prominently in the theological controversies of the fourth century. Ancient authorities identify the two, and modern arguments to the contrary are not convincing. For a listing of the ancient authorities, see C. J. Hefele, *A History of the Councils of the Church* (Edinburgh: T. & T. Clark, 1876), 2: 336–37.

88. The third canon declares, "If any one teaches a slave, under pretext of piety, to despise his master, to forsake his service, or not to serve him with good-will and entire respect, let him be anathema" (Hefele, *Councils*, p. 328). The context, and the Synodal Letter of the council, indicate that the "pretext of piety" was joining a monastic community. As to the date of the Council of Gangra, there has been much debate. A likely date would be on or about A.D. 345.

89. See, for instance, *Contra gentes* 21, 38, 43; *De inc. Verbi* 9, 10, 13, 55; *Orat. alt. contra Arr.* 79; *Orat. tert. contra Arr.* 5. Except where otherwise stated, all references to the works of Athanasius are from *PG*.

90. Setton, *Christian Attitude* (n. 52 above), pp. 73–75. Much of this section on Athanasius's attitude toward the emperor is derived from Setton's work.

91. Quoted in Setton, *Christian Attitude*, pp. 78–79.

92. *Hist. Arianorum* 52, *NPNF* 2d ser.

93. Setton, *Christian Attitude*, p. 80.

94. *Hist. Arianorum* 61, *NPNF,* 2d ser. As Athanasius comments, the purpose of all this was to intimidate the opposition: "They thought by treachery and terror to force certain persons into their heresy" (ibid., 62). Cf. *Hist. Arianorum* 72; *Ep.* 47.

95. *Ep. fest.* 1.11; 5.3; *Ep.* 45.

9/The Cappadocians

The region of Cappadocia, among the mountains of Anatolia, has always been a harsh land. Since ancient times it was known for its majestic and stark landscapes and for its rugged people, who were famous for the horses they reared. The very name *Cappadocia* came from the Persian *Katpatuka*, or "land of fine horses." Besides horses, Cappadocia's plateaus abounded in goats, sheep, and camels, while olive trees covered the hillsides and wheat and vines claimed the best agricultural land. Under Roman rule, and especially after the founding of Constantinople, easier access to large markets increased the monetary value of land, which tended to be concentrated in ever-fewer hands.[1] By the fifth century, practically all the land was either in imperial hands or in the hands of wealthy magnates.[2] During the fourth century, this process was already quite noticeable. Taxes on some agricultural properties were so onerous that lands were simply abandoned, thus adding their former owners to the masses of the poor and reducing the total agricultural output of a region already prone to shortages.[3] Such taxes, as well as the pressure and competition of wealthy landowners, meant that previously independent farmers were often deprived of their lands and forced either to work for the new owners or to join the ranks of the urban poor.

Drought and famine contributed to the worsening pattern. This was particularly true of the year 368, when we are told that the parched earth cracked, so that the sun baked its very heart and once-mighty rivers could easily be forded by children.[4] As is often the case, evil times provided the opportunity for the powerful to increase their power. Farmers whose seed had dried in the ground had to sell their lands or were forced to borrow money, which in the end amounted to the same, since at prevailing interest rates most debtors lost the land they had offered as security on their loans.

Given such conditions it is no wonder that among the Christian writers of the fourth century few equal the concern for economic matters shown in the works of the so-called Cappadocian Fathers: Basil of Caesarea, his brother Gregory of Nyssa, and their friend Gregory of

Nazianzus. Of the three, Basil, who was bishop of the capital city of Caesarea, took the lead in attacking the evils of the time. He was not particularly original in his understanding of economic matters. Much of what he wrote had been said earlier, either by Christians such as Clement of Alexandria, Tertullian, and Cyprian, or by Stoic and Cynic philosophers.[5] Its significance, therefore, lies not in its originality but rather in its witness to a continuing tradition of teaching on these matters—as well as in the verve and vehemence of Basil's exhortations. Each of the three, while agreeing with the others on the essential, brought a different emphasis to the subjects at hand. Basil was the man of action, who organized relief for the poor on a sound institutional basis. Gregory of Nyssa made an important contribution to the development of Christian social and economic thought by relating it to the doctrine of creation. Gregory of Nazianzus based his outlook on our common human nature and its implications for human solidarity. It is also significant that by their time, partly as a result of the monastic movement, Basil and others founded institutions that sought to put in practice those traditional teachings. To this we shall return.

Conditions of poverty in fourth-century Cappadocia are eloquently described by Basil and his colleagues. In 382, long after the drought had passed, but when various social upheavals created similar results, Gregory of Nyssa described the life of the poor:

These days have truly produced a multitude of people without dress or shelter . . . We are not lacking in sojourners and exiles, and pleading hands are extended to us everywhere. These people's shelter is the open sky. Their roofs are porticoes and crossroads and abandoned corners in the public squares. They find refuge in holes among the rocks, as if they were owls or bats. They wear rags for clothing; their only harvest is the goodness of those who give them alms; their food, whatever falls from anybody's table; their drink, the springs, as it is with the beasts; their hand is their cup; their storehouse, a fold in their clothing, if this is not torn so that even what is put in it is lost; their knees are their table; and the ground is their only bed.[6]

Numerous passages in the writings of the Cappadocians describe the effects of hunger in painful detail.[7] However, by far the most dramatic description of the plight of the poor in the fourth century appears in a sermon by Basil in which he depicts the horror of a father who has to sell a child into slavery:

What can he do? He looks at his children and knows that there is no alternative but to take them to the marketplace and sell them. Think of the struggle between fatherly love and the tyranny of hunger. Hunger threatens with a most horrible death; nature calls him to die with his children. Repeatedly he has set out to do what he must do, and repeatedly he has turned back, but in the end he has been overcome by the inescapable need and violence.

What thoughts must be in his mind! Whom shall I sell first? The eldest? His rights hold me back. The youngest? I pity him for his innocence, for he knows nothing of sorrows. This one is the living image of its parents. That one has a special gift for letters. Woe is me! What shall I become? How will I set aside my natural love? If I keep them all, I will have destroyed all of them. If I give up only one, how will I dare look upon the rest?[8]

Some modern readers may find such a situation difficult to believe. Yet for a father to sell one or more of his children in order to feed his family was not unheard of in Basil's time. Indeed, the words just quoted are taken from a homily in which he is trying to move his readers to compassion and generosity toward the poor. An example taken from an unbelievable or even an infrequent situation would have defeated its purpose.

However, long before reaching such dire straits, those on their way to poverty often sought relief by borrowing money. Given the practices of money lenders, this seldom proved more than a temporary respite leading to greater poverty. The law limited interest rates to 12 percent, but some usurers lent money at exorbitant rates.[9] Actually, the main business of usurers was not so much earning interest on their capital as it was expropriating lands and other property that had been offered as security against loans that could not possibly be paid. For this reason the Cappadocians, like many of their contemporaries, attacked usury as one of the root causes of poverty.

In a sermon against usury, Gregory of Nyssa describes the typical situation: the poor man waits at the lender's doorstep precisely because he is poor and hopes that the other's wealth will help him. The lender, to whom the poor comes as to a friend, is in truth an enemy. He finds his supposed friend wounded and wounds him even more, loaded with anxiety and adds one more anxiety to his burden.[10]

As usual, Basil is more forceful.[11] His sermon On Usury is primarily addressed to the poor, trying to persuade them that borrowing money is no solution to their problems. However, almost in passing, Basil includes a number of biting remarks about the rich who lend money on interest. It is most inhuman, says Basil, that when someone is in need another will take advantage of that situation to make money, "increasing his opulence at the price of the sufferings of the poor."[12] Like his brother Gregory, Basil paints the picture of a man who goes to another asking for a loan. The other says that he is sorry; he has no money; he himself is poor. Then the borrower mentions the magic words *interest, surety,* and *mortgage,* and the lender suddenly remembers that he has some money entrusted to him by an anonymous friend to be loaned at an outrageous rate of interest. Since the man in need is his friend, he claims, he will give him a cut rate. The result is that the man in need, who came looking for a friend, has in fact entrusted himself to an enemy; he came looking for medicine and was given poison.

Basil says to the lender, "Do you not know that you are increasing your sins more than you can increase your money through usury?" And to the borrower, "If you have the money to pay, why not solve your present problem using that? And if you do not have it, you are simply heaping evil upon evil . . . Now you are poor, but free. If you borrow, you will not become rich, and you will lose your freedom."[13]

Playing on the double meaning of the word *tókos* as both "interest" and "offspring" or "birth," Basil declares that interest receives this name because of the evil and pain it begets. He then compares the money of the usurer with crops and beasts:

When their time comes, seeds germinate and animals grow; but interest begins to reproduce from the moment it is begotten. The beasts become fertile soon, but cease reproducing equally soon. Capital, on the other hand, immediately produces interests, and these continue multiplying into infinity. Everything that grows stops growing when it reaches its normal size. But the money of the greedy never stops growing.[14]

To ask for interest on a loan is to be like a farmer who not only gathers the harvest but also digs under the root trying to recover the seed. On the other hand, to give to the poor, either as a loan without interest or as an outright gift, is to lend to God. God is the guarantor of money given to the poor, so that it can properly be said that one who gives to the poor in fact lends to God (Prov. 19:17), not in the sense that God will reward the giver with more material wealth, but in the sense that it will be taken into account on judgment day. Thus it is the height of infidelity to trust a rich person as a guarantor of a loan and not to trust God by practicing liberality toward the poor.[15]

It is impossible to know how this particular sermon of Basil was received. We do know that he and a number of his colleagues were able to induce significant liberality, at least from a number of their parishioners—a matter to which we shall return.

Gregory of Nyssa, on the other hand, was well aware that some among his hearers would not like his views on usury. They would object that they in fact provided a necessary service for the poor and that if Gregory insisted on his position, they would simply have to stop lending money. To such objections, Gregory responds that they are typical of people blinded by their wealth so that they will not understand what they are being told:

They threaten not to lend to the poor, and to close their doors to the needy. What I tell you is first of all to give, and then I call you to lend. Lending is another form of giving, but only when it is without usury or interest . . . For the same punishment awaits the one who lends not and the one who lends with usury.[16]

Usury, however, is not the ultimate cause of poverty. The ultimate cause of poverty is greed. Even the drought and famine of 382 Basil blames on greed. God is punishing the inhabitants of the area, he says, because they have been greedy. In earlier times, their flocks had produced many lambs, but the poor were still more numerous than the sheep. The granaries were bursting with grain, and their owners showed no mercy for those who lived in want.

Who has fed the orphan, so that now God would give us bread as to orphans? . . . Who has taken care of the widow, burdened by the needs of life, so that now their own needs will be taken into account? . . . Destroy the contract with heavy interests {tókoi} so that the earth may bring forth {téke} its produce.[17]

It is the rich, with their unwillingness to share, who have brought this calamity upon the entire area, just as Achab's sin brought destruction to the entire camp. Indeed, the rich have everything except the ability to feed themselves, for all their wealth is not enough to produce a single cloud or a few drops of rain.[18]

Gregory of Nazianzus agrees, detailing the sins that had brought about such natural calamities as the lack of rain:

One of us oppressed the poor, taking his lands and moving the boundaries, . . . as if he alone were to inhabit the earth. Another polluted the earth with interests and rents, reaping where he did not sow . . . not tilling the soil, but exploiting the sufferings of the needy . . . Another had no mercy for the widow and the orphan, and did not feed the hungry . . . It is for these reasons that God's wrath is unleashed upon the children of unbelief, and the heavens either remain closed or they open only to our hurt.[19]

In short, the main cause of hunger and want in the world is the unwillingness of the rich to share with those in need. Such unwillingness creates misery: first, by provoking the wrath of God upon society, as we have just seen; and, second, by accumulating goods in the hands of the rich while the poor do not have even what is necessary to live. The devil uses his wiles to convince the rich that they need all sorts of things that in truth are not necessary and by creating useless things to be desired.[20]

The rich must realize first of all that what they have is not really theirs but God's. They cannot take it with them when they die. Indeed, the only wealth that survives death is that acquired through loving one's neighbor and through properly administering God's gifts. Proper administration requires a clear distinction between the necessary and the superfluous. All that is not necessary is superfluous and therefore must not be retained as long as others lack the necessities of life. To do otherwise, to claim that one has exclusive right to something that another needs, is tantamount to theft and even homicide. These are views all three Cappadocians share. Let us look at some of the passages in which they are expressed.

Basil declares that "the superfluous must be distributed among the needy"[21] and then goes on to compare the rich with a man who arrives at the theater before the rest and on that basis lays claim to the entire place, not allowing others in. Such a man thinks that simply because he got there first he can claim exclusive ownership of what was intended for common use. If, instead of that, "each were to take what they need, and to leave the rest for the needy, no one would be rich; but also no one would be poor."[22] In consequence, Basil can indict the unrepentant rich with harsh worlds:

What is a miser? One who is not content with what is needful. What is a thief? One who takes what belongs to others. Why do you not consider yourself a miser and a thief when you claim as your own what you received in trust? If one who takes the clothing off another is called a thief, why give any other name to one who can clothe the naked and refuses to do so? The bread that you withhold belongs to the poor; the cape that you hide in your chest belongs to the naked; the shoes rotting in your house belong to those who must go unshod.[23]

Obviously, the rich never think that they have too much. They find excuses to justify their greed. If they desire their neighbor's house, they say that it casts a shadow or that it is noisy or that it attracts people of ill repute. "Even the sea will not overreach its bounds, nor will the night go beyond its appointed time; but the greedy know no limit." And the reason for this is not purely psychological. Economically and politically those who manage to enslave some can then use that power to commit further evil and to enslave others. Thus the power of oppressors, like the money of the usurer, continues increasing, apparently with no bounds. "Nothing resists the violent power of wealth; everything yields to its tyranny." And, if any dare protest, they are beaten, indicted, condemned to servitude, put in prison.[24]

It is clear that Basil had no illusions about the social order in which he lived nor about the much-touted Roman system and sense of justice. As we shall see, on occasion he appealed to that sense. Yet he repeatedly reminded his flock that, even when that system fails and the oppressive rich escape human justice, there will be another court, whose judge will not be swayed by the power and prestige of the rich.

What will you tell the Judge, you who dress up your walls and leave humans naked? You who groom and adorn your horses and will not look at your naked brother? You whose wheat rots, and yet do not feed the hungry?[25]

In a similar vein, Gregory of Nazianzus confesses that he wishes that love of others (philanthropía) were optional and not a requirement.[26] But precisely because it is a commandment from the Lord, "I must not be rich while they go begging, nor enjoy good health without attempting to heal their wounds, nor have abundant food, good clothing and a roof under which I can rest, unless I offer them a piece of bread and give them, as I can, part of my clothing and shelter under my roof."[27]

Likewise, Gregory of Nyssa affirms that, were we to live according to God's will that we share with each other, "poverty would no longer afflict humankind, slavery no longer debase it, shame would no longer distress it, for all things would be common to all."[28] But the opposite actually takes place, for people see others lacking bread and give them nothing. The wealth in a single household could relieve the misery of many, just as water from a single source can irrigate vast fields, but too often, even in households having more than can possibly be used, a miserly spirit stops the flow.[29]

Like Clement and many others before them, the Cappadocians are concerned also with the salvation of the rich. What the rich are to do with their wealth is to share it; for sharing has such wealth come to them. Basil interprets the words of Jesus to the rich young man as telling him that he has not really obeyed the commandments. Had he done so, he would not be rich, for "any who love their neighbor as themselves will have no more than their neighbor."[30] In fact, the so-called rich are really poor, for they have nothing they can call their own. Yet because they are rich in the passing wealth of the world, they are in the strange position of being able to loan to God, who is truly rich, by giving their wealth to the poor.

The Cappadocians, however, do not regard the poor simply as a means for the salvation of the rich. Their writings show a genuine concern for the poor. This is the reason Basil, in contrast to Clement, declares that in giving one should take care that the gift goes to the truly needy. If the purpose of the gift is primarily the good of the giver's soul, then the recipient makes little difference as long as the giver is generous and sincere. If, on the other hand, its purpose is also to meet the needs of those who suffer, then it is important to determine that need and the best possible use of the resources available. Therefore Basil, quoting the passage in Acts saying that the believers laid their gifts "at the foot of the apostles" (Acts 4:35), recommends careful management of what is available for the needy.[31] Instead of everyone giving to whom they please, specific people should be named to manage available resources, and individual donors should make their gifts through them.[32] As we shall see, Basil put this theory into practice.

Gregory of Nazianzus builds his call to sharing on the notion of our common humanity. His speech on love for the poor begins with the affirmation that we are all partners in poverty, because we all depend on God's grace.[33] No matter how strong, we all share in the common weakness of humanity, for we are all one. Therefore, we have no reason to rejoice or even to feel relieved because that weakness had brought others down ahead of us. No matter why they have lost their goods— Gregory lists loss of parents, exile, the cruelty and tyranny of the powerful, the inhumanity of tax collectors, bandits, and confiscation,[34]— their plight simply shows us our common inheritance.

In order to show the scope of this common human nature, Gregory describes the lot of lepers. They are the most despised among the poor. They are people whom others shun. And yet they are just like us. We all share a common humanity. Thus we must share of ourselves with them. In a way, we already partake of a common reality with them. Material sharing—and, in the case of lepers, using our healthy bodies to assuage their pain—is simply the expression of a common reality that we cannot obliterate. Thus while Gregory does believe, with all Christian tradition before him, that the rich can be saved only by mak-

Doesn't mention P.Juleman

ing their wealth available to the needy, his call for such sharing is based on a much wider base than the concern for the salvation of the rich.

The same is true, perhaps to a greater degree, of Gregory of Nyssa. As we have seen, he too could condemn the rich for retaining what was not theirs while others suffered want. Yet his philanthropic thought is based, not on the salvation of the rich, nor even on the needs of the poor, but on the dignity of the human creature. The reason God made the human creature last of all was that the entire creation was intended as a palace for its human rulers. All the things that God made beforehand are called "wealth," and their purpose was for the enjoyment of the human creature. Here Gregory points out that all other things God created through a simple command—for instance, "Let there be light"— whereas the human creature was the result of divine self-counsel: "Let us make man . . . "[35]

The image of God to which this divine self-counsel refers is the ability to command. "Thou art, o human," declares Gregory, "an animal with the power to command."[36] The human being, the crown of creation, has a dignity that must be respected. For this reason Gregory decried slavery in some of the strongest words used in the ancient church on this topic. Only irrational creatures are subject to servitude, and it is the height of folly to think that one can purchase another human being, the very image of God, for a few coppers, when in fact that image is of such worth that the whole of creation would not suffice to pay for it.[37]

In that original creation, there was no death or disease or "yours and mine," all of which resulted from sin. On the contrary, there was open and spontaneous sharing.[38] In this fallen world, by contrast, the serpent makes its way by tempting us to break the bounds of the necessary. Slowly we move beyond the daily bread to wish for more and better foods, and eventually we come to the conclusion that we need better furniture and cups and silver beds and fine covers and sheer curtains with gold thread, and before we even realize it we are slaves of greed.[39] We have enslaved the image of God in us to the power of the serpent. In brief, by oppressing or ignoring the poor, we are showing contempt, not only for the image of God in them, but also for the same image in us.

Instead, we should not only preserve that image but also cultivate in us the likeness of God. The divine image is our rationality. The likeness is cultivated by acting in ways that reflect the goodness of God. "For as you practice goodness you are clothed in Christ, and as you become like Christ you become like God."[40] Thus one reason for sharing with the needy is that by so doing the likeness of God in us becomes clearer.

Like Gregory of Nazianzus, Gregory of Nyssa believes that a primary reason for sharing what we do not need with others who do need it is our shared humanity. The needy are ultimately one with those who have more than they need. There is but one common humanity, and we all partake of it.

We must remember what we are, and about whom we are speaking. We are humans speaking about humans. We have a common nature, and there is nothing to set us apart from it. We have all come into life along the same route; we all have the same needs of food and drink in order to live; our bodies are built the same way, and their functions are the same; and at the end of life all our bodies are all equally dissolved.[41]

The Cappadocians, and many others in their time, sought ways to bring all of this theory into practice. Along these lines, the work of Basil has been studied in most detail.[42] It has been pointed out that Basil did not try to undo the social and economic inequalities of his time by either ecclesiastical disciplinary action or governmental intervention.[43] Such a statement is true only if properly understood. Basil did not invoke the power of the church by excommunicating the rich who refused to give to the poor, but, as the texts quoted above amply show, he brought the power of the pulpit to bear heavily on them. The principle that giving must be voluntary, clearly enunciated from the earliest times in the life of the church, was still followed. Basil and the other Cappadocians made it clear that those who gathered an unnecessary surplus while others were poor and starving did so at their own risk. They must also pay a heavy price in ridicule and contempt, for Basil and the others made them appear both callous and laughable. Thus, while it is true that the church issued no sentences of excommunication against the rich, it is also true that these leaders showed not the slightest inclination to soften the harsh words of Scripture for the benefit of the rich. It is important to remember that when the Cappadocians spoke of giving to the poor they did not mean setting aside a small portion of one's wealth for that purpose. They spoke of ridding oneself of all that was not strictly necessary. When Gregory of Nazianzus's brother Cesarius died, his heirs made no objection to his desire that his entire inheritance be given to the poor. And there are numberless testimonies of people who did exactly as Basil and his friends told them, retaining for themselves only what was strictly necessary.

The matter of governmental intervention is somewhat different. The Cappadocians, and Basil in particular, did repeatedly use the power of the state to try to correct injustices and to improve the lot of the needy. They lacked a comprehensive vision or theory of the manner in which government policies enrich some and impoverish others, and therefore one does not find in their writings grand schemes of social reform like those of more recent times. Yet they repeatedly saw the impact of specific government action on individuals and even on entire towns, and they tried to correct the injustices they perceived. Basil spoke openly of what he considered corrupt and tyrannical government officials.[44] In his list of reasons why people become poor, Gregory of Nazianzus lists, in one breath with the depredations of thieves and bandits, the cruelty of rulers, the inhumanity of government officials, and confiscatory policies.[45] Several of Basil's letters are addressed to public officials, asking them to reverse specific policies or decisions that bring suffering to the poor.[46] When the miners of Taurus were taxed beyond their capacity to pay, when work animals were requisitioned by the state, and when new assessments threatened ruin for small landowners, Basil intervened. Thus it is not true that, while he preached vehemently in favor of the poor, he did nothing on their behalf at the level of government policies. What is true is that he considered the state and the basic outlines of its political and social structures as given realities that he did not seek to change.

Finally, a word must be said about the manner in which Basil and others around him organized the work of the church on behalf of the poor. The church distributed food to the poor during the famine of 369, before Basil himself was a bishop,[47] and he later continued the practice, especially in time of famine. His friend Gregory of Nazianzus describes this work:

He indeed could neither rain bread from heaven by prayer, to nourish an escaped people in the wilderness, nor supply fountains of food without cost from the depth of vessels which are filled by being emptied . . . But he did devise and execute with the same faith {as produced these miracles in the Old Testament} things which correspond to them, and tend in the same direction. For by his word and advice he opened the stores of those who possessed them, and so, according to the Scripture dealt food to the hungry, and satisfied the poor with bread . . . He gathered together the victims of the famine with some who were slightly recovering from it, . . . and obtaining contributions of all sorts of food which can relieve famine, set before them basins of soup and such meat as was found preserved among us.[48]

On a more permanent basis, Basil founded on the outskirts of Caesarea a center that later came to be known as the Basiliad.[49] Similar centers had been established elsewhere by others.[50] The importance of Basil's foundation lies both in its influence on other similar programs and in the relatively detailed knowledge of its functioning that has come down to us, thus giving us a glimpse of the organization of Christian charity in the fourth century. Gregory of Nazianzus describes Basil's establishment as follows:

Go forth a little way from the city, and behold the new city, the storehouse of piety, the common treasury of the wealthy, in which the superfluities of their wealth, aye, and even their necessities, are stored, in consequence of his {Basil's} exhortations, freed from the power of the moth, no longer gladdening the eyes of the thief . . . where disease is regarded in a religious light, and disaster is thought a blessing, and sympathy is put to test.[51]

Apparently, when Gregory speaks of a "new city" he is not exaggerating. The picture drawn from Basil's own correspondence is of a large complex of buildings that provided shelter for travelers, medical care for the ill—especially those, such as lepers, whom society at large despised—food for the hungry, and occupation for many who otherwise would be unemployed. Since Basil exhorted his clergy to collect clothing for the poor, one may surmise that such clothing was also available at the Basiliad.[52] He also speaks of the need to build facilities for people in different occupations.[53] This may have been a way to provide work for some of the poor who sought refuge in the establishment. It clearly also was an attempt to bring the establishment closer to self-sufficiency, although Basil continually sought contributions from the wealthy for the support of the Basiliad.[54]

This institution and several smaller ones to which Basil refers in his epistles were his way of putting into practice his theory that the management and distribution of gifts for the poor ought to be placed in expert hands. He encountered opposition, apparently because some among the rich wished to be given public credit for their liberality, and this could not be done if their gifts were channeled through the church.[55] But emulation also followed, and Basil's establishment became a model after which hundreds of institutions were founded.

Scholars have frequently discussed the Cappadocians' social class and how this may have affected both their views on economic matters and their ability to influence authorities through their intervention. There is no doubt that the families of Gregory of Nazianzus and of Basil and his brother Gregory of Nyssa were wealthy landowners. Gregory of Nazianzus referred repeatedly to his family estates,[56] and upon retirement he was able to live quite comfortably on his inheritance. There is much more evidence of large landholding by Basil's family.[57] Scholars have also debated at length the precise social standing of this particular family. Some have claimed that they came from the ancient Iranian aristocracy that had settled in the region centuries earlier; others, that they were of senatorial rank. Most probably they belonged to the higher echelons of the curial class, which was charged with municipal government throughout the empire. If so, they were exceptionally wealthy for that class, particularly at a time when it was in decline throughout most of the empire.[58]

How did the Cappadocians manage their wealth? Unfortunately, we have no exact figures. Gregory of Nazianzus kept enough for a comfortable retirement. We are told that Basil sold his property and gave it to the poor, but no sources indicate that he lived in poverty. On the contrary, some of that property remained in the hands of his family, and Basil continued receiving part of its income. Thus, when particular circumstances such as famine required it, he was able to make further contributions for works of charity.

It is significant that, although the Cappadocians retained some of their wealth, and although they had bitter enemies who sought every opportunity to attack them, there is no record that such enemies criticized them for not practicing what they preached on economic matters. Nor are there indications that the rich whom they chastised in their preaching and who found other reasons to criticize them responded by pointing to the wealth that the preachers still retained. The inevitable conclusion is that, although modern critics may find an inconsistency between the Cappadocians' preaching and their practice on this point, such supposed inconsistency did not exist in the minds of their contemporaries. How can that be explained?

The obvious answer is that the sharing of wealth that the Cappadocians preached was not a dogmatic and legalistic selling of all possessions to give to the poor. They did not cherish voluntary poverty as a goal in itself. The primary purpose of their teaching on economic matters was the relief of suffering and not the salvation or the peace of mind of the wealthy. Naturally, the wealthy can have no peace of mind and cannot be saved without responding to the needs of the poor. Yet what the wealthy are to do is not simply to clear their conscience by giving all away indiscriminately. That would elicit admiration and would make them feel good, but it would not necessarily be the best way to manage their wealth on behalf of its real owners, the poor. The goal must be to help the poor as much as possible. Here one is reminded of Basil's counsel, that whatever is made available for the poor should be carefully and expertly managed by specialists. That goal can best be served, not by one magnanimous act of giving all away, but by the much more difficult practice of making all available to respond to whatever needs might arise.

NOTES

1. R. Teja has done an excellent study of social and economic conditions in Cappadocia during the time we are considering: *Organización económica y social de Capadocia en el siglo IV, según los Padres Capadocios* (Salamanca: Universidad de Salamanca, 1974). Teja discusses both agricultural production and land distribution on pp. 23–43.

2. See the description of conditions by the time of Justinian in J. B. Bury, *History of the Later Roman Empire (395-565)* (London: Macmillan and Co., 1923; reprint, New York: Dover, 1958), 2:341–42.

3. Basil's Epistle 83 deals with precisely such a case.

4. Basil, *Hom. in temp. famis* 2. Except as otherwise noted, all citations to the Cappadocian Fathers are from *PG*.

5. This has been shown some time ago by A. S. Dirking, *Basili Magni de divitiis et paupertate sententiae quam habeant rationem cum veterum philosophorum doctrina* (Guestfalus: Aschendorff, 1911). Dirking centered his attention on Basil's three homilies against the rich and came up with a striking number of parallelisms in earlier authors. See his charts on pp. 35, 41, 45, 46, 48, 49, and 50.

6. Gregory of Nyssa, *De paup. amandi* 1.

7. Basil, *Hom. in temp. famis* 7:
The most horrible of all deaths is hunger, the disease of the starving, the worst human misery. The point of a sword kills quickly; a raging fire soon puts an end to life . . . But hunger is a slow disease . . . The flesh clings to the bones like a spider's web. It loses its color, which disappears as the blood becomes thin. Nor is it white, for it turns black as it dries up . . . The knees no longer support the body, but drag it along. The voice is thin and weak. The eyes are weak and useless in their sockets, like a dry nut in its shell . . .

8. *Hom. in illud Luc.: "Destruam . . . "* 4. Selling one's child into slavery was eventually forbidden. *Cod. Theod.* 3.3.1, in *Theodosiani Libri xvi*, ed. Th. Mommsen (Berlin: Weidmann, 1962).

9. John Chrysostom (*In Matt. hom.* 51, *PG*) speaks of annual rates as high as 50 percent.

10. *Orat. contra usurarios.*

11. For Basil's views on usury, see S. Giet, "De s. Basile à s. Ambroise: La condamnation du prêt à interêt au IVe s.," *RScRel* 32 (1944): 95–128; G. Lozza, "Plutarco, s. Basilio e gli usurari," *Koinonia* 4 (1980):139–60.

12. *Hom. ii in Ps. xiv* 1.

13. *Hom. ii in Ps. xiv* 1–2.

14. *Hom. ii in Ps. xiv* 3.

15. *Hom. ii in Ps. xiv* 5.

16. *Orat. contra usurarios.*

17. *Hom. in temp. famis* 4.

18. *Hom. in temp. famis* 4.

19. *Oratio xvi* 18.

20. Basil, *Hom. in divites* 2; Greg. of Nyssa, *De paup. amandi* 1. At this point one cannot help but reflect on Basil's comment on the "invention of so many useless things," and the structure of our own economy, which is sustained through a process of constantly creating new needs.

21. *Hom. in illud Luc.: "Destruam . . . "* 1.

22. *Hom. in illud Luc.: "Destruam . . . "* 7. On the practice of reserving seats in theaters and other public places for the rich and powerful, see R. MacMullen, *Corruption and the Decline of Rome* (New Haven: Yale University Press, 1988), p. 65.

23. *Hom. in illud Luc.: "Destruam . . . "* 1. In another passage (*Hom. in temp. famis* 7), he accuses those who do not feed the hungry of homicide: "One who can remedy this evil and out of greed refuses to do so, can justly be considered a murderer."

24. *Hom. in divites* 5.

25. *Hom. in divites* 4.

26. Gregory of Nazianzus, *Orat. xiv, De paup. amore* 39.

27. Gregory of Nazianzus, *Orat. xiv, De paup. amore* 19.

28. Gregory of Nyssa, *De Beat. orat.* 5.

29. *De paup. amandi* 1.

30. *Hom. in divites* 1.

31. See A. M. Busquet, "S. Basilio predicador de la limosna," *Paraula cristiana* 19 (1934): 16–31.

32. *Hom. i in Ps. xiv* 5.

33. *Orat. xiv, De paup. amore* 1.

34. *Orat. xiv, De paup. amore* 1.

35. *De hom. opificio* 2.

36. *In verba, "faciamus hom."* 1.

37. *In Eccl. hom. iv.* Basil's attitude toward slavery left much to be desired, for he had little to say against the institution itself, and he even ordered that runaway slaves seeking refuge in monasteries be returned to their masters (*Reg. fus. tract.* 11). On this subject, as well as on the question of how Basil's attitudes toward the poor can be reconciled with his conservative views on slavery, see R. Teja, "San Basilio y la esclavitud: Teoría y praxis," in *Basil of Caesarea: Christian, Humanist, Ascetic*, ed. P.J. Fedwick (Toronto: Pontifical Institute of Medieval Studies, 1981), 2:393–403. See also I. Karayannopoulos, "St. Basil's Social Activity: Principles and Praxis," in ibid., 2:375–91. On the other hand, while Basil contrasts with Gregory in their respective concern over slavery, he does agree with his younger brother on underscoring the dignity of the needy. Commenting on the Psalms, he repeatedly urges the poor to hold their head high before the rich and not to fear them nor cringe before them (*In Ps. xlviii* 1, 10).

38. *In Eccl. hom. vi* 4.

39. *De orat. dominica* 4. Cf. *De paup. amandi* 1.

40. *In verba "faciamus hom."* 1.

41. *De paup. amandi* 2.

42. Y. Courtonne, *Un témoin du IVe siècle oriental: Saint Basile et son temps d'après sa correspondence* (Paris: Les Belles Lettres, 1973); J. Bernardi, *La prédication des Pères Cappadociens: Le prédicateur et son auditoire* (Paris: Presses Universitaires de France, 1968); M. M. Fox, *The Life and Times of St. Basil the Great as Revealed in His Works* (Washington, DC: Catholic University of America, 1939); B Gain, *L'église de Cappadoce au IVe siècle d'après la correspondance de Basile de Césarée (330–379)* (Roma: Pontificium Institutum Orientale, 1985); S. Giet, *Les idées et l'action sociale de saint Basile* (Paris: J. Gabalda, 1941); B. Treucker, *Politische und sozialgeschichtliche Studien zu den Basilius-Briefen* (München: Kommission für Alte Geschichte und Epigraphik, 1961).

43. L. Vischer, *Basilius der Grosse: Untersuchungen zu einem Kirchenvater des vierten Jahrhunderts* (Basel: F. Reinhardt, 1953), p. 165.

44. *Ep.* 85, 237, 247.

45. *Orat. xiv de paup. amore* 6.

46. *Ep.* 85, 88, 110, 303, 308, 310, 312.

47. *Ep.* 31.

48. Gregory of Nazianzus, *Oratio xliii* 35, *NPNF,* 2d ser.

49. Well studied by Gain, *L'église de Cappadoce* (no. 42 above), pp. 277–89.

50. Such as Eustathius of Sebaste (see Epiphanius, *Haer.,* 75) and the Armenian patriarch Narses, according to Faustus of Byzantium, quoted by V. Langlois, *Collection des historiens anciens et modernes de l'Arménie* (Paris: Firmin Didot, 1869), 2:239. Narses had been in Caesarea before Basil was a bishop, and the relationship between his vision and that of Basil is not clear. Also, apparently there were similar institutions in Constantinople under Constance II, more than ten years before Basil launched his project.

51. *Oratio xliii* 63.

52. *Ep.* 286.

53. *Ep.* 94.

54. He even dared ask for land for this purpose from emperor Valens, who considered him an enemy. See Theodoret, *Hist. Eccl.* 4, 16, *NPNF,* 2d ser

55. Cf. *Ep.* 94.

56. *Ep.* 7; *Oratio xviii* 20; *Carm.* 2.1.1, 3, 11.

57. Most of this evidence comes from his brother Gregory of Nyssa, *V. Macr.* In one passage (in W. Jaeger's edition, *Opera Gregorii Nysseni*; Leiden: E. J. Brill, 1952-; 1:380) Gregory seems to imply that one of the family's properties was so extensive that it took three days to cross. The passage, however, could also be interpreted in a different manner. In any case, the family did have property—how extensive, it is impossible to tell—in three neighboring provinces. Cf. *V. Macr.* (Jaeger, 1:376, 393). On the land holding of the Great Cappadocians and their friends and correspondents, see Teja, *Organización,* (n. 1 above), pp. 35–37. The list is impressive.

58. For summaries of the controversy over the social order to which Basil and Gregory belonged, see T. A. Kopecek, "The Social Class of the Cappadocian Fathers," *CH* 42 (1973): 453–66.

10/ Ambrose and Jerome

T he authors who have most recently occupied our attention were natives of the Greek-speaking eastern portion of the Roman Empire. They studied in Greek schools and wrote in Greek. We now turn to the West, where Latin was the language most commonly spoken, and to writers who not only wrote in that language, but also had been formed in the traditions stemming from ancient Rome.

Ambrose

The dominant figure in fourth-century Western theology until the time of Augustine is Ambrose, who was bishop of Milan from 373 until his death in 397. An aristocrat by birth and a high official in government until his election as bishop, Ambrose was noteworthy both as a preacher and as a staunch defender of orthodoxy. As a preacher, he was instrumental in the conversion of Augustine. As a defender of orthodoxy, he resisted the attempts of Empress Justina and others to gain a foothold for Arianism in Milan.

As a theologian, however, Ambrose did not offer originality. Indeed, probably his main contribution was keeping the West abreast of theological developments in the East. His treatise *On the Holy Spirit*, much appreciated by his Latin readers, was an adaptation—some parts only a translation—of works on the same subject by Didymus the Blind and Basil the Great.[1] His six books on the six days of creation, the *Hexaemeron,* is also highly dependent on Basil. His treatise *On the Sacraments* drew heavily on the catechetical orations of Cyril of Jerusalem. And an entire book of his *Commentary on Saint Luke* is taken from Eusebius of

Caesarea. Occasionally, passages in his sermons and epistles repeat almost word for word passages from Basil the Great.

It is not surprising, then, that much of his teaching on economic matters merely repeated what had been said before. What is surprising is that he did set his own stamp on much of what he had to say on the subject.

From Christian as well as Stoic and Cynic tradition Ambrose draws the notion—seen repeatedly in previous pages—that those we call rich are not really such. On the contrary, the more the rich have, the more they want, and want is a sign of poverty.[2] "What is the rich, but a bottomless pit for wealth, an unsatiable thirst and hunger for gold."[3] Some are rich even though they own little, and others are poor though wealthy, and therefore it is correct to speak of "a man of wealth," for it is the man who belongs to the wealth, and not the wealth to the man.[4]

But the fool does not own even what he thinks he has. Does he possess riches, do you think, if he broods over his wealth day and night and is tormented by a wretched miser's worries? He is actually in need; although he appears wealthy in the opinion of others, he is poor in his own. He makes no use of what he has, but, while grasping one thing, he longs for another. What enjoyment of riches is there when there is no limit to one's longing? No one is rich if he cannot take from this life what he has, because what is left here is not ours but another's.[5]

Another common theme that Ambrose takes up is that riches are not in themselves evil. What is evil is greed. Greed so clouds the senses that people begin to confuse profit with piety and are convinced that money comes to them as a reward for wisdom.[6] "The wealth does not commit the crime; the will does."[7] Indeed, for Ambrose avarice is so central a sin that on occasion he can even speak of the primal sin as "original greed."[8] As we shall see, greed is what destroyed and continues destroying the original commonality of goods. Greed is also the main motivation of the rich, and for this reason much evil can be attributed to wealth, although always remembering that the evil lies not in the wealth itself, but in the wealthy who are controlled by avarice. This is what makes wealth a poison with no other antidote than almsgiving.[9] This is also why wealth deletes the likeness of God in humans and in its stead places the likeness of the devil.[10] But, above all, greed is the reason for much injustice and exploitation, and thus Ambrose can condemn those who speculate with the nourishment of the poor:

Thou makest much of the want of corn, the small supply of food. Thou groanest over the rich crops of the soil; thou mournest the general plenty, and bewailest the garners full of corn; thou art on the lookout to see when the crop is poor and the harvest fails. Thou rejoicest that a curse has smiled upon thy wishes, so that none should have their produce. Then thou rejoicest that thy harvest has come. Then thou collectest wealth from the misery of all, and callest this industry and diligence, when it is but cunning shrewdness and an adroit trick of the trade . . . Thy gain is the public loss.[11]

Greed, however, works at all levels. The very rich are like a shark that eats many fishes, both large and small. In the belly of a shark one finds a multitude of fish, some of which have in turn devoured others smaller than they. Likewise, in the property of the rich one finds possessions both large and small, all of which they have devoured, dispossessing both the poor and others who were not as wealthy as they.

In general, Ambrose apparently believes that almost all methods of acquiring wealth are unjust. That is certainly true of trade, which he regards with the abhorrence of a Roman aristocrat brought up in traditional values. Trade is based on lying and cunning, for the seller tries to make the merchandise appear more valuable than it is, and the buyer does the exact opposite.[12] He goes so far as to declare that to use the sea for commerce is to twist its purpose, for the sea was given in order to produce fish and not in order to be sailed.[13] As we shall see, on both of these issues—trade and the purpose of the sea—his views contrast sharply with those of John Chrysostom. For Ambrose, travel to distant lands to procure what is not available locally is one more consequence of greed, of not being content with what is readily at hand.

The only source of wealth of which Ambrose occasionally approves is agriculture. As a true Roman aristocrat, he stands in the tradition of Columella and Cato. He can well understand and approve of Naboth's reluctance to give up his inheritance.[14] Agriculture is also commendable in that it produces wealth without taking it away from another, which is more than can be said of other means of acquiring wealth.[15]

In any case, avarice leads the rich to turn wealth away from its purpose, which is sharing. Wealth is only valuable as it moves for the benefit of others. Water, which is useful and necessary, becomes putrid and grows worms if it is left stagnant. A well from which water is never drawn loses its quality. Likewise, stored wealth is useless and no more than a pile of dirt, but if it is used it can become precious.[16] Since the heart is where one's treasure is, those who bury their treasure also bury their heart.[17] Hidden money is base and evil, but money that faith impels to be distributed is valuable.[18] This is true, not only of private wealth, but also of the wealth of the church. Ambrose defends his actions in using the treasures of the church in Milan to redeem captives:

So I once brought odium on myself because I broke up the sacred vessels to redeem captives . . . {For} it was far better to preserve souls than gold for the Lord. For He Who sent the apostles without gold also brought together the churches without gold. The Church has gold, not to store up, but to lay out, and to spend on those in need. What necessity is there to guard what is of no good? . . . Is it not much better that the priests should melt it down for the sustenance of the poor, if other supplies fail, than that a sacrilegious enemy should carry it off and defile it? Would not the Lord Himself say: Why didst thou suffer so many needy to die of hunger? Surely thou hast gold? . . . It had been better to preserve living vessels than gold ones.[19]

Storing and accumulating wealth and using it for luxury and pleasures both cause much suffering. Ambrose connects the two and describes the plight of the poor and its connection to the avarice and luxurious living of the rich in terms reminiscent of Basil:

You strip people naked and dress up your walls. The naked poor cries before your door, and you do not even look at him. It is a naked human being that begs you, and you are considering what marbles to use for paving. The poor begs you for money and gets none. There is a human being seeking bread, and your horses chew gold in their bits. You rejoice in your precious adornments, while others have nothing to eat. A harsh judgement awaits you, oh rich! The people are hungry and you close your granaries. The people cry and you show your jewels. Woe to one who can save so many lives from death, and does not![20]

In other passages he quotes Basil almost word for word. At one point he describes the anguish of a father who has to sell a son in order to save the rest of the family,[21] and elsewhere he decries the cunning with which a usurer appears to be a friend of those in need.[22]

Yet not all in Ambrose's works is derived from earlier authors. At one point his words are clearer than most of his predecessors. He names as unjust an order in which the poor produce the wealth but never enjoy it. If there is any merit in gold, such merit is not in those who own it but in the mines where people are condemned to forced labor. "The poor find the gold, and to them it is denied. They work seeking, they work to find what they will not possess."[23] Those who employ others must pay them their just wages, for they too are salaried laborers in Christ's vineyard, and they will wish to receive their wages in heaven. Not to pay a laborer the wages necessary to sustain life is tantamount to homicide.[24] This is as close as Ambrose—or any of the ancient Christian writers—comes to determining what a just wage is. Note that the measure of a just wage is not in the productivity of the laborer, nor in the skill required to do the job, but in what is necessary to sustain life.

Ambrose saves his most radical words for his discussion of property. The tradition that extols common property and generally condemns private ownership finds in him its greatest exponent. The most important texts on the matter—although many others appear—are the following:

In the beginning people practiced the natural policy, after the example of the birds, so that both work and honors were common, and people knew how to divide among themselves the obligations as well as the rewards and power, so that no one was left without reward, not free from labor. This was a most beautiful state of things . . . Then the lust after power came in, and people began claiming undue powers, and not relinquishing those they had.[25]

Why do you {the rich} drive out of their inheritance people whose nature is the same as yours, claiming for yourselves alone the possession of all the land? The

land was made to be common to all, the poor and the rich. Why do you, oh
rich, claim for yourselves alone the right to the land?[26]

The world has been made for all, and a few of you rich try to keep it for
yourselves. For not only the ownership of the land, but even the sky, the air,
and the sea, a few rich people claim for themselves . . . Do the angels divide the
space in heaven, as you do when you set up property marks on earth?[27]

When you give to the poor, you give not of your own, but simply return what
is his, for you have usurped that which is common and has been given for the
common use of all. The land belongs to all, not to the rich; and yet those who
are deprived of its use are many more than those who enjoy it.[28]

God our Lord willed that this land be the common possession of all and give its
fruit to all. But greed distributed the right of possessions. Therefore, if you
claim as your private property part of what was granted in common to all human beings and to all animals, it is only fair that you share some of this with
the poor, so that you will not deny nourishment to those who are also partakers
of your right {by which you hold this land}.[29]

Greed is the cause of our want. The birds have abundant natural food because
they have received in common that which is necessary for their nourishment,
and they do not know how to claim private ownership. By claiming the private,
we {humans} lose the common.[30]

Why do you consider things in the world as possessions {proprium}, when the
world is common? Why do you consider the fruits of the land private, when the
land is common? . . . Birds, who own nothing, lack nothing.[31]

Nothing graces the Christian soul so much as mercy; mercy as shown chiefly
towards the poor, that thou mayest treat them as sharers in common with thee
in the produce of nature, which brings forth the fruit of the earth for use to
all.[33]

But this is not even in accord with nature, for nature has poured forth all things
for all men for common use. God has ordered all things to be produced, so that
there should be food in common to all, and that the earth should be the common possession of all. Nature, therefore, has produced a common right for all,
but greed has made it a right for a few.[33]

Much has been written on these passages, some studies trying to
show that Ambrose is a forerunner of modern socialist views and others
that he supports private property.[34] In truth, however, Ambrose is best
understood as part of the tradition to which he belonged and which he
is expressing.

Clearly, his rejection of private property is not a dogmatic principle
he applies in every situation. In discussing the episode of Naboth's vineyard, he gives no indication that Naboth had no right to this land. On
the contrary, what disturbs him is that Ahab is violating that right. Furthermore, in his repeated calls to the rich to share their wealth, he takes
for granted that they have power over their wealth and that their giving
will be voluntary. On this basis, some interpreters have claimed that
Ambrose's communistic passages are simply left over from the ancient

tradition of a primitive golden age of communal property and are not intended to apply to contemporary society.[35] The main difficulty with such an interpretation is that in most of the texts quoted above Ambrose is speaking of the primal community of property as the basis for concrete action today. Thus, for instance, the rich are called to share with the poor the produce of their land precisely because in some sense the poor have a right to that land. Ambrose is not speaking only of a past utopia but also of a present obligation.

To interpret Ambrose as if he were simply speaking of a bygone age when property was held in common is to ignore the real impact of his doctrine. That doctrine contrasts sharply with the Roman legal understanding of property. The notions that some things can be *privately* owned, as if the owner had no obligation toward anyone else, and that they can be *absolutely* owned, as if the owner were free to do anything with them, are what he most strongly rejects. His are not a series of loose attacks on greed, supported by an occasional reference to a primal commonality of property. On the contrary, he is at odds with the very foundation of Roman law which he practiced and which he knew quite well; Ambrose offers a different foundatin—one, however, that still bears the imprint of his Roman upbringing.

Ambrose's critique of the Roman notion of property is based on his understanding of justice—another fundamental Roman concept. He agrees with the ancient view that justice is a social rather than a private matter.[36] "Justice, then, has to do with the society of the human race, and the community at large. For that which holds society together is divided in two parts, justice and good-will, which is also called liberality and kindness."[37]

The Christian view of justice, however, differs from that of the pagan, for "that very thing is excluded with us which philosophers think to be the office of justice," namely not to do evil "except when driven to it by the wrongs received." Then, and most importantly for our argument, Ambrose disagrees also with the second item in the traditional definition of justice, which is "that one should treat common, that is, public property as public, and private as private." This Ambrose rejects, for he knows the excesses to which this notion of justice connected with absolute rights of private property can go. He therefore continues, "But this is not even in accord with nature, for nature has poured forth all things for all men for common use."[38] It is significant to note that he bases this understanding on "nature." He knows that the Stoics held similar views, and he is ready to claim that they simply drew them from Moses. But he is also willing to argue that the world itself is organized in such a way that common property and not private should be the rule.

To the pagan notion of justice as hurting only those who deserve it, and of distinguishing between private and public property, Ambrose opposes a loftier and broader view of justice. Justice is one of the two elements holding society together, the other being liberality or kindness.

Since justice has a social function, it cannot be self-serving. "She, existing rather for the good of others than of self, is an aid to the bonds of union and fellowship {*communitas*, the Latin translation of *koinonía*} amongst us."[39] Also, justice cannot exist apart from the other pillar of society, liberality or kindness. This is why justice as revenge is not real justice. This is also why justice is not served when people treat some things as common and others as private, "For as long as we want to add to our possessions and to heap up money, to take into our possession fresh lands, and to be the richest of all, we have cast aside the form of justice ... How can he be just that tries to take from another what he wants for himself?"[40] "No virtue is more fruitful than equity or justice, which benefits others rather than self, and places common interests before its own."[41] As a student of Ambrose has said, "The Stoic {and also traditionally Roman} justice, with its nice balancing of what is due to self and to others, is put out of court, and in place thereof unlimited unselfishness or altruism is substituted."[42]

Thus justice and the original commonality of goods are interlocking pieces, for true justice seeks the common good through sharing possessions, and the original commonality defines God's purpose, which the just must reflect. This is why Ambrose condemns the rich who use civil "justice" in order to despoil the poor. "What are you doing with the {legal} book, and letters, and the notarized document, and the I.O.U.'s, and the bonds of law? Have you not heard? 'Break every bond of injustice.'"[43] No matter what civil justice and documents might say, all that anyone has belongs to God. And, since God intends commonality, what the rich have and do not need belongs to the poor.

Jerome

Jerome is without any doubt the most dazzling—and the most biting—Christian author of the fourth century. His letters and other writings were widely read during his lifetime, and he therefore greatly influenced the shaping of the Christian mind. His translation of the Bible, the *Vulgate*, became the most commonly used version in the Western church for centuries.

On economic issues, however, Jerome is disappointing both for his lack of originality and because his views on wealth and its use do not appear to have the broader theological grounding that we have found in Ambrose and that we will find later, particularly in Chrysostom and Augustine. Most of his comments on wealth and its use are what one would expect from an ascetic who was also deeply influenced by Stoicism. Still, the very fact that much of what we have found so far appears also in Jerome, often with little or no theological grounding, indicates the degree to which such views were part of general Christian teaching.

Jerome agrees with the long-standing Christian tradition that whatever we have is not properly ours. "Only those things are truly ours that thieves cannot take nor tyrants wrest away from us, and which will follow us beyond death."[44] To Eustochium, his friend and disciple, he writes, "You must flee from greed, not merely by not coveting what belongs to another, as the laws of the state forbid, but also by not retaining your own property, which in truth is not yours."[45] "Take care not to augment alien wealth while your Lord begs."[46] "We may, indeed, take a man's own riches to be those which do not come from some one else, or from plunder; . . . But the sense is better if we understand a man's 'own riches' to be those hidden treasures which no thief can steal and no robber can wrest from him."[47]

The difference between these passages, however, and what we have found in writers such as Basil and Ambrose is that the primary reason things are alien to us is death, not justice or the rights of the poor. In each of the texts quoted above it is clear, if not from the text itself then from its context, that what Jerome means by saying that all material wealth is alien to us is that death sets a limit to our ownership. As we would say today, "You can't take it with you." The only treasures that are worth keeping—or that can be really kept—are those that last beyond death. While this theme appears also in Basil and Ambrose, their denial of the absolute conception of property is also grounded on God's ultimate ownership and God's concern for the needy. This theme does appear occasionally in Jerome's writings. For instance, he writes to Hebydia that "if you have more than is needful in order to eat and be dressed, give it away, acknowledge yourself a debtor in it."[48] Jerome does not explain the nature of this debt or to whom it is owed, but since this is a common theme in early Christian teaching it would appear that he is saying that Hebydia owes either to God or to the poor whatever she does not need for herself. Also, on at least one occasion Jerome declares that it is an iniquity "not to give to brothers for their use what God has created for all."[49]

A further element that must be taken into account is that Jerome, more than any of his predecessors, insists on the distinction between the commandments and the counsels of perfection. While this distinction appears in other ancient Christian writers, it does not play in them the fundamental role that it plays in Jerome. When Basil and Ambrose speak of the manner in which Christians ought to deal with wealth, they are most often speaking and writing as pastors and addressing the entire Christian community. On the other hand, Jerome's primary perspective is that of a monk. Much of his advice, both to other monastics and to a number of other correspondents, deals with the monastic life and with whether to embrace it. A question his correspondents often asked was how one could be a Christian without giving all one has, as Jesus said to the rich man. Thus for him the distinction between the commandments and the counsels of perfection is crucial, for one of those counsels is "go, sell all you have, and give to the poor."

The distinction between commandments and counsels means that when Jerome speaks of the manner in which someone ought to deal with wealth his response depends on whether that person is simply trying to obey the commandments of Christ or also the counsels of perfection, in other words, whether that person is a monastic or not. Jerome insists that Jesus' words to the rich man do not impose an obligation but only an invitation to a higher perfection.[50]

And if you wish to be perfect, He does not set upon you the yoke of an obligation, but leaves it up to your free decision. Do you wish to be perfect and be at the highest summit of virtue? Do as the apostles, sell all you have, give it to the poor and follow the Savior. Follow, alone and bare, after virtue alone, bare virtue. Do you wish not to be perfect, but to reach the second level of virtue? Divest yourself of all you have, give it to your children and to your relatives. No one will despise you if you choose the lower level, as long as you acknowledge that the first course is the most perfect.[51]

With varying degrees of perfection, Christians will commit their wealth also at various levels. Two things, however, are absolutely necessary. First, one must not become a servant of wealth through greed.[52] Second, one must seek to meet the needs of others.[53] Jerome does not elaborate beyond what we have found repeatedly in other writers.

Finally, a number of items deserve at least passing attention. First is the matter of who are those "others" whom a Christian must succor. We have seen some ancient writers declare that one should help all who are in need, without asking questions about their condition or merit; others have said the opposite, that one must carefully select the recipients and the means of almsgiving. Jerome himself is of a divided mind on the subject. At one point he counsels that in almsgiving one should prefer Christians to unbelievers, and that among Christians one should give to saints rather than sinners.[54] He even declares that when Jesus said "the least of these my brethren" he did not mean any who are needy, but "the poor in spirit," by which Jerome seems to mean those who have embraced poverty willingly, the monastics.[55] On the other hand, he also points out that those who refuse to give to people who appear to be unworthy risk not giving to the worthy.[56]

Jerome counsels a friend about how to use her money in words that might well apply today:

Others may build churches, may adorn their walls when built with marbles, may procure massive columns, may deck the unconscious capitals with gold and precious ornaments, may cover church doors with silver and adorn the altars with gold and gems. I do not blame those who do these things; I do not repudiate them. Everyone must follow his own judgment. And it is better to spend one's money thus than to hoard it up and brood over it. However your duty is of a different kind. It is yours to clothe Christ in the poor, to visit Him in the sick, to feed Him in the hungry, to shelter Him in the homeless.[57]

Finally, it is important to mention that, although Jerome does not develop his theological outlook on riches and their use as did Basil, Ambrose, and many others, he does on occasion exhibit a profound distrust of wealth and the wealthy. This seems to arise from a combination of his ascetic inclinations and his firsthand knowledge of the life of the aristocracy in Rome. In any case, his sayings on the subject do not lend themselves to building a coherent whole. He declares, for instance, that it is true that Abraham, Isaac, and Jacob were rich, but that they were unable to enter the Kingdom while they were rich.[58] The passage, though interesting, is obscure. Does Jerome mean that they somehow gave up their wealth? Nothing in the text warrants such an interpretation. Does he mean that they did not enter until after their death, or until after the advent of Jesus, and that by then they were no longer rich? In that case, Jerome is hardly saying anything of great significance, beyond the commonplace statement that the rich cannot take their riches to heaven.

Another tantalizing yet disappointing passage appears in the letter to Hebydia quoted above. Commenting on the phrase "unrighteous mammon" in Luke 16:10, Jerome declares, "Rightly did he call it unrighteous, for all wealth comes from iniquity, and no one can find unless another loses. For that reason I agree with the popular saying, that to be rich one must either be unjust or be the heir of an unjust person."[59] This passage could either be pregnant with condemnation for most economic pursuits, or it could be no more than an isolated rhetorical exaggeration. Again, Jerome, brilliant in his use of words, disappoints us when we ask for the precise meaning of those words and their place in his total outlook.

Other Western Theologians

While Ambrose and Jerome overshadowed other Western theologians until the advent of Augustine, the views of a few others should be recorded. Hilary, bishop of his native city of Poitiers until his death circa A.D. 367, is best known for his treatises in connection with the Arian controversy. Yet his writings also include passages on the use of wealth, and these uphold views and positions that we have already found in other Christian writers. Like his predecessors, he condemns usury—he, like they, means any loan on interest—which takes advantage of the needs of the poor in order to augment their oppression. If those who have resources they do not need are not willing to be generous with them and give them to those in need, they should at least be willing to loan them without expecting to make a profit.[60]

According to Hilary, the possession of wealth is not wrong, for without such it would be impossible to share with others,[61] an argument we have found as early as the second century. It is possible to own things properly by using them for the good of others and thus gaining eternity.[62] Yet it is also true that Christians should not seek to become wealthy, for one cannot do so without partaking in the evils of the world.[63]

Yet Hilary makes a place for the commonality of property, and he also rejects the purely legal notion of ownership:

Let no one regard anything as theirs, or as private. On the contrary, to all of us were given, as gifts from the same Father, not only the same beginning of life, but also things in order that we might use them. We must emulate God's goodness poured upon us, following the excellent example of the Lord who has given us all these things. Therefore, in order to be good, we must consider all things as being common to everybody, and not allow ourselves to be corrupted by the pride of luxury of the world, nor by greed after wealth, nor by seeking after vainglory. On the contrary, we are to submit to God and remain in the love of every common life, living in communion.[64]

In Zeno, bishop of Verona at approximately the same time when Ambrose was bishop of Milan, we find a critique of civil justice similar to that in Ambrose, although the surviving texts are briefer.[65] Christians who think that justice consists in keeping one's own and not seeking after what is another's—who, according to Zeno, are the vast majority—are simply forgetting the higher commandment of Christ, to sell, give to the poor, and follow him. Furthermore, they err in thinking they can truly speak of some things as theirs. "Tell me, what things are yours, when we read that among those who feared God all things were common." In any case, civil justice cannot be trusted, for the legal confiscation of property "has become an industry," so that the powerless are legally robbed of what they have, which, as Zeno says, is worse than having it taken by outright violence.[66]

The anonymous author usually known as Ambrosiaster, probably a contemporary of Ambrose, also tries to redefine justice, which he describes as "liberally giving of one's own to the poor."[67] "Since God gives, humans must distribute to those who lack: that is justice."[68] At this point, Ambrosiaster also declares that those who give freely will receive more, since God will see to it that they will have even more to give. In any case, justice for this anonymous writer, as for Ambrose, is closely connected both with mercy and with the commonality of goods:

Mercy is also called justice. The one who gives knows that God gives all things in common, since the sun shines on all, and it rains on all, and God gives the earth to all. Therefore one shares the wealth of the land with those who have not, so that they not be deprived of the benefits coming from God. Thus, a just person is one who does not keep for self alone what one knows has been given for all.[69]

NOTES

1. Jerome, who had no liking for Ambrose, translated Didymus's work, and in the preface to his translation he declared that he had preferred to translate it rather than to imitate "certain persons and adorn myself, like an ugly rooster, with borrowed feathers." *PL.*
2. *De Nabuthe Jez.* 4, *PL:* "Oh you rich! You do not know how poor you are, nor how poor you make yourself by considering yourself rich! The more you have, the more you will want. And no matter how much you acquire, you will still be a pauper. Profit does not quench avarice, but rather inflames it."
3. *De Nabuthe Jez.* 28, *PL.*
4. *De Nabuthe Jez.* 63, *PL.*
5. *Ep.* 38.6, *FOTC.*
6. *Ep.* 2.15, *FOTC.*
7. *In Luc.* 5.69, *PL.*
8. See A. O. Lovejoy, *Essays in the History of Ideas* (New York: G. P. Putnam's Sons, 1948), P. 296.
9. *De Elia* 76, *PL.*
10. *De officiis* 1.244, *NPNF,* 2d. ser.
11. *De off.* 3.6, *NPNF,* 2d ser.
12. *De off.* 3.37, 57, 65–66, 71–72, *NPNF,* 2d ser.
13. *De off.* 3.19, *NPNF,* 2d ser.
14. *De Nabuthe Jez.* 13, *PL.*
15. *De off.* 3.40, *NPNF,* 2d ser.: "Agriculture is good indeed, for it supplies fruits for all, and by simple industry adds to the richness of the earth without any cheating or fraud."
16. *De Nabuthe Jez.* 52, *PL.*
17. *De Nabuthe Jez.* 58, *PL.*
18. *In Psalm.* 37.24, *PL.*
19. *De off.* 2.136–37, *NPNF,* 2d ser.
20. *De Nabuthe Jez.* 56, *PL.*
21. *De Nabuthe Jez.* 21–25, *PL.*
22. *De Tobia* 9–11, *PL.*
23. *De Nabuthe Jez.* 54, *PL.* Note the ironic contrast between the rich in whose ownership of the gold there is no merit, and the mines, where the merit is, but where people instead of being rewarded are punished.
24. *De Nabuthe Jez.* 92. Cf. *Ep.* 19.3.
25. *In Haxaem.* 5.15.52, *PL.*
26. *De Nabuthe Jez.* 2, *PL.*
27. *De Nabuthe Jez.* 11, *PL.*
28. *De Nabuthe Jez.* 53, *PL.*
29. *In Psalm.* 118.8.22, *PL.*
30. *In Luc.* 7.124, *PL.*
31. *De viduis* 5, *PL.*
32. *De off.* 1.11.38, *NPNF,* 2d ser.
33. *De off.* 1.18.132, *NPNF,* 2d ser.
34. See, for instance, O. Schilling, "Der Kollektivismus der Kirchenväter," *TheolQuar* 114 (1933):481–92; D. Franses, *Radicalisme in de eersten eeuwen der Kerk* (Hertogenbosch: Teulings, 1936); G. Squitieri, *Il preteso communismo di S. Ambrogio* (Sarno: Tip. M. Gallo, 1946); S. Calafato, *La proprietà privata in S. Ambrogio* (Torino: Marietti, 1958); L. J. Swift, *"Iustitia* and *Ius privatum:* Ambrose on Private Property," *AmJPhil* 100 (1979):176–87.
35. So O. Schilling, *Reichtum und Eigentum in der altkirchlichen Literatur* (St. Louis: Herder, 1908), p. 146.

36. Cicero, *De off.* 1.1.7.
37. Ambrose, *De off.* 1.28.130, *NPNF,* 2d ser.
38. *De off.* 131–32, *NPNF,* 2d ser.
39. *De off.* 136, *NPNF,* 2d ser. In 2.49 he speaks of justice as "being a good guardian of another's rights and protector of its own, thus maintaining for each his own." But he makes clear that he is speaking of the way justice is traditionally and popularly understood. Also, in *De Nabuthe Jez.* 40, when arguing that one should not judge the merits of the needy, but respond to their need, he uses the term *justice* in the more traditional sense: "Do not inquire after justice" (*PL*).
40. 137, *PL.*
41. *De parad.* 18, *PL.*
42. F. H. Dudden, *The Life and Times of St. Ambrose* (Oxford: Clarendon, 1935), 2:552.
43. *De Nabuthe Jez.* 45, *PL.*
44. *Com. in Eccl.* 3, *PL.*
45. *Ep.* 22.31, *BAC.* The *NPNF,* 2d ser. apparently takes this to mean that Eustochium's wealth is no longer hers, since she has taken up the monastic life, and thus translates: "not keeping your own property, which has now become no longer yours." The Latin does not seem to warrant that translation: *sed quo tua quae sunt aliena non serves.*
46. *Ep.* 54.12, *BAC.* Again, the translation of the *NPNF* gives a different meaning: "See to it that you do not, when the Lord your God asks an alms of you, increase riches which are none of His." The Latin says: *Cave ne mendicante Domino tuo alienas divitas augeas.*
47. *Ep.* 71.4, *NPNF,* 2d ser.
48. *Ep.* 120.10, *BAC,*
49. *Ep.* 121.6, *BAC.*
50. *Ep.* 130.14, *NPNF,* 2d ser. "Christ's words are 'if thou wilt be perfect.' I do not compel you, He seems to say, but I set the palm before you, I shew you the prize; it is for you to choose whether you will enter the arena and win the crown."
51. *Ep.* 120.1, *BAC,*
52. *Com. in Mat.* 1.6.24, *PL.*
53. *Com. in Eph.* 2.4, *PL.*
54. *Ep.* 120.1, *BAC.*
55. *Com. in Mat.* 4.25.40–41, *PL.*
56. *Com. in Eccl.* 11, *PL.*
57. *Ep.* 130.14, *NPNF,* 2d ser.
58. *Com. in Mat.* 3.19.23, *PL.*
59. *Ep.* 120.1, *BAC.*
60. *In Psalm.* 14.15, *PL.*
61. *Comm. in Mat.* 19.9, *PL.*
62. *Comm. in Mat* 19.9; *In Psal.* 51.21; 143.23, *PL.*
63. *Com. in Mat.* 19.9, *PL.*
64. *Com. in Mat.* 4.2, *PL.* The last words of the quote are: *communione vivendi in omnis communis vitae caritate teneamus.*
65. On the teachings of Zeno (and on those of Gaudentius of Brescia, Chromatius of Aquileia, and Maximus of Turin), see L. Padovese, *L'originalità cristiana: Il pensiero etico-sociale de alcuni vescovi norditaliani del IV secolo* (Roma: Editrice Laurentianum, 1983).
66. *Tract.* 3.5–6, *PL.*
67. *Com. in i Cor.* 15.34, *PL.*
68. *Com. in i Cor.* 10–11, *PL.*
69. *Com. in i Cor.* 9, *PL.*

¹¹/John Chrysostom

No preacher in the entire history of the church has been as acclaimed as John Chrysostom. Indeed, the very name by which he is known by posterity is not his own but was given to him more than a hundred years after his death by reason of his eloquence: Chrysostom, "the golden-mouthed." All who know his name know that he was a great preacher; yet few are aware of the place that economic issues occupy in his sermons. His concern for those issues was so great that it has been said, without much exaggeration, that "one hardly finds in his hundreds of homilies one in which he does not defend . . . the right of the needy to help and succor."[1]

Chrysostom never wrote a systematic treatise on issues of faith and wealth, as did Clement of Alexandria. Yet the materials on this subject are so abundant in his sermons and writings and his perspective is so broad that he may be said to be the culmination of early patristic teaching on these issues. Unfortunately, the lack of a systematic treatise from his pen on the subject means that we must collect and organize into a coherent whole some of the thousands of statements that appear in his writings.

Before we do so, however, let us learn about his background and his work. John was born in Antioch into a family of means sometime around the middle of the fourth century. His father died shortly after his birth, and he was reared by his mother, Anthusa, who saw to it that he received both the best education available and proper instruction in the Christian faith. He was baptized when he was some twenty-three years old, and he soon declared that he wished to follow the monastic life. After delaying his departure in deference to his mother, he tried the monastic life for six years. Convinced by ill health that this was not his calling, he returned to Antioch, where he was ordained a deacon in 381 and a presbyter in 386. Bishop Flavian, aware of his unique gifts, appointed him to preach at the main church in the city, which he did for twelve years.

John was content as a pastor and preacher when he was abducted by imperial command in order to be made bishop of Constantinople. It was a post he did not want, and it would bring him much heartbreak. Constantinople at that time was both a city of luxury and a city of wretched poverty. All the goods of the world flowed to Constantinople, as they had done earlier to Rome. Most members of the court were rich absentee landowners who brought to the city much of the income from their farms. The greatest of them was the emperor himself. The wealthy spent prodigally on luxuries, extravagant feasts, and sumptuous residences. Meanwhile, the vast majority of the population lived in wretched tenements, often several stories high and leaning on each other. They were peasants who had been uprooted by the land-grabbing greed of the powerful; laborers who had moved to the city during a time of much construction and were now condemned to the most demeaning working conditions—when work was available; sailors and drifters brought by the false allure of the great city; women who had no other means of survival than prostitution.

As he had done in Antioch, Chrysostom now did in Constantinople. His income as bishop of the imperial capital was large, and he devoted it to helping the poor and to constructing buildings for the care of the sick and the needy. He also continued to preach on their behalf. The difference was that in Constantinople, much more than in Antioch, many among the rich resented his preaching. Foremost among them was Empress Eudoxia, who decided that what the eloquent preacher said about luxury and its connection with cruelty to the poor was addressed directly to her. Eventually, after many vicissitudes, Chrysostom was exiled, first to Cucusus in Lesser Armenia and then to the remote village of Pityus, beyond the Black Sea. Enroute to that last place of exile he died, a martyr of his preaching on behalf of the poor.

Chrysostom's teaching on social and economic matters, like that of Gregory of Nyssa and Gregory of Nazianzus, is based on his understanding of human nature. Being human and being humane belong together to such an extent that one who has no mercy is no longer human.[2] Humans are capable of becoming inhumane, of denying and destroying their own nature. In such cases the soul is dead, and we are no longer human.

For whence is it clear that we have a soul? Is it not from its operations? When then it doth not perform the things proper to it, is it not dead? When, for instance, it hath no care for virtue, but is rapacious and transgresseth the law; whence can I tell that thou hast a soul? Because thou walkest? But this belongs to the irrational creatures as well. Because thou eatest and drinkest? But this too belongeth to wild beasts. Well then, because thou standest upright on two feet? This convinceth me rather that thou art a beast in human form . . . Whence then can I learn that thou hast the soul of a man, when thou kickest like the ass, when thou bearest malice like the camel, when thou bitest like the bear, when thou ravenest like the wolf, when thou stealeth like the fox, when thou art wily as the serpent, when thou art shameless as the dog? Whence can I learn that thou hast the soul of a man?[3]

To be unmerciful, therefore, is to deny the very essence of what it means to be human. And what is true of all humans is even more true of those who call themselves Christians. The very essence of Christianity is caring for others, and therefore to fail to do so is to contradict one's own Christian nature.

Do not tell me that you cannot watch after others. If you are Christians, what is impossible is for you not to watch after them. Just as there are in nature things that cannot be denied, so is it in this case, for it has to do with the very nature of being a Christian. Do not insult God, as you would were you to say that the Sun cannot shine. If you claim that a Christian is not able to be of service to another, you insult God and call God a liar.[4]

Chrysostom's theology is built on the presupposition of a greater continuity between creation and redemption than much later theology, especially Western, held. Thus mercy and mutual service are the mark of both being human and being a Christian. The created order has been organized by God in such a way that it moves all of creation toward its intended goal. Human solidarity is born both out of our created similarity and out of our created differences, for both are intended to bring us together.

First we are taught love in the very manner in which we were created, for God, having created a single human being, decreed that we should all be born from it, so that we might all see ourselves as one and seek to keep the bond of love among ourselves. Secondly, God wisely promoted mutual love through our own trade and dealings. Notice that God filled the earth with goods, but gave each region its own peculiar products, so that, moved by need, we would communicate and share among ourselves, giving others that of which we have abundance and receiving that which we lack.

The same is true of each of us individually, for God did not grant all knowledge to all, but rather medicine to one, construction to another, art to a third, so that we would love each other because we need each other.[5]

Thus Chrysostom, like Lactantius, argues that the basis for society is our mutual need. However, the emphasis differs, for while Lactantius argued that solidarity is the defense that God has given us—like antlers to the deer—Chrysostom sees the goal, not in defense or survival, but in solidarity itself. We are weak, and God has intended that it be so precisely in order that we may come together. The purpose of all trade, as well as of every contract, is communication, and not vice versa. From the point of view of God's plan for creation, we do not communicate in order to trade but trade in order to communicate. On this point his views contrast with those of Ambrose, who felt that long-distance trade resulted from undue desire for things that nature has not made available, and that people should be content with what their region produces.

In consequence, riches in themselves are not evil, but they too are intended for communication—for sharing. Riches are good only when they are used.[6] When they are accumulated they are no longer even true riches. "Wealth that is locked up and buried is fiercer than a lion and causes great fright. But if you bring it out and distribute it among the poor, the fierce beast becomes a lamb."[7] Wealth is not bad if it is used properly. What is evil is greed and love of money.[8] Given the nature of wealth as something that must be shared in order to be real, Chrysostom can claim that "not to give part of what one has is in itself a theft."[9]

In this context, Chrysostom can repeat the common assertions about the nature of true wealth. "Rich is not the one who has much, but rather the one who gives much."[10] Truly rich is not the one who has all sorts of things, but rather the one who has no great needs.[11] The others, those who are constantly seeking to accumulate greater wealth, are neither rich nor fortunate. They are like someone who is always thirsty and therefore has to drink much. Just as such a person is never satiated, so are the rich forever wanting, forever poor.[12] Or they are like brigands who attack people on the roads and in the fields and then hide their ill-gotten gains in caves. Such brigands may have all sorts of luxury items, and for a while they may enjoy their feasts, but people will not envy them, for the punishment that awaits them is much greater than their present pleasures. Likewise, the rich and the greedy are like bandits who take the wealth of others and hide it in their caves. And they too, like brigands, ought to be pitied rather than envied, for the punishment that awaits them is great.[13] Or, in still another image, those who appear to the world as rich are no more than actors wearing a mask on stage. All one has to do is remove their mask and enter into their conscience to find that they are poor in virtue. Furthermore, even if no one removes their mask in this life, death will put an end to the masquerade, and their true nature will be revealed.[14]

Chrysostom's thought on wealth and its use must be understood from the point of view of his fundamental notion that true wealth is by nature outgoing. Wealth is really such only when it moves out. One could say that wealth is by nature "expansive," but in our modern world that would be understood in the sense that wealth tends to accumulate and to expand its power, which is exactly the opposite of what Chrysostom intends. Wealth, like light, has value only when it goes out and spends itself. "A light that instead of banishing darkness would augment it would not be called 'light.' Likewise, I would not call 'wealth' one that, instead of banishing poverty, increases it."[15] Wealth is difficult to retain, for the more one seeks to retain it the more it escapes, or rather, the more it turns into something else. It is like seed, which piled up rots and is lost, whereas spread over the fields it multiplies and brings forth more of its kind.[16] How does one spread this seed? By using it to destroy poverty, just as one spreads light by using it to destroy darkness. Just as seed is best employed in the belly of the earth, so is wealth best employed in the belly of the hungry.[17]

This "expansive" nature of true wealth is the basis for Chrysostom's comments both on the question of private property versus communal and on the need for the rich to share with the poor. Let us look at these two in order.

Chrysostom's entire call for the sharing of wealth clearly presupposes private property, at least to a degree. He uses Job and Abraham repeatedly as examples of people who were both rich and just, and he never questions that they had a right to their property. In attacking usury, he declares that there are righteous means of making money, such as agriculture, cattle and sheep raising, and manual labor.[18] Sometimes he even seems to imply that the division of society between the rich and the poor is similar to the division of labor, so that each, the rich and the poor, have their proper functions.[19] On the other hand, the main thrust of his work leans in the opposite direction, arguing that God's intention for creation was the commonality of property.

Tell me, then, whence thou art rich? ... The root and origin of it must have been injustice. Why? Because God in the beginning made not one man rich, and another poor. Nor did He afterward take and show to one treasures of gold, and deny to the other the right of searching for it: but he left the earth free to all alike. Why then, if it is common, have you so many acres of land, while your neighbor has not a portion of it?[20]

This passage points in two directions that we must pursue. First, commonality of goods and not private property is the order of creation. Second, private property, particularly when it reaches the level of wealth, is somehow connected with injustice. Chrysostom frequently joins these two subjects or alludes separately to one or the other. Quoting a few of hundreds of texts on the matter illustrates his views:

But is this not an evil, that you alone should have the Lord's property, that you alone should enjoy what is common? Is not "the earth God's, and the fullness thereof"? If then our possessions belong to one common Lord, they belong also to our fellow-servants. The possessions of one Lord are all common ... Mark the wise dispensation of God. That He might put mankind to shame, He hath made certain things common, as the sun, air, earth, and water, the heaven, the sea, the light, the stars; whose benefits are dispensed equally to all as brethren. ... And observe, that concerning things that are common there is no contention, but all is peaceable. But when one attempts to possess himself of anything, to make it his own, then contention is introduced, as if nature herself were indignant, that when God brings us together in every way, we are eager to separate ourselves by appropriating things, and by using those cold words "mine and thine."[21]

The rich have that which belongs to the poor, even though they may have received it as an inheritance, no matter whence their money comes.[22]

From that church {in the early chapters of Acts} those tasteles words of "mine" and "yours" were banished ... Neither did the poor envy the rich, nor were there any rich. All was common. No one said that they owned anything. It was not as it is now ... The rich who had prepared for themselves food and nourishment invited the poor, and they had a common table, a common banquet, a common feast in the very church.[23]

Let us not become more beastly than the beasts. For them, all things are common: the earth, the springs, the pastures, the mountains, the valleys. One does not have more than another. You, however, who call yourself human, the tamest of animals, become fiercer than the beasts and shut up in a single house the sustenance for thousands of poor people. And even so, it is not only our nature that is common to us all, but also many other things: the sky, and the sun, and the moon, and the choir of stars, and the air, and the sea, and the fire, and the water, and the earth, and life, and death, and growth, and old age, and sickness, and health, and the need to eat and be clothed. Also common to us all is the spiritual, the sacred table and the body of the Lord and his precious blood, and the promise of the Kingdom ... Is it not then absurd, that we who have so many great things in common ... will be so greedy when it comes to riches, and rather than maintaining that commonality we become fiercer that the wild beasts?[24]

Whence, then, does such great inequality arise? It arises from the greed and the arrogance of the rich. But I ask that in the future you act in a different manner: closely bound together in those things that are common and most needful, let us not be rent asunder by those that are earthly and lower, such as riches and poverty.[25]

In short, a contradiction, or at least a tension, appears in Chrysostom's teachings. On the one hand, he holds that God's purpose is the commonality of goods; on the other, he takes for granted that there will be rich who must share their wealth with the poor.

The seeming contradiction becomes less marked when we realize that beneath it lies a rejection of the traditional Roman notion of property and an attempt to substitute a different view for it. As we have seen, at the core of the Roman legal system was the right of private property conceived in absolute terms, including not only the use of property but even its abuse. What Chrysostom in fact proposes is a different view of property, a view limited to use and directed toward the communication that is the goal of creation.

In several passages Chrysostom uses the etymological connection between *chrémata* (wealth) and *chrésis* (use) in order to argue that our power over wealth is not one of dominion or true ownership but only one of use.

This wealth is not a possession, it is not property, it is a loan for use {*chrésis*}. For when thou diest, willingly or unwillingly, all that thou hast goes to others, and they again give it up to others, and they again to others. Goods {*chrémata*} are named from use {*kechrésthai*, a derivative of *chrésis*}, not from lordship, and are not our own, and possessions are not a property but a loan. For how many masters has every estate had, and how many will it have![26]

What the rich have is in fact no more than a deposit or a trust, a further reason they must be careful, lest the deposit that has been entrusted to them make them guilty of mismanagement.[27] It in fact belongs to the Lord, who has entrusted it to the rich so that they may distribute it among the needy. Therefore if they use on themselves more than necessary they will have to render account for having embezzled what was not theirs.[28] This is why, commenting on the rich man and Lazarus, Chrysostom comes to the conclusion that "not giving to the poor of what one has is to commit robbery against them and to attempt against their very life, for we must remember that what we withhold is not ours, but theirs."[29]

That what we have is not true ownership but only use also leads to Chrysostom's second basic point regarding property, namely, that it should be directed toward sharing and communication. In a way, just as artisans must know how to practice their trade, there is a proper practice of the "trade" of the rich, and this derives precisely from the nature of wealth:

Riches are called such {chrémata} so that we might not bury them, but use them properly. Every artisan knows his craft well. But the rich? The rich know not how to work iron, nor how to build a ship, nor weaving, nor building, nor any such thing. Let the rich then learn their own trade properly, which is to employ their wealth correctly, and giving alms to the needy, and they will know a craft which is better than any other.[30]

Chrysostom's disagreement with Roman law on these matters may be seen in his comment that he laughs at wills in which someone leaves the ownership of a house or of a field to one heir and its use to another. The fact is, Chrysostom argues, that we never have anything more than the use, for even though we claim to be owners death will eventually dispossess us—a particularly poignant irony when the person speaking about ownership as full dominion is writing a will and thus considering the eventuality of death.[31]

Thus Chrysostom's main objection to the traditional notion of property is that its supposedly absolute nature needs to be limited. There is no such thing as absolute property, what the old Romans would have called quiritarian property. Ownership is not really such but is rather a loan, and it is a loan made with a purpose. When that purpose is ignored, the loan is misused. This in turn leads us to Chrysostom's second objection to the traditional notion of property. Not only is property limited in that all that we really can have is its usufruct; it is also limited in that even the usufruct must be managed according to its proper goal. That goal, as has already been pointed out, is communication, solidarity, the unity and concert of all of humanity. Both common ownership and private property—such as is allowed—have been established by God with that purpose.

Chrysostom details his views in a passage that brings together both private and common ownership. He begins by asserting that the most necessary things God has given abundantly to all: water, air, fire, and so forth. The rich and the poor alike enjoy the same sunlight and the same air, and one does not have more of them than the other. On the other hand, things that are not as important as light, water, and air are subject to private ownership.

Why is it, that God has made common the most important and necessary to sustain our life, and yet money, which is of lesser importance and value, is not common? And again I ask, why? In order to protect both life and virtue. If things that are absolutely necessary were not common, the rich, greedy as they are, would probably choke the poor to death. For, since they behave with their money as they do, their conduct would be even worse if they also had the management of those other things. On the other hand, if money were also the common property of all, and equally accessible to all, there would be no opportunity for almsgiving and no motivation for charity.[32]

As we read these lines, it is easy, from our twentieth-century perspective, to see the shortcomings of the argument. Clearly, hunger exists in our society, as it did in Chrysostom's time, because food and land, which are clearly necessities of the first order, are not equally available to all. Yet this should not obscure Chrysostom's point, which is that both the commonality of goods and private property are ordered toward a further end. While, as we have seen from several texts quoted above, the commonality of goods best serves that end, private ownership of some things is also justified—can only be justified—insofar as it serves that end: solidarity, or, as Chrysostom would say, communication.

Thus the worst possible use of private property is seeking independence. As we have seen repeatedly, Chrysostom insists that true wealth is such that not to share it contradicts its very nature. Furthermore, to be dependent on each other is part of the human lot as designed by God, and it is useless to seek to avoid it. In a passage that says much about our modern quest after "security," Chrysostom says,

Why then tremblest thou at poverty? and why pursueth thou after wealth? "I fear," saith one, "lest I be compelled to go to other men's doors and to beg from my neighbor." And I constantly hear many also praying, and saying, "Suffer me not at any time to stand in need of men." And I laugh exceedingly when I hear these prayers, for this fear is even childish. For every day and in every thing, so to speak, do we stand in need of one another. So these are the words of an unthinking and puffed up spirit, and that doth not clearly discern the nature of things . . . If thou be rich, thou wilt stand in need of more, yea of more and meaner. For just in proportion to thy wealth dost thou subject thyself to this curse . . . For if thou art desirous of being exceedingly independent of every one, pray for poverty; and then if thou art dependent on any, thou wilt be so only for bread and raiment.[33]

According to Chrysostom, the rich deceive themselves when they think that it is only the poor that need them, and not vice versa. To illustrate this, he suggests that his hearers imagine two cities (by which he means two societies), one holding only rich people and the other only poor. Place them both on an equal footing at the start and see which is better able to support itself. The city of the rich will have no one to do the traditional chores of the poor: no field laborers, no carpenters, no builders, no bakers, no smiths. The city of the poor will have none of the things traditionally associated with wealth: no gold, no silver, no jewels, no silk. Which of the two cities will fare better? When the time comes to raise food, which city will be able to do it? When the time comes to bake or to build or to weave, which city will be able to meet its needs? Evidently, that of the poor. Chrysostom concludes, "When will the city of the poor have need of the rich? Clearly, when the time comes to destroy it," for the rich will bring with them the quest after luxury, pleasures, and ease, which will destroy the city.[34] The obvious conclusion is what Chrysostom has pointed out repeatedly, namely, that when it comes to independence and self-sufficiency the poor are much closer to it than the rich. At one point, Chrysostom even asks, "What are the rich for in the world, since they are useless?" His response is that those who simply accumulate wealth are indeed useless, but that those who use it justly by sharing it do have a function, which is precisely sharing and distributing wealth among the needy.

This interdependence of all humanity lies behind Chrysostom's harsh words to the rich. There are numerous indications in his sermons—and many others in the accounts of various incidents in his life—that the rich often accused him of opposing them.[35] Chrysostom denied such charges. On occasion, he did chastise the poor as well as the rich and declared that covetousness and greed exist at all levels of society.

Let us therefore, both poor and rich, cease from taking the property of others. For my present discourse is not only to the rich, but to the poor also. For they too rob those that are poorer than themselves. And artisans who are better off, and more powerful, outsell the poorer and more distressed, tradesmen outsell tradesmen, and so all who are engaged in the marketplace. So that I wish from every side to take away injustice. For the injury consists not in the measure of the things plundered but in the purpose of him that steals.[36]

The reason he speaks so much of the obligations of the rich, says Chrysostom, is that the poor do not have as many nor as great opportunities to practice evil as the rich do.[37] Both the poor and the rich are his children, and he loves them both. Yet when the rich oppress the poor he will attack them, both for the sake of the poor, who suffer physical harm, and for the sake of the rich, who suffer even greater spiritual harm.[38] To those who accuse him of being against the rich, he declares,

As long as you will not cease devouring and destroying the poor, I shall not cease accusing you of it . . . Leave my sheep alone. Let my flock be. Do not destroy it; and if you do, do not complain that I accuse you.[39]

As shepherd of a spiritual flock, his weapons are words, not stones, and with words he will attack the oppressing rich. Or rather, he will call them to join his flock, for he loves them.

I am not against the rich, but for them. Even though you may not think so, in speaking as I do I speak in your favor. How so? Because I free you from sin, I free you from a life of plunder, I make you a friend of all, and loved by all.[40]

Thus we see the larger context of Chrysostom's often-quoted harsh words against the rich. They must be understood within an entire theological framework that begins with God's purpose both in creation and in redemption, namely, human solidarity and communication. From this it follows that the traditional Roman view of property as absolute dominion must be rejected in favor both of common property and of a narrowly defined and clearly limited private property. Private property is really not such; it is rather a usufruct or a loan given to its owners as administrators for the goal of human solidarity. This both limits the rights of owners and places them under great responsibility, for to misuse wealth is tantamount to embezzlement from God—and from the poor, whom wealth is supposed to help. Thus both the physical welfare of the poor and the salvation of the rich are at stake, and Chrysostom can claim that he attacks the rich precisely because he loves them, because they are part of his flock, because he is their pastor.

This does not make his demands any less stringent. On the contrary, he declares that the wealthy have no right to use for themselves anything more than what is strictly necessary. The superfluous they hold only in trust, and to use it for themselves violates that trust. His main call is not to ascetic practices of renunciation, but to proper stewardship.

For neither am I leading thee to the lofty peak of entire poverty, but for the present I require thee to cut off superfluities and to desire a sufficiency alone. Now the boundary of sufficiency is the using those things which it is impossible to live without. No one debars thee from these; nor forbids thee thy daily food. I say food, not feasting; raiment, not ornament . . . And let him that can be satisfied with pulse and can keep in good health, seek nothing more; but let him who is weaker and requires to be dieted with garden herbs, not be hindered of this. But if any be even weaker than this and require the support of flesh in moderation, we will not debar him from this either. For we do not advise these things to kill and injure men, but to cut off what is superfluous; and that is superfluous which is more than we need. For when we are able even without a thing to live healthfully and respectably, certainly the addition of that thing is a superfluity.[41]

This distinction between the necessary and the superfluous appears repeatedly in Chrysostom's sermons as the main guideline for the proper use of wealth.[42] Giving alms is not enough, for there must be a proportion between one's means and one's giving, a proportion determined precisely by the distinction between the necessary and the superfluous.[43] The wealthy must not think that they can spend lavishly on their own desires and claim that they are merely spending their own money. What they spend needlessly is part of the common inheritance that God has given to all.[44] Just as shoes that are too large make walking difficult, too large a house hinders the way to heaven.[45]

Within this framework, Chrysostom's harsh words appearing throughout his sermons are a sincere call to repentance. Two quotes provide their flavor:

Is it not murder, pray, and worse than murder, to hand the poor man over to famine, and to cast him into prison, and to expose him not to famine only, but to tortures too, and to countless acts of insolence? For even if you do not do these things yourself to him, yet you are the occasion of their being done, you do them more than the ministers who execute them. The murderer plunges his sword into a man at once, and after giving him pain for a short time, he does not carry the torture any farther. But do you who by your calumnies, by your harassings, by your plottings, make light darkness to him, and set him upon desiring death ten thousand times over, consider how many deaths you perpetrate instead of one only? And what is worse than all, you plunder and are grasping, not impelled to it by poverty, without any hunger to necessitate you, but that your horse's bridle may be spattered over with gold enough, or the ceiling of your house, or the capitals of your pillars. And what hell is there that this conduct would not deserve, when it is a brother, and one that has shared with yourself in blessings unutterable, and has been so highly honored by the Lord, whom you, in order that you may deck out stones, and floors, and the bodies of animals with neither reason, nor perception of these ornaments, are casting into countless calamities? And your dog is well attended too, while man, or rather Christ, for the sake of the hound, and all these things I have named, is straitened in extreme hunger. What can be worse than such confusion? What more grievous than such lawlessness as this? What streams of fire will be enough for such a soul? He that was made in the image of God stands in unseemly plight, through thy inhumanity; but the faces of the mules that draw thy wife glisten with gold in abundance.[46]

Nay, this itself will even the more weigh thee down, when thou indeed abidest in a three-storied dwelling whilst He owns not even a decent shelter; when thou [liest] upon soft couches whilst He hath not even a pillow. 'But,' saith one, 'I have given.' But thou oughtest not to leave off so doing. For then only wilt thou have an excuse, when thou hast not what [to give], when thou possessest nothing; but so long as thou hast, (though thou have given to ten thousand) and there be others hungering, there is no excuse for thee. But when thou both shuttest up corn and raisest the price, and devisest other unusual tricks of traffic; what hope of salvation shalt thou have henceforth? Thou hast been bidden to give freely to the hungry, but thou dost not give at a suitable price even. He emptied Himself of so great glory for thy sake, but thou dost not count Him deserving even of a loaf; but thy dog is fed to fullness whilst Christ wastes with hunger.[46]

While Chrysostom calls the rich to radical obedience on economic matters, he also responds to some of the objections that the rich may raise, that the poor are not always worthy. As we have already seen, he does not exempt the poor from the obligations of sharing with those who are even less fortunate than they. He is willing to concede that, just as the greatest temptation of the rich is pride, so is lying the greatest temptation of the poor.[48] Yet the rich have no right to take that as an excuse for not giving.

'But he fakes all that weakness and trembling,' you tell me. And, saying so, you do not fear that a bolt of lightning will strike you from heaven? Forgive me, but such words make me burst with wrath. You who fatten yourselves and enjoy your ease, you who drink well into the night, and then cover yourselves with soft blankets, . . . you dare demand a strict account from the needy who is little more than a corpse, and you fear not the account you will have to render before the court of Christ, terrible and frightful? If the poor fake, it is out of need that they fake, for it is your merciless inhumanity and your cruelty that forces them to do so.[49]

Nor do the well-to-do have the right to accuse the poor of sloth or to refuse to aid them on the basis of Paul's saying that those who do not work should not eat.

Paul's rules are not only for the poor, but also for ourselves. I shall say something that is harsh and will enrage you; yet I say it not to hurt, but to correct. We point our finger at the idleness of the poor, and yet we ourselves often work at things that are worse than idleness . . . You who often spend the day in the theatres and in merryments, you who gossip about the whole world, think that you are not idle. And then you look at someone who spends the entire day asking and begging, in tears and suffering, and you dare ask for an account![50]

Apparently also in Chrysostom's time some said they would rather withhold their giving until they could decide who among the poor were worthy. To such excuses Chrysostom replies, first, that it is better to give to some who may be unworthy and not to miss the worthy, than to try to give only to the worthy and risk missing them. Second, "Alms are to be given, not to the way of life, but to the human being; we must have compassion, not because the poor are virtuous, but because they are needy."[51].

With Chrysostom we reach the fullest and most cohesive development of Christian doctrine on wealth and economic responsibility in the period we are studying. On a number of subjects, such as usury, he essentially repeats what his predecessors said before, and for that reason we have not dwelt on them. Naturally, since his views are expressed in hundreds of sermons rather than in a single systematic treatise, at some points they are not entirely coherent. For instance, occasionally Chrysostom will draw on the theme that almsgiving is like lending to God.[52] This theme, which we have already found in earlier Christian writers, and which is based on Proverbs 19:17, "He who is kind to the poor lends to the Lord," clearly contradicts what he says in many other sermons, that all we have is already a loan or a trust from God. Such minor inconsistencies, however, should not detract from the total coherence and theological grounding of Chrysostom's economic teachings.

NOTES

1. Sierra Bravo, *Doctrina social y económica de los padres de la Iglesia* (Madrid: COMPI, 1976), p. 306.
2. *Hom. in Matt.* 52.5, *NPNF,* 1st ser. "Unless one has this, one has fallen away from being a man." *Hom. in ii Cor.* 16.5, *NPNF,* 1st ser. "For such a one {as practices mercy} is in the highest sense a man."
3. *Hom. in ii Cor.* 6.3, *NPNF,* 1st ser.
4. *Hom. in Act. Apost.* 20.4, *PG.*
5. *Hom. de perfecta caritate* 1, *PG.* Cf. *Hom. in i Cor. xxxiv* 7, *NPNF,* 1st ser.
   He {God} likewise made us to stand in need of one another, that thus he might bring us together, because necessities above all create friendships. For no other reason neither suffered He all things to be produced in every place, that hence he might compel us to mix with one another ... And accordingly that we might easily keep up intercourse with distant countries, he spread the level of the sea between us, and gave us the swiftness of the winds, thereby making our voyages easy.
6. *Hom. in Act. Apost.* 1.2, *PG.*
7. *Hom. de Sat. et Aur.* 2, *PG.*
8. *Hom. ad pop. Antioch.* 1.5, *PG.*
9. *De Lazaro* 11.4, *PG.*
10. *Hom. ad pop. Antioch.* 2.5, *PG.*
11. *De Lazaro* 2.1, *PG.*
12. *De Lazaro* 2.1. We have found this theme earlier in Plutarch, from whom Chrysostom may well have borrowed it.
13. *De Lazaro* 1.12, *PG.*
14. *De Lazaro* 2.3, *PG.*
15. *Hom. in i Cor.* 13.5, *PG.*
16. *In Psalm.* 48.2.3, *PG.*
17. *In Psalm.* 48.2.3. This is also the reason Chrysostom deplores the fact that the church has received endowments for the care of the poor. Such endowments both force the leaders of the church to be involved in business in ways that are not appropriate and excuse later generations from the need to give. The only reason the church must keep such endowments is the hardness of heart of the present generation. *Hom. in Mat.* 85.3, *NPNF,* 1st ser. "But now there are fields, and houses, and hirings of lodgings, and carriages, and muleteers, and mules, and a great array of this kind in the church on account of you, and your hardness of heart. For this store of the church ought to be with you, and your readiness of mind ought to be a revenue to her; but now two wrong things come to pass, both you continue unfruitful, and God's priests do not practice their proper duties."
18. *Hom. in Mat.* 56.6, *PG.*
19. *Hom. in ii Cor.* 17.2, *PG.*
20. *Hom. in i Tim.* 12, *NPNF,* 1st ser.
21. *Hom. in i Tim.* 12, *NPNF,* 1st ser.
22. *De Lazaro* 2.4, *PG.*
23. *In dict. Pauli,* "Oportet ... " 2.3, *PG.* Cf.*Hom. in Act. Apost.* 7.2, *PG.*
24. *In Psalm.* 48.4, *PG.*
25. *Hom. in Joh.* 15.3, *PG.*
26. *Hom. in i Tim.* 11, *NPNF,* 1st ser.
27. *De Lazaro* 6.8, *PG.*
28. *De Lazaro* 2.4, *PG.*
29. *De Lazaro* 6, *PG.*
30. *Hom. in Matt.* 49.4, *BAC.*
31. *Hom. ad pop. Antioch.* 2.6, *PG.*
32. *Hom. ad pop. Antioch.* 2.6, *PG.*
33. *Hom. in ii Cor.* 17.3, *NPNF,* 1st ser.
34. *Hom. in i Cor.* 34.5, *NPNF,* 1st ser.

35. In his homilies one finds frequent references to the rich who make such complaints as "How long will you turn your tongue against us? How long will you war against us?" *Hom. de Sat. at Aur.* 2, *PG.*

36. *Hom. in i Thes.* 10, *NPNF,* 1st ser.

37. *Hom. in i Cor.* 13.4, *NPNF,* 1st ser.

38. *De Eutrop.* 2.3, *PG.*

39. *In Psalm.* 48.4, *PG.*

40. *In Psalm.* 48.4, *PG.*

41. *Hom. in ii Cor.* 19.3, *NPNF,* 1st ser.

42. *Hom. in Gen.* 37.5; 55.4, *PG.*

43. *Hom. in Mat.* 52.3, *NPNF,* 1st ser.

44. *Hom. in i Cor.* 10.4, *NPNF,* 1st ser.

45. *Hom. ad pop. Antioch.* 2.5, *PG.*

46. *Hom. in Rom.* 11.5, *NPNF,* 1st ser.

47. *Hom. in ii Cor.* 17.3, *NPNF,* 1st ser.

48. *Hom. in ii Cor.* 13.4, *NPNF,* 1st ser.

49. *Hom. in i Cor.* 21.6, *PG.*

50. *De eleem.* 6, *PG.* Cf. *Hom. in Mat.* 35.3–4; *Hom. in i Cor.* 11.6, *NPNF,* 1st ser.

51. *De Lazaro* 2.6, *PG.*

52. *Hom. de poen.* 7.6, *PG.*

12/Augustine

No theologian, except perhaps Paul, has been more influential in the Western church than Augustine. He brought together many different strands of thought and wove them into a system that entirely dominated Christian theology at least until the thirteenth century and has continued to be influential to this day. Augustine is the great teacher of the West, through whose eyes much Western theology, both Catholic and Protestant, has read the New Testament.

In social and economic matters, he both agreed and disagreed with other Christians before him and what was being said even in his own time by Chrysostom and others. Yet in the chaos that followed after his death, his views became so dominant that much of what had been said earlier was forgotten. Therefore, in order to understand the later course of Christian views on issues of faith and wealth, we must see their source in Augustine. And in order to understand Augustine we must keep in mind the wider scope of his theology and world vision.[1]

Augustine's valuation of the world and of creatures was heavily influenced by his Neoplatonic outlook. It led him to see the world as a hierarchy of being, from the lowest echelons of materiality to the highest levels of rationality and spirituality. This is the natural order established by God, which exists not only in creation in general, but also within us.

And the eternal law is the divine order or will of God, which requires the preservation of natural order, and forbids the breach of it. But what is this natural order in man? Man, we know, consists of soul and body; but so does a beast. Again, it is plain that in the order of nature the soul is superior to the body. Moreover, in the soul of man there is reason, which is not in a beast. Therefore, as the soul is superior to the body, so in the soul itself the reason is superior by the law of nature to the other parts which are also found in beasts; and in reason itself, which is partly contemplation and partly action, contemplation is unquestionably the superior part.[2]

In this hierarchy all is good. Nothing is in itself evil. Evil is not a substance but is rather the corruption or misuse of what is by nature good. This perspective allows Augustine to repeat what we have found in earlier writers, that the evil in wealth lies not in the riches themselves but in the avarice that often accompanies wealth."Avarice is not a fault inherent in gold, but in the man who inherently loves gold, to the detriment of justice, which ought to be held in incomparably higher regard than gold."[3] However, although gold and silver and possessions are good, they do not make the owner good.[4] One can do good with them, but merely having them makes one no better than another who does not have them. When the evil have gold the needy are oppressed, judges are bribed, and laws are subverted; when the good have it the poor are fed, the naked are covered, the oppressed are set free.[5] The difference is not in the gold itself but in the attitudes of those who possess and use it.

At this point an important distinction comes into play. All things are good, but some goods are to be used and others are to be enjoyed.[6] When we change this order and try to use what is to be enjoyed or enjoy what is to be used, evil arises.

There are some things, then, which are to be enjoyed, others which are to be used . . . Those things which are objects of enjoyment make us happy. Those things which are objects of use assist, and (so to speak) support us in our efforts after happiness, so that we can attain the things that make us happy and rest in them. We ourselves, again, who enjoy and use these things, being placed among both kinds of objects, if we set ourselves to enjoy those things which we ought to use, are hindered in our course, and sometimes even led away from it; so that, getting entangled in the love of lower gratifications, we lag behind in, or even altogether turn back from, the pursuit of the real and proper objects of enjoyment.[7]

Naturally, what Augustine means here by enjoyment (*fruitio*) is much more than mere pleasure. He means finding true and final happiness in a thing. Only that is worthy of enjoyment which can produce true joy and satisfaction. All the rest must be used in order to attain what can truly be enjoyed. "To enjoy a thing is to rest with satisfaction in it for its own sake. To use, on the other hand, is to employ whatever means are at one's disposal to obtain what one desires."[8]

This distinction is so crucial that "every human evil or vice consists in seeking to enjoy things that are to be used, and to use things that are to be enjoyed."[9] Only rational beings are capable of this distinction, for the beasts have no notion of instrumentality. They eat in order to eat, not because they seek an ulterior goal. Humans, on the other hand, have the capacity to distinguish between an instrument and the goal for which it has been made, and therefore they also have the capacity to pervert their relationship to the instrument so that it becomes an end in itself, or, as Augustine would say, of enjoying rather than using it.

Strictly speaking, God is to be enjoyed, and all creatures are to be used for the enjoyment of God. The fundamental vice of humanity consists precisely in enjoying things and using God to obtain things. This is the evil of "those perverse creatures who would fain enjoy money and use God, not spending money for God's sake, but worshipping God for money's sake."[10] Avarice lies here, in this confusion. The greedy seek to enjoy their possessions and sometimes even to use God in order to increase their wealth. In so doing, they fall into crass idolatry, for only God is to be enjoyed, and all things are to be used in order to attain that enjoyment.

Human beings, however, exhibit another perversion in our relationship with things. Besides attempting to enjoy things, one can also misuse them. Although things are intended to be used, not every use is appropriate to them. Improper use Augustine calls "abuse."[11] Use has to do with utility, and utility requires proper use. Therefore, those who abuse, or do not use well, do not really use at all.[12] "Gold and silver thus belong to the one who knows how to use them, for it is commonly said among people that one is worthy of owning something when one uses it well. On the other hand, whoever does not use justly does not legitimately possess, and if whoever does not legitimately possess claims possession, then this will not be the claim of a just owner, but the lie of a shameless usurper."[13]

Since the proper use of things is for enjoying God, and since proper possession requires proper use, we possess truly and justly only what we use in order to enjoy God. It is significant that here Augustine has dealt with the three basic rights that ancient Roman law equated with private property: the right to use, the right to enjoy, and the right to abuse. The third Augustine completely rejects, for abuse or improper use is a violation of the true nature of property as Augustine understands it. The second he also rejects as appropriate to anything one can "own" in the legal sense. Things, no matter whether privately owned or not, are not to be enjoyed; they are instruments to achieve the true enjoyment of God. Finally, he radically redefines the right to use, for it is no longer the right to use for whichever ends the owner determines, but only the right to use things for their proper end, the enjoyment of God.

The proper use of material goods requires a clear distinction between the necessary and the superfluous. A few material things are truly necessary: food, clothing, and shelter. Augustine is willing to concede that some people, accustomed as they are to delicate foods and certain comforts, may truly have come to need them. Even so, much that the rich have is superfluous. If it is superfluous, if they cannot use it directly to sustain their life in order to enjoy God, to retain it is to misuse it. This is even more true since what is superfluous to them is necessary to the poor.[14] Therefore, the Christian knows that "not to give to the needy what is superfluous is akin to fraud."[15] And Augustine can say, "From those things that God gave you, take that which you need, but the rest, which to you are superfluous, are necessary to others. The superfluous goods of the rich are necessary to the poor, and when you possess the superfluous you possess what is not yours."[16] In any case, since all belongs to God, when one gives what is superfluous this should not be called liberality; it is a mere act of restitution.[17]

The proper use of all that one does not need is, as so many had said before Augustine, to share it with the poor. Here we find once again the themes of lending to God, of atoning for sin, and of transferring wealth from earth to heaven.

On the subject of lending, both to God and to humans, Augustine says little that is new. Lending money on interest is evil. On the contrary, one should give freely; if one cannot give, then one should lend without expecting a profit in return. Furthermore, one should not importune the debtor for payment.[18] However, although Augustine proscribes lending with interest to others he commands lending to God, promising a high rate of return. While lending to another for profit is evil, lending to God by giving to the poor earns us the way to heaven. Therefore, says Augustine, "Give the temporal and receive the eternal; give the earthly and receive the heavenly."[19] "Since God pays the merciful bountifully, anyone who performs an act of mercy makes a loan to God."[20]

That almsgiving is a way of atoning for sin was a common view in Augustine's time. He affirms that almsgiving together with prayer and fasting are the means by which one purges the small sins that we all commit daily.[21] Apparently, this practice had become so common that Augustine felt there was the danger that some would continue sinning, even to the point of stealing what was not theirs and then trying to atone for it through almsgiving. Needless to say, Augustine has harsh words for such views and practices.[22]

On the matter of transferring one's wealth to heaven, much of what Augustine says is commentary, with some imaginative illustrations, on Jesus' command to store up treasure in heaven rather than on earth. Suppose you were living in a house and saw the walls crumbling. Wouldn't you hasten to carry out your possessions before the house falls? Likewise Christians who look at the world and see its ruin approaching must hasten to transfer their possessions out of this crumbling world and into everlasting heaven.[23] And children who store their money in banks where they cannot see it, but who still continue adding to their treasure, should be an example of faith to Christians, who must also continue placing their treasure in heaven, even though they cannot see it.[24] Naturally, this is to be done by acts of mercy, especially by giving to the poor—although Augustine speaks more than most of his predecessors of giving money to build churches. By giving to the poor, one uses one's perishable wealth to build up an imperishable treasure in heaven.

Augustine's concentration on life eternal and on the enjoyment of God means that at times the poor appear to be no more than stepping stones—in Augustine's categories, instruments to be used—toward the goal of salvation. "What are the poor to whom we give but bearers carrying our wealth to heaven? Give, therefore to your bearer, who hauls your gift to heaven."[25]

This last quote points to one of the greatest flaws in Augustine's theological outlook. Up to this point, ideas found in Augustine are similar to those of Basil, Ambrose, and Chrysostom, except they are grounded on a Neoplatonic view of the hierarchy of being and therefore emphasize the need to use material wealth in order to gain spiritual blessing. Augustine's Neoplatonic framework, however, carries him much further. Ultimately, issues of poverty and wealth are not important in themselves, for they concern the material, and our goal is much higher than that. All creatures, including the poor, are instruments for attaining the enjoyment of God. One may object that Augustine explicitly says we should not wish that there be needy in order to have an opportunity for works of mercy.[26] Yet, this is an isolated text among many where Augustine speaks of the function of the poor in giving others an opportunity for charity and service. In any case, even in this text his main concern is not the poor themselves but the giver's attitude, which must be one of love and must exclude paternalism.[27]

Exactly what Augustine means by "the poor" is not altogether clear. He exhorts the poor who are tempted to steal out of need, not to steal but to trust in God, which might indicate that he is speaking of the entirely dispossessed.[28] In any case, the disparity between rich and poor and the resulting suffering of the latter are not a tragedy nor an evil, but something God has created in order to carry forth the plan of salvation. "God made the poor to test the human in them, and made the rich to test them through the poor. God has done everything properly, . . . and we must believe that it was good, even though we do not understand why it was done."[29] "It is Christ, God of the prophets, who not only creates the rich by most graciously giving them goods, but also the poor by most justly withholding or taking away from them."[30] "Who made the two? The Lord made the rich so they could find help in the poor, and the poor to test the rich."[31]

Both the rich and the poor, as well as wealth and poverty, have a place in God's plan. While this results in the theory that God has somehow willed the poor to be such, one positive result is that the poor are seen, not only as objects of charity, but also as subjects who have something to contribute to others. Augustine does not depict the poor as simply waiting to receive from the rich but as also having something to give, both to the rich and to others who are also poor. To the rich, they can contribute precisely by receiving. The wealth of the rich is a burden that impedes their progress to heaven. The poverty of the poor is also a burden. When the rich give to the poor, both burdens are shared, so that in a sense the poor also give to the rich.[32] But the poor also can contribute to others in need. One who can see may offer to help the blind, another whose legs are healthy may aid the lame, and a third can bury the dead.[33]

All of this is highly theoretical, and Augustine is apparently aware that in spite of all he says about giving up the superfluous, few will follow his advice. What, concretely, does he suggest that his flock do with their wealth? He tells them to set aside at least a tenth of all their possessions and income for the poor. After all, he declares, the Pharisees did as much, and the justice of Christians should be higher than that of Pharisees![34] Naturally, this must not be understood as contradicting all he has said about giving up everything superfluous, but rather as a concession to a flock that is not quite ready to take the drastic steps its pastor would rather recommend.

On the other hand, Augustine also uses the distinction between the commandments and the counsels of perfection. It allows him to say that Christ does not command all to sell all they have and give it to the poor, but only those who wish to be perfect.[35] Augustine, like all his orthodox contemporaries, rejects the notion that total renunciation or communal life are required of all Christians.[36] At the same time, he does believe that the highest order of life on earth is precisely that of those who give up their wealth and choose to live in a monastic community. Once people have decided to live in such a community, they must not continue calling things their own but must have all things in common.[37] In this context, he uses the example of the old Roman Republic, whose citizens remained privately poor in order to enrich the city; he declares that Christians who do likewise in order to enjoy the company of angels have nothing to boast about, since the ancient Romans did something similar for a much smaller reward.[38] The monastic life allows Christians to divest themselves of all that is superfluous and thus to be true possessors of what they have—both their limited material goods here on earth and their treasure in heaven. In this context one must read Augustine's passages that exalt the practice of common property. He says, for instance,

Any who wish to serve the Lord must not rejoice in the private, but in the common. The earliest Christians made common property of their private goods. Did they lose what was theirs? . . . It is because of our private possessions that there are disagreements, enmity, dissension, wars . . . [39]

Yet by his time this was not a call for all Christians to share their possessions but rather an argument in favor of the monastic life, which in turn functioned as a constant reminder to the rest of the church that material possessions are not the ultimate goal in life.

However, at another point Augustine had to deal more concretely with the issues of property and property rights. The Donatist controversy forced Augustine to think through the relationship between civil and ecclesiastical authority at various levels. One pressing question was the issue of property rights and how they relate both to natural law and to civil law. The churches and other properties of the Donatists had been confiscated as part of the empire's attempt to suppress them. The Donatists were accusing the Catholics of having robbed them and Augustine in particular of holding properties that in fact belonged to the Donatist church. Augustine defends himself at length, and in so doing he sets down his view that God has granted civil authorities the power to set and determine property rights.

Failing everywhere else, what do they now allege against us, not finding what to say? 'They have taken away our houses, they have taken away our estates.' . . . Behold, there are those estates; by what right dost thou assert thy claim to them? By divine right, or by human? Let them answer: Divine right we have in the Scriptures, human right in the laws of kings. By what right does every man possess what he possesses? It is not by human right? For by divine right, 'The earth is the Lord's, and the fullness thereof.' The poor and the rich God made of one clay; the same earth supports alike the poor and the rich. By human right, however, one says, 'This estate is mine, this house is mine, this servant is mine.' By human right, therefore, is by right of the emperors. Why so? Because God has distributed to mankind these very human rights through the emperors and kings of this world. Do you wish us to read the laws of the emperors, and to act by the estates according to these laws? If you will have your possession by human right, let us recite the laws of the emperors; let us see whether they would have the heretics possess anything. 'But what is the emperor to me?' thou sayest. It is by right from him that thou possessest the land. Or take away rights created by emperors, and then who will dare say, 'That estate is mine, or that slave is mine, or this house is mine'? . . . For there are to be read well known laws, in which the emperors have directed that those who, being outside the communion of the Catholic Church, usurp to themselves the name of Christians, and are not willing in peace to worship the Author of peace, may not dare to possess anything in the name of the Church . . . Say not then that the possessions are thine; because it is to those same human rights, by which men enjoy their possessions, thou hast referred them.[40]

From this text it is clear that according to Augustine not only has God made some poor and some rich, but God has done this through the civil order. The result is that there is no moral authority to which the Donatists can appeal, for the emperor's authority is derived from God, and things belong to whomever those laws assign them. Augustine's argument is not entirely without foundation; he says that there is no other authority by which property rights are assigned than that of the emperor. The Donatists may refuse to accept the authority of the emperor, but in that case no other authority exists to which they can appeal in order to claim their rights. And if they do accept the authority of the emperor, they have to relinquish their claims, for the emperor has decided against them.

In another text,[41] writing to an acquaintance of his youth who now had joined a fairly moderate Donatist group, Augustine argues that things can be owned according to either divine or human right. According to divine right, all things belong to the just. According to human law, they belong to those to whom the kings of the earth assign them. It is clear that according to human law these properties do not belong to the Donatists, for the emperor has decided that they do not. As to divine law, the Donatists, being unjust, have no recourse to it. "But we have worked in order to acquire these goods," the Donatists may say. To this Augustine replies with a quote from Proverbs 13:22 "From the labors of sinners will the just eat."[42] He does not support those who have taken the condemnation of the Donatists as an opportunity to seize their property for themselves, for they are holding what in fact belongs to the poor and to the church. Yet he does argue that, the Catholic church being the true Church of Christ, all these properties are rightly given for it to administer.

Ultimately, matters of property rights are thus to be determined by the state. Clearly, Augustine's claim that "by divine right" all things belong to the just plays no significant role in his argument, except to deprive the Donatists of any claim to an authority higher than the emperor. Since, by Augustine's definition, the Donatists are not just, this avenue of appeal is not open to them. Presumably, had the imperial decisions gone in the opposite direction, Augustine and his party could have claimed that divine law was still on their side.

The main issue, however, is that in spite of all his exhortations to individuals on economic matters, when it came to applying these principles to the social order Augustine reverted to his Roman legal upbringing. His mother was probably of Berber background, and it was her faith that he eventually embraced. But his father was a Roman official, and it was his view of the social order that Augustine shared in his response to the Donatists, and the Circumcellions in particular. He could preach and teach that those who loaned money ought not to demand payment or collect interest, but when the poor rebelled and destroyed the extortionate letters of credit by which the rich held them in bondage he thought it a great crime. He could affirm that apart from the outward dress of their wealth the poor and the rich are equal; yet when "land-owners of honorable birth and gentlemanly breeding" were harshly treated he could call on the support of the state to restore an order in which the poor were treated with equal harshness.[43]

By "divine law" all things belong to the just, Augustine would say. And he would add that those who misuse or abuse things are not their true owners. But by human law, which is an extension of the divine, all things belong to those to whom the existing order confers them. If the result is that some are poor and some are rich, that is God's doing and not for us to question.

NOTES

1. This is not the place to discuss Augustine's theology, even in outline. I have tried to do this in *A History of Christian Thought*, 2d ed. (Nashville: Abingdon, 1987), 2:15–55.
2. *Contra Faust. Manich.* 22.26, *NPNF*, 1st ser.
3. *De civ. D.* 12.8, *NPNF*, 1st ser. Cf. *Ser.* 61.10; *In Psalm.* 59.9. Except where a different source is given, all references to Augustine's writings are from *PL*.

4. *Ser.* 48.8.
5. *Ser.* 340.9.
6. The consequences of this distinction for social ethics are explored by R. Canning, "The Augustinian '*uti/frui*' Distinction in the Relation between Love for Neighbour and Love for God," *Aug.* 33 (1983): 165–231.
7. *De doct. Christ.* 1.3, *NPNF*, 1st ser. Cf. *De civ. D.* 11.25, *NPNF*, 1st ser.: "And this seems to be the difference between them, that we are said to *enjoy* that which in itself, and irrespective of other ends, delights us; to *use* that which we seek for the sake of some end beyond."
8. *De doct. Christ.* 1.3, *NPNF*, 1st ser.
9. *De lxxxiii quaest.* 30,.
10. *De civ. D.* 11.25, *NPNF*, 1st ser.
11. *De doct. Christ.* 1.4, *NPNF*, 1st ser.
12. *De lxxxiii quaest.* 30,.
13. *Ser.* 50.4,.
14. *Ser.* 61.12, Cf. *Ser.* 39.6, On the theme of poverty in Augustine's sermons, see P. Vismara Chiappa, *Il tema della povertà nella predicazione di Sant' Agostino* (Milano: A. Giuffrè, 1975).
15. *Ser.* 206.2,.
16. *In Psalm.* 147.12,. Cf. *Ser.* 107.4, Those who are so concerned with gathering enough to live should "set aside in their mind what they need to live, and think about who should have the rest, lest, trying to save in order to live, they will reap their own death."
17. *In Psalm.* 95.15,.
18. *Ser.* 239.5,. It is interesting to note, however, that in this text Augustine is not referring to the destitute who owe money, but to someone who owns a house and other possessions. The lender is told not to force the borrower to sell house or possessions.
19. *In Psalm.* 36.3.6,.
20. *De serm. Dom. in Monte* 1.20.68.
21. *Ser.* 9.17; 43.1.
22. *De civ. D.* 21.27.2.
23. *Ep.* 122.2.
24. *In Psalm.* 48.5.12.
25. *Ser.* 60.8.
26. *Tract. in ep. Io. ad Parth.* 31.5.
27. *Tract. in ep. Io. ad Parth.* 8.
28. *In Psalm.* 61.16. Cf. *Ser.* 32.15; 85.6–7.
29. *In Psalm.* 124.2, *PL*.
30. *Contra adv. leg et proph.* 2.9.37.
31. *Ser.* 39.6.
32. *Ser.* 61.12; 164.9. *De disc. Christ.* 7.8.
33. *Ser.* 91.9. *In Psalm.* 36.2.13.
34. *Ser.* 85.5. *In Psalm.* 146.17.
35. *Ep.* 157.25, 30.
36. *Ep.* 23.
37. *Reg. serv. Dei* 1.
38. *De civ. D.* 5.18.2.
39. *In Psalm.* 131.5.
40. *In Evang. Iohan.* 7.25–26, *NPNF*, 1st ser.
41. *Ep.* 93.12.50.
42. RSV: "The sinner's wealth is laid up for the righteous."
43. *See his Ep.* 185.15 quoted above, p. 160.

RETROSPECT

13/Retrospect

As we look back at the story just surveyed, we are struck both by the continuity of certain themes and by the vast difference between the world of Augustine and that of the earliest Christian preachers. Let us look first at the themes showing continuity, sometimes almost to the point of unanimity, and then at some of the more significant developments during the four centuries we have been studying.

Common Views

The first point of agreement is obvious but still merits mention. All the authors we have surveyed agree that issues of faith and wealth belong together. Not a single voice—we have studied practically all the foremost leaders of the church during a period of almost four hundred years—favors the argument, so often heard in modern times, that these issues ought to be kept separate and that preachers or religious teachers should leave them to others. Presumably some of Chrysostom's wealthy hearers who protested the content of his sermons might have voiced such views. Probably Empress Eudoxia did so. What is clear is that not one major Christian leader held that issues of faith and wealth should be kept separate.

On the outlines of the actual relationship between faith and wealth there is also remarkable unanimity, to the point that certain themes appear again and again almost as if one author had been copying from another. This is true both of themes drawn from Scripture and of those derived from the classical wisdom of Greece and Rome. Usury, by which is usually meant any loan on interest, is universally condemned in the early church. The one possible exception is Clement of Alexandria, who may have held that the proscription of loans on interest applies only to loans to other believers, but even this possibility is based only on a debatable interpretation of a single text. At least some among the clergy made loans on interest, even at outrageous and illegal rates, which is proved by the seventeenth canon of the Council of Nicea forbidding such practices.[1] Still, Christian writers throughout the first four centuries are practically unanimous in their rejection of usury as well as of any loan on interest, and for this they draw both on Old Testament law and on the Greco-Roman tradition that held usury in contempt, even though a moderate rate of interest was legal according to civil law.

3) The reinterpretation of "rich" and "poor," so that the seemingly rich are in truth poor in virtue and poor in joy, is another theme borrowed heavily from pagan writers. Images drawn from classical authors, such as the seeker of wealth being similar to a person who is always thirsty, appear repeatedly in early Christian writers and preachers. So does the theme that excessive wealth brings nothing but worry, and that a moderate level of poverty leads to a happier life.

4) More exclusively Christian is the notion that on giving to the poor one lends to God—a notion derived from the book of Proverbs but soon developed into an entire theological rationale for almsgiving.[5] Not surprisingly, the idea that the rich are at a disadvantage when it comes to entering the Kingdom, probably derived from the very words of Jesus, is common in early Christian literature.[6] So is the theme that one who can help another and fails to do so renders oneself guilty of whatever happens to that other person, including homicide.

In spite of the unanimously negative attitude toward accumulating wealth, writers share an equally unanimous positive attitude toward the things themselves that constitute wealth. Since wealth can mean both things and their accumulation, some authors, such as Clement of Alexandria, at times appear almost to contradict themselves. Yet, in a church beset by gnostic notions about the evil of material creation, it was important to insist that all things, including those that are usually counted as wealth, are good. At the same time, however, the very authors who defend the value of things—and even of wealth—against the gnostics also insist on the evil of accumulating such things. The evil, as they say, is not in things themselves, but in the person who accumulates them and loves them inordinately. To this view we shall return, for it led to significant developments in the attitude of Christians toward wealth and the wealthy.

9) Most remarkably, there is a surprising level of agreement on whether property should be private or held in common. The sort of sharing described in the early chapters of Acts was not abandoned as quickly nor as easily as we sometimes assume. On the contrary, it continued at least until well into the second century and probably, in some mitigated forms, throughout most of the third. At the same time, as the church grew in numbers, and as it came to include a wider variety of economic levels in its membership, the voluntary nature of such sharing was un-

derscored, and in some instances emphasis shifted from commonality of goods—*koinonía*—to almsgiving.

(11) By almsgiving, however, the writers of the first four centuries do not mean the practice of giving loose change to beggars. On the contrary, the criterion they most often use is that one should keep for oneself only what is necessary and give the superfluous to the needy. Augustine encapsulates this principle by declaring that what is superfluous to some is necessary to the poor. At the same time, those who propose this principle are willing to concede, as do both Chrysostom and Augustine, that out of custom or weakness some may find certain things necessary that others who are poorer would consider superfluous. In such cases, the teachers and pastors we have been studying are flexible enough not to set stringent rules but to let believers determine what in their own case is necessary and what is superfluous, although some advise that believers should not make this decision strictly on their own but rather guided by a spiritual mentor. Augustine also suggests the tithe as a minimum measure.

(12) On the commonality of property, a fairly frequent notion among the theologians is that in creation God intended all things to be common, and that private property exists because of our fallen condition. Such views often combine the stories of the garden of Eden with the ancient myth of an original golden age. What stands between Eden and us is sin, and hence the frequent connection between the notion of private property and sin. Private property, whereby some can keep the produce of the land from others, is, as Ambrose would say, the result of usurpation—words that come close to the modern socialist dictum that private property is theft.

(13) At the same time, all our authors take private property for granted. Clement of Alexandria is the first to argue that if no one possessed anything, it would be impossible to obey Jesus' commandment to give to the poor. One cannot give what one does not have, he argues—the most common argument we have found in defense of private property. Even when that argument is not explicitly stated, it is clear that the Christian writers of the first four centuries, in calling believers to give, are assuming the existence and continuation of private property.

(14) The writers, however, place drastic limitations on such private property. These limitations contrast with the prevailing view of Roman law, which considered property rights absolute, to the point that, in earliest Roman law, private property was not subject to taxation. Christian teachers consistently reject such an understanding of property rights. For them, all property in some sense is alien. By this they mean several things. First, and most consistently among early Christian authors, all property is alien to its owners because it ultimately belongs to God. This has important implications for the question of its proper use, to which we shall turn next. Second, property is alien because we cannot claim

more than a temporary ownership of it, an ownership ended always by death. Along these lines some authors comment on the number of owners an estate has had before its present owner and how many more it will have in the future. Third, some of the authors would say that property is alien because it is the result of injustice—so, among others, Irenaeus and Jerome.

The rights of ownership, according to the Christian writers, are further limited by the proper use of wealth. In the ancient Roman tradition, an owner had the right to determine such use. Christian teachers unanimously declare that it is not so. Precisely because all property is alien, not every use is legitimate. The authors differ on the criteria by which they determine proper use. The criterion most often used is sufficiency, meaning that owners of property or wealth should use for themselves only enough to meet their needs. What surpasses the measure of sufficiency is superfluous and should be shared with others whose primary needs are not being met. Clement and others offer the criterion of usefulness. By this they mean that wealth should not be spent on useless things or things that could be just as useful with less ostentation. Thus Clement reminds his readers that an iron knife cuts better than one made out of gold or silver; Chrysostom and others mock those whose horses wear golden bits. Augustine introduces the contrast between use and enjoyment, declaring that all possessions are to be used for the ultimate purpose of enjoying God. In a more practical vein, he suggests the tithe as a measure of the minimum that should be shared with others.

In spite of these differences, all agree on the fundamental criterion that wealth is to be shared. This principle works at more than one level, for it is both the basis of economic life and the reason those who have more than they need must share it with the needy. With respect to economic life, Ambrose stands practically alone in condemning trade, as he declares that God made the sea for fishing and not for sailing long distances in search of what the local area does not produce. Almost all other writers, however, agree that human interchange, both in goods and in other relationships, is part of the order created and intended by God. Chrysostom, in contrast with Ambrose, praises God for creating the sea so that people can travel long distances and meet each other's material needs through trade. Lactantius declares that just as God gave antlers to the deer to defend itself, humankind has been given each other, so that through social life, mutual support, and trade we may defend ourselves.

The principle that wealth is created in order to be shared, however, is used much more frequently and insistently to remind Christians of the need to share with the less fortunate. To accumulate wealth is to pervert it, not only because real wealth must always be moving and active, but also because the purpose of wealth is to meet human need. Therefore, those who accumulate wealth as if it were an end in itself or

who accumulate it in order to live in comfort and ostentation are mis-
using wealth. Along these lines several authors declare that those who
accumulate wealth are no longer rightful owners of it, or even that those
who keep for themselves what the poor need are no better than thieves.
This line of argument repeatedly leads the authors to conclude that the
intended use of wealth is the common good. Private property is justifi-
able only to the extent it is used for sharing, to promote the equality
that the present order does not foster.

Writers of the first centuries use particular theological foundations
in discussing communal property. Most often their arguments point to
the past, to the original golden age, and not so much to the future, to
the eschatological Kingdom of God.[2] Perhaps more precisely, when most
of the writers seek a model of social order that their readers should
emulate, they find that order in the past and not in the future. The
eschatological argument, with the exception of the very early proclamation, tends to be more individualistic. Some writers indeed offer the
eschaton as a reason for sharing wealth. Yet this is not because the
expected Kingdom is one in which there will be equality, but rather
because only those who have shared their wealth on earth will be admitted into heaven.

Significant Developments

The tendency toward an individualistic eschatology appears early
in the proclamation of the church, and it becomes more marked as time
progresses. From Clement's concern about how the rich can be saved,
eschatology moves to Augustine's view that all creatures, including the
poor, are to be used to enjoy God.

Changes in eschatology parallel a similar tendency to interiorize the
criteria for the use and possession of wealth. Condemnation of excessive
wealth in the earliest documents is directed mostly toward the possession
itself as an obstacle in the Christian life. Little is said about the distinction between being wealthy and the avarice that often accompanies
wealth. For Hermas, for instance, the obstacle to Christian obedience
lies in wealth itself. The rich must have wealth cut away from them
before they are suited to the tower that the angels are building. A few
decades later, Clement of Alexandria emphasizes avarice and not wealth
itself as the obstacle to salvation. Still, Clement says quite clearly that in
a situation in which so many are needy only undue love of wealth will
lead the rich to refuse to share their possessions. Thus, while the evil
lies in the will, rather than in things themselves, the accumulation of
things is necessarily accompanied by an evil desire. This is the most
commonly held view throughout the period we have been studying.
Authors such as Basil and Chrysostom, while agreeing that the evil of

wealth lies in the corruption of the will that results in greed, do not allow this to become an easy way out. The wealthy cannot claim that although they have a vast accumulation of riches they are detached from them, are not avaricious, and therefore are guiltless. The wealthy who withhold their resources from the poor, they would say, misuse their possessions and render themselves guilty of theft, and in some cases even of homicide.

By the time of Augustine, however, this emphasis has shifted even further. What is important is the attitude of the soul, which must be one of detachment from things. Although Augustine continues the earlier Christian tradition by declaring that what is superfluous should be shared with the needy, he emphasizes the inner attitude of the will. Things are to be used, not enjoyed. This means that too much preoccupation with things must be avoided. Through this teaching the burden of conscience tends to be lifted from those who, precisely because they are in comfortable circumstances, do not have to worry too much about material things; it tends to be placed increasingly on those whose material needs are so pressing that preoccupation with them is nearly inescapable. The practical consequences of this may be seen in Augustine himself and his reaction to the Donatist threat, particularly to the unrest caused by the Circumcellions. That gentlemen are forced to perform manual labor or that letters of indebtedness are destroyed is a great crime and shows an undue preoccupation with material things. Yet that the same gentlemen oppress the poor and that the letters of indebtedness manifest their concern with material things apparently is less important.

Further Questions

Some obvious questions arise from this survey of developments. The first is why these views of the earliest Christian writers have been generally ignored in textbooks and courses on church history and the history of Christian thought. The question is not idle, and it becomes more significant when realizing that most of the texts quoted in the preceding chapters are not taken from obscure authors or from obscure writings of otherwise well-known authors. On the contrary, they have been drawn from those whom Christian tradition has dubbed the Fathers of the Church, that is, from those whose writings are constantly scrutinized in order to discover the nature of early Christian teaching.

One obvious answer is that matters such as the origin, nature, and use of wealth are not considered theological issues, and therefore when historians of doctrine have read these texts in the past they have not been looking for such matters. True as that may be, it simply leads to a further question: why have such matters not been considered properly theological issues, when it is clear that the ancient writers themselves considered them of great theological significance? The almost inescapable conclusion is that they have not been considered theological issues because the church at large has avoided them. This is not to say that issues of wealth and its relationship to faith have not been an important consideration throughout the history of the church. It means rather that they have been conveniently placed at the margin, as the concerns primarily of monastics and others who seek to live the Christian life at a higher plane of commitment than the rest of the church. In more recent times, by defining them as issues of social ethics, and therefore as the subject matter of a different discipline, we have tended to define them as nontheological issues.

It is clear that this process gained momentum in the fourth century, as the growth of the monastic movement coincided with the increasing numbers of those who were joining the church. Monasticism found theological justification in the distinction between commandments, which must be obeyed, and counsels of perfection, meant for those who follow the monastic life. Using this distinction made it possible to conceive of the church as composed of two sorts of Christians. To obey only the commandments is good. To follow also the counsels of perfection is better. Matters of faith and wealth were thus separated into a convenient division of labor, whereby monastics upheld the ancient traditions of limited and shared wealth, while others could freely accumulate wealth and then use part of it to support monastics, and also for almsgiving, progressively understood as giving food or small change to the impoverished.

Were we to continue reviewing the history into the Middle Ages, we would find statements on the limits to property and on the rights of the poor that are as radical as anything found in the first four centuries. These statements, however, come almost exclusively from the monastic milieu. Thus the monastics were fulfilling their function of keeping the ancient tradition alive, while both individual Christians and the church at large—its laity as well as most of its hierarchy—were free to strive after wealth in ways and to a degree that earlier Christians would have found scandalous. Still, the very existence of the monastic movement performed a function, constantly reminding the church at large of the incompatibility between radical Christian obedience and the quest after personal economic profit.

For theological reasons, the Reformation did away with the monastic movement. Monasticism, the Reformers held, undermined both the sanctity of the common life of the laity and the very notion of justification by faith that was the cornerstone of the Reformation. But monasticism was abolished also for economic reasons. The desire to confiscate the lands and other properties of monastic orders played an important role, for instance, in the actions of Henry VIII abolishing monasticism. Monasticism, however, lost ground for a deeper reason. To an age of burgeoning private wealth through trade and industrial development, the monastic was of life was a painful reminder of values and traditions that were no longer cherished. The accumulation of wealth—"capital" it was now called—become the main goal of entire societies that also considered themselves Christian. The collaboration between Christianity and capitalism developed most rapidly in societies and churches where the monastic movement was no longer present to serve as a reminder— even though at times a very imperfect reminder—of earlier Christian views on the relationship between faith and wealth.

Thus if matters of wealth and its proper use have been generally ignored in textbooks and courses on church history and the history of Christian thought, it has been because historians and theologians, conditioned by their times as we all are, had been taught not to consider such matters as property theological themes.

Our final question can only be mentioned and very tentatively explored in these pages. What is the relationship between the items discussed in the previous chapters and the other theological issues being debated at the time? Or, in other terms, were we to restore issues of faith and wealth to their proper place at the heart of the self-understanding of the ancient church, how would that affect our reading of the history of Christian thought?

It is clear that connections exist between the matters we have been discussing and the main issues debated among Christians during the first four centuries of the Christian era. Such connections need to be researched in greater detail and more carefully nuanced. At especially two points further research and reflection are likely to affect our entire understanding of the history of Christian thought.

The first of these is the challenge of gnosticism and the church's response to it. Historians have moved from understanding gnosticism as a series of complex cosmogonies and speculations to seeing it as a way of salvation. Perhaps it is time that we add another dimension to our understanding of gnosticism and the church's opposition to it. Ignatius was concerned about the heretics in Antioch, not only because they held strange doctrines, but also because they cared not for the widow, the orphan, or the oppressed. Clement and others insisted on the positive goodness of the things constituting wealth because the gnostics denied it. Thus the early Christian doctrine of creation took shape in the middle of a debate about the value and use of things, and it was also, at least partly, an attempt to offer guidance in their use and management. Significantly, as we move into later centuries the doctrine of creation remains one of the pillars on which most of the authors we have studied build their arguments on the proper use of wealth. Thus it is clear that the doctrine of creation and its development should not be studied apart from its connection with issues of the proper management of created things, in other words, with issues of faith and wealth.

A second and more tantalizing field of inquiry is the connection between matters of faith and wealth and the Arian controversy. Two things are clear. First, while both sides in the controversy—and even some who did not actively participate, such as Eusebius of Caesarea—employed the image of the emperor to speak of God, Athanasius and the Nicene party did so in a particular way. Athanasius underscores, not only the imperial majesty of God, but also the point that this universal emperor has deigned become one of us, or, as he would have said, come to live in our city. In short, the Arians viewed God as clothed in absolutely transcendent majesty. Athanasius by contrast, viewed God as choosing solidarity with oppressed humanity.

Second, some of the more radical statements of the fourth century on the rights of the poor, on the commonality of property, and on the injustice of excessive wealth were made by authors whom historians repeatedly quote as among the staunchest opponents of Arianism: Basil the Great, Gregory of Nazianzus, Gregory of Nyssa, Ambrose. These theologians have often been faulted by historians—especially Western historians—for speaking of the relations among the three persons of the Trinity in terms similar to the relations among three human beings. Gregory of Nyssa, for instance, speaks of the relations among Peter, James, and John as an adequate means of viewing the distinctions in the Trinity. Without discounting the inadequacy of such imagery, could one assert that part of what is at stake here is not only the relationships among the three divine persons but also the relationships among human persons? Could it be that, in rejecting subordinationism as a proper way of understanding relations within the Godhead, the Cappadocians are also pointing to a different way of understanding relations in human society? I have not researched the matter; I am not even certain that the materials exist with which to arrive at anything more than very tentative conclusions. Yet, the question should be asked: could it be that the conflict between Arianism and the Nicene faith was also a conflict between two different understandings of the proper order of society?

All of these questions may interest the historian and should be explored. Ultimately, however, they must not be allowed to obscure or postpone the more urgent and fundamental issues facing Christians today; we must no longer ignore the witness of earlier Christians on those issues. They lived in a world in which contrasts between the rich and the poor were staggering; we live in a world populated by a few who have millions and by millions who have nothing. For them, these issues were indissolubly connected with the meaning of salvation. Has the world changed so much that what they had to say is no longer relevant? I believe not. Has our commitment waned to such an extent that we can no longer take seriously the questions they pose to our use of the world's resources? I hope not.

NOTES

1. "Inasmuch as many enrolled among the clergy, following covetousness and lust of gain, have forgotten the divine Scripture, which says 'He hath not given his money

upon usury,' and in lending money ask the hundredth of the sum [as monthly interest], the holy and great Synod thinks it just that if after this decree any one be found to receive usury . . . he shall be deposed from the clergy and his name stricken from the list" (*NPNF,* 2d ser.).

2. This point has been noted with reference to sexual ethics and to matters of employment and participation in the life of society by D. R. Cochran, "The Relation between Ethics and Eschatology in the Ante-Nicene Fathers," *AngTheolRev* 22 (1940): 309–25.

Index